TALKING
ANIMALS
AND OTHERS

Walter R. Brooks

TALKING ANIMALS AND OTHERS

The Life and Work of Walter R. Brooks,
Creator of Freddy the Pig

MICHAEL CART

THE OVERLOOK PRESS
Woodstock & New York

This edition first published in the United States in 2009 by
The Overlook Press, Peter Mayer Publishers, Inc.
Woodstock & New York

WOODSTOCK:
One Overlook Drive
Woodstock, NY 12498
www.overlookpress.com
[for individual orders, bulk and special sales, contact our Woodstock office]

NEW YORK:
141 Wooster Street
New York, NY 10012

Cataloging-in-Publication Data is available from the Library of Congress

Book design and type formatting by Bernard Schleifer
Manufactured in the United States of America
ISBN 978-1-59020-170-1
FIRST EDITION
3 5 7 9 8 6 4 2

For my great-nephews
Rhett, Wyatt, and Andrew
and
for Aladdine Joroff and
friends of Freddy everywhere

Contents

Preface

This book has been a long time in the making. Nearly twenty-five years ago I was musing, one day, on how important the Freddy books had been to me as a child, how they may even have saved my life. *Saved my life?* How is that? Well, first of all, by never failing to make me laugh. In the years since I was a child, researchers have learned a great deal about the therapeutic value of laughter. I could have saved them a lot of time and money if they had only asked me about how much better I always felt after spending time in the precincts of a Freddy book. Of equal, if not greater, importance to me was the fact that the Bean Farm and its Centerboro environs had also offered me a safe place I could retreat to when the real world became a bit—or a *lot*—too much to bear, as it so often did back then. The world Walter had created became my sanctuary. His vision of paradise became mine, too. No, I couldn't physically go there. But I could go there in my imagination and, it sometimes seemed, perhaps with just a little extra effort, I might—just might—be able to blink and, presto, actually find myself there, surrounded by my friend Freddy and *his* friends. Such dreams can keep a kid going.

Thinking about this, I found myself wishing there were some way I could express my appreciation to Walter R. Brooks for all that he had done for me. Sadly, I had never had the opportunity to meet him and thank him in person, since he had died in 1958 when I was only seventeen. What kind of life had he led, I wondered? What kind of person had he been? All of a sudden I realized there was a way I *could* thank him: I could write a book about him, a biography that would incorporate an assessment and appreciation of his work!

But where to begin? I had grown up to become a library director and, as a researcher, I had already unearthed what meager material existed about this extraordinary man. But there was so little it was hardly enough for a modest-sized article. How could I find more? Well, as I've just mentioned, I was a library director, so I immediately sat down and wrote a letter to another library director, the director of the Roxbury, New York Public Library. Why Roxbury? Well, my earlier research had told me that this village in the Catskills was where Walter had lived the last ten years of his life. But this is where the story gets a bit weird and makes me wonder if this project might have been a bit . . . *fated*. For somehow—though to this day I have not been able to determine how—I seemed to know that Walter had married twice and that his second wife had been considerably younger than he. Might she possibly still be alive these twenty-five or so years after his passing? Well, that's the question I asked the Roxbury librarian. And in very short order I got the answer in a reply to my letter. Yes, indeed, Dorothy (Mrs. Walter R.) Brooks was still very much alive and, in fact, was a member of the library's board of trustees! And her home address was enclosed.

I immediately wrote to Mrs. Brooks, enclosing a copy of an article I had published several years earlier about the Freddy books. I explained that I would be in New York State that fall and wondered if I could possibly come to Roxbury to meet her?

She replied as quickly as the librarian had. Of course I could visit. She'd be happy to meet me. And so, reader, she did! Our first visit went so well that it was followed by many more. In fact, my fall trips to Roxbury and other places in New York where Walter had studied and lived became something of an annual pilgrimage. Each time I went I found out more about my childhood hero. And finally I had amassed enough information to write the biography that follows.

I could not, however, have done it without the extraordinary help of Dorothy Brooks. From the beginning, she supported this project and gave me complete access to Walter's files and papers. She was endlessly patient with my seemingly endless questions and put me in contact with others who had known her late husband, especially her longtime friend Pauline Hopkins. One of my greatest pleasures was being present on those occasions when Pauline would visit Dorothy from her home on Cape Cod and being then privileged to hear them reminisce. They both became not only sources and resources but also treasured friends. And one of my greatest sadnesses was losing first Dorothy, and then, several years later, Pauline (or Polly, as everyone called her).

One evening, several years after we first met, Dorothy and I were sitting at her kitchen table in Roxbury. I had just finished another lengthy interview with her for the biography I was already at work on and there was a momentary silence. Then Dorothy looked over at me and said, with a smile and a nod, "I think Walter would have approved."

My fondest wish is that she, too, might have approved—of the book that follows.

Dorothy Brooks and her cat, Dennis the Menace

Part I
THE LIFE

Walter R. Brooks, urban sophisticate

1

The Book That Began It

THE YEAR WAS 1927. A TACITURN CALVIN COOLIDGE WAS in the White House; a soft-spoken Charles A. Lindbergh was making aviation history by completing the first nonstop solo flight across the Atlantic; and out in Hollywood the Warner brothers were making some history of their own: by releasing the first feature-length sound movie, *The Jazz Singer*, they were forever transforming silent films into "talkies." Meanwhile, across the continent in New York, Alfred A. Knopf was making some noise of his own by publishing a children's book about another kind of "talkies"—talking animals! Titled *To and Again,* the book launched a series of twenty-five antic animal adventures that would become classics of twentieth century children's literature and would, in the person of their protagonist—a pig of many parts named Freddy—give children's literature one of its enduringly great characters.

Walter R. Brooks, the author of this soon-to-be landmark series, was a sophisticated, forty-one-year-old advertising man turned magazine editor, who lived in New York's bohemian Greenwich Village, affected tweed suits, and was known to use an elegant cigarette holder when he smoked and—an ardent "wet" during this Prohibition era—drank.

Though *To and Again* was his first children's book, he was already a published author of one serialized novel and some twenty-five stories and articles for adults. Over the years that followed he would publish nearly two hundred more, the best known among them being brittle, witty comedies with urban settings, including twenty-five that starred another talking animal, a raffish horse named Ed, who—as "Mr. Ed"—would inspire the eponymous, cult classic television sitcom of the sixties.

Given Walter's worldliness, it may seem ironic that it should be the twenty-five Freddy books with their gentle, character-driven humor and their lovingly realized rural and small-town settings that remain his most significant accomplishment. Or is it? Maybe not. For it often seems there were two Walter R. Brooks—one, the Manhattan sophisticate described above and the other, a man who—one hot, lonely summer in Washington, DC—sat down and wrote *To and Again* simply for his own amusement. In doing this, the second Walter R. Brooks recaptured the innocence of a happy childhood spent in the uncomplicated, late-nineteenth-century world of small-town Rome, New York.

Sadly, that world ended in 1901 when, at fifteen, Walter's home was, as he later tersely put it, "broken up" and he was sent to prep school in Peekskill, New York, then to college in Rochester, New York, and finally to medical school in New York City. What this meant for his emotional life may be moot but surely it is significant that his adult writing is typically informed by a degree of emotional distance, a cerebral, often satiric remove from his characters. But such an attitude is cheerfully absent from the Freddy books, which are filled with the kinds of characters who populated his childhood and whom he recalled from the affectionate closeness of his heart.

It is almost as if, in the Freddy books, Walter were telling himself comforting stories that enabled him to return to this simpler time. And this may also explain the artfully artless style in which these books are written, a style which—for the time—was modestly revolutionary. For in employing an easy, conversational voice, Walter rejected the stilted "British" English in which most American children's books were still being written in the 1920s (and which informed all of his own early work for adults) and dared, simply, to write as people actually talked. But why not? This was a man whose hobby was learning foreign languages—he spoke or read, by some accounts, at least six. To some of his readers, the occasional grammatical irregularities and especially the wonderfully idiosyncratic regionalisms and exclamations ("Great potatoes!") that enliven his style might, themselves, have sounded like a foreign language. But, to Walter himself, they were as familiar and comfortable as slippers, for they evoked the sounds of conversation he heard as a child in pre-twentieth-century upstate New York.

Nevertheless, his liberties with the formalities of language outraged some early reviewers, including the librarian who huffed—of an early Freddy book—"Slang of the comic strip type and bad grammar are frequently found in the conversational parts. Libraries can do without [this book]."

A more sensible view was expressed by the children's book author Margery Williams Bianco (*The Velveteen Rabbit*), who, in her own review of *To and Again* noted, "This is a story all children will enjoy, full of just the sort of humor and adventure they appreciate."

The book that began it: the first "Freddy"

The very fact that *To and Again*—this droll tale of normally hard-working farm animals on vacation in Florida[1]—was light-hearted and filled with humor was another revolutionary element, since children's books of the time tended to take themselves seriously as opportunities for edifying—not amusing—young minds. This was the sort of cant that Walter detested and, although he wasn't writing for children—but for himself—his book, when it was finally published by Knopf, arrived as a breath of fresh air in the hitherto stultifyingly serious atmosphere of children's literature. Its gentle rudeness would endear it to generations of children to come—*and* their parents.

The commercial success of the Freddy books would change Walter's life, making it possible for him to abandon full-time editorial work and to focus, instead, on his own writing. But their critical success—*To and Again* was named one of three "books of

---

1. Why Florida? Thanks to a land boom throughout the 1920s, the state was at the forefront of the popular consciousness (see the Marx Brothers' movie, *The Cocoanuts*, for example). Also, Walter's cousin Lucy wintered in Palm Beach every year.

the year" by the prestigious *Horn Book Magazine* and was praised by that arbiter of excellence in children's literature Anne Carroll Moore—would change not only children's literature but also the lives of the countless children who looked forward with breathless anticipation to each year's carefully crafted new "Freddy." And some of them (present company included) were so inspired by Walter's marvelous use of language and manifest love for words that they grew up to become writers and other professional wordsmiths themselves.

For a man who loomed so large in the imaginations and reading lives of so many children (and of their parents who delighted not only in the author's inventive language but also in his satirical puncturing of the pompous and the powerful), Walter offered an unimposing physical presence, being slight in stature (he was only five feet, six inches tall), small-featured, and with a tendency to plumpness; the only thing about him that was thin was his sandy-colored hair.

What did distinguish him, even as a boy, was his extraordinary set of eyebrows! Darker than his hair and far more expressive than the straight line of his mouth, they were eternally arched as if the blue eyes beneath them were looking askance and with secret amusement at a world that took itself far too seriously. "Here, let me help you with that," his expression seems to be saying to a sober-sided world. But it was his work, informed by a sense of humor that could be as dry—and intoxicating—as a good martini, that actually provided the license for laughter.

Though half a century now has passed since the publication of the final Freddy book, the series remains extraordinarily fresh and, well, *funny*. This is a remarkable gift to readers and Walter R. Brooks was a remarkable man who came from a remarkable family. In fact, to begin to understand and to appreciate him we need, first, to examine the context of his childhood and the antecedents who established it.

Himself an amateur genealogist whose personal files contain evidence of his own lifelong fascination with the history of his family, Walter would surely approve of such a strategy. And so, because the past is so manifestly prologue, it's back to the nineteenth century we now go.

2

The Past Is Prologue, Part I

I T SNOWED—AND THEN SOME—IN THE SMALL UPSTATE TOWN of Rome, New York, the morning Walter R. Brooks was born. It was Saturday, January 9, 1886, and according to the local newspaper, the *Sentinel*, the snow was "the worst on record, a storm which no part of the country escaped." By noon a foot of what the paper picturesquely called "the fleecy element" had fallen, and "stages from all points were about half an hour behind and railroad traffic was considerably interfered with."

To those of lively imagination it might seem that the wild weather was Nature herself taking notice of the birth of a man who would grow up to write so memorably about the natural world. This whimsical notion is reinforced by the *Sentinel*'s further report of another natural occurrence that accompanied the author's advent. "A rare celestial sight," it wasn't a star in the East—perish the sacrilegious thought—but instead a rare conjunction of the planet Saturn and the third-magnitude star Mu Geminorium.

If Walter had been born several thousand years earlier in another Rome, the one of Classical antiquity, the storm and celestial phenomenon that accompanied his birth might have been hailed by soothsayers as having significance for his later life. But this was upstate New York in the late nineteenth century and there is no record of any latter-day seer's having made such observations. Nevertheless, the Classical analogy is also invited by the existence of a handsome marble bust of Dr. Walter Rollin Brooks, Walter's paternal

The noblest Roman, Walter's Grandfather Brooks

grandfather and namesake; for it depicts him—in the prevailing fashion of the time—as a toga-clad Roman senator.

Not in fact a politician but a pastor of the Hamilton, New York Baptist Church from 1859 to 1873, Dr. Brooks was also a member of the faculty of Madison University, the precursor to today's Colgate. There the bust sits atop a filing cabinet in a lonely corner of the university archives, staring sightlessly at a beautifully carved wooden desk that the university's Archivist Emeritus Harold Williams once speculated might actually have belonged to Dr. Brooks.

So: an unprecedented snowstorm, a rare celestial sight, a toga-clad bust of a long-dead clergyman, an American town called Rome—are these merely random elements of the first days of a literary life or do they cohere and give them form and portentous meaning? For any biographer, but especially for the biographer of an author, there is a temptation to invest such events with symbolic value for the sake of transforming what might be the merely ordinary into the artful.

Yet it does seem *somehow* significant that remarkable natural phenomena should have visited the birth of this man who would love the natural world and would write so amusingly and eloquently about it in both his books for children and his short stories for adults, and whose grandfather was not only a minister but also a university lecturer in natural history (zoology, geology, biology, and botany) and who also taught a course on the relation of religion and science.

And isn't it interesting that the planet Saturn should have made such a dramatic appearance at the birth of a man who, like his namesake grandfather, would be noteworthy as an adult for his saturnine countenance? "My fun is confined to my writing," an unsmiling Walter told a newspaper reporter in 1938. "I'm not continually trying to be funny, thank goodness."

If each individual's life is, at least in part, the cumulative genetic product of all those lives that have ancestrally preceded it, surely the character, personality, and interests of Walter's grandfather and other ancestors influenced his own. Similarly, the human drama and tragedy that touched so many of those earlier lives must have contributed to Walter's later evolution as an author who chose not to cry but to laugh at the world. Finally, Walter's forebears' significant influence on the religious, intellectual, political, and commercial life of nineteenth-century America might well have contributed to Walter's becoming a uniquely *American* writer who celebrated in his work the traditional American values and enduring small-town ethic that his own ancestors had helped create and, further, whose humor was so firmly rooted in the Yankee tradition of iconoclasm and deflation of authority figures.

Consider, then, in this familial context his paternal grandfather, Walter Rollin Brooks, who was born on August 3, 1821, in Nelson Flats, New York, a charming town in central New York near Cazenovia and southeast of Syracuse. In those long-gone days the village was distinguished for "its good hotels, its noble farms, good and substantial farm building, and fine family mansions of the old style."

More than a century later Walter wrote to the town clerk of Nelson: "I wonder if you can help me find some information I have been looking for for some time. My grandfather (same name as my own) was born in Nelson in 1821. I believe him to have been a grandson of Roger Brooks who was a cabinet-maker in Nelson and was reported to have come there with a large number of families from Pownal, Vermont, in 1796. Are there any town records that would shed light on the question?"

Clerk Louis E. Smith's reply was succinct: "We have nothing on the records for the date you mentioned that I can find."

This may have been due to the fact that Walter had the date wrong. It was 1794, not 1796, when Roger Brooks emigrated from Pownal in southwestern Vermont to this central

New York village named for the famous commander of the British Fleet, even though the nearest body of water was the landlocked Cazenovia Lake and—some years later—the man-made Erie Canal.

Walter *was* right about the profession, though, for Roger Brooks was, indeed, a cabinetmaker and a good one, whose handicraft "gratified the aesthetic tastes of the early settlers."

One of Roger's four sons, Jesse, married a local woman named Olivia Lyon on July 29, 1817, and four years later the couple became the parents of Walter's grandfather (to avoid confusion this grandfather will hereafter be referred to as "Dr. Brooks"). Subsequently, sometime between 1825 and 1830, the young family moved to Mayville in extreme western New York State, where Dr. Brooks's five younger siblings (three boys and two girls) were born (an older brother had been born in 1818).

It was also there, on the banks of beautiful Lake Chautauqua, that the future Dr. Brooks emerged as a "boy preacher" before becoming, at age seventeen, a member of the class of 1843 at Madison University. Now Colgate, Madison then housed a Baptist theological seminary and was located in Hamilton, New York, only twenty-seven miles east of Nelson. Failing to graduate because of problems with his eyes, the first Walter returned to Mayville, where, in 1842, he was ordained and, the same year, married Susan E. Curtice. The first of their three sons, Arthur, was born on July 4, 1843. Their second, Charles H., followed on May 13, 1845. After three years in Mayville the young minister began a series of brief pastorates at Sardinia, New York (1846–47), and then in Perry (1848–1856), which is approximately forty-five miles southwest of Rochester. It was there on July 4, 1849, that Walter's father, William Walter, was born. It was also there that Madison University granted Dr. Brooks the A.M. degree in 1852. Four years later, at the end of 1856, Dr. Brooks responded to a call from the American Baptist Home Missionary Office and jour-neyed west to Madison, Wisconsin, to become pastor of the First Baptist Church there.

Tragically, less than three months later, after a brief ten-day illness, his young wife Susan died of typhoid pneumonia.

Cared for in his bereavement by a sister, who also took care of his three young sons, Dr. Brooks faithfully remained in Madison for two more years, though he was often depressed and his prayers and sermons were notably gloomy. One of these, "A Prayer of Submission," survives:

> My heart, darkened and torn with its grieves and fears flees as a bird to its mountain, to Thee. In Thee, from whom my trial cometh, alone is there refuge for my soul. Thou hast created the affections which life wounds and bereaves; Thou wilt look pitifully upon the bleeding of their wounds. Lo, I submit myself to Thy will, venturing only to implore with humility Thy mercy, to temper for me Thy deserved judgments and that whatever it shall please Thee to take away from me, it may please Thee to leave me the comfort of Thy peace.

Finally, another summons came, this one calling him back to his old college town of Hamilton, where, on January 1, 1859, he became pastor of the First Baptist Church.

Like his grandson, Dr. Brooks, now thirty-eight, was of medium height and his appearance was unimposing, except for one singular feature: "his head," we are told, "bespoke no ordinary brain."

Though universally regarded as brilliant—one observer said he had a mind "thirty years in advance of its time"—the young minister often appeared sad; his voice from the pulpit, "a solemn monotone" and his manner, introspective.

Apparently as much a philosopher as a preacher, he was less concerned with the conduct of life than with "large, eternal truths: God, man, sin, redemption (and) eternal life." "In fact," one admirer recalled, "no

Dr. Walter Rollin Brooks

thinker has stood higher than Dr. Brooks in the range and loftiness of his thinking."

Too lofty, perhaps, for while Walter was once quoted as calling his namesake a "fire and brimstone Baptist preacher," the opposite was the case, some complaining that because Dr. Brooks did not appear "to take any special pains to adapt his preaching to habits of mind in the people," his sermons sailed over the heads of his congregation.

But not over those of the university administrators who embraced the new arrival and named him Secretary of the Education Board in 1859 (an office he filled until his death in 1888), a Member of the Corporation in 1864, and Secretary of the Board of Trustees from 1865 to 1873 and again from 1883 to 1888. "He had a beautiful hand," archivist Williams recalled in 1986, "and his minutes were a joy."

Perhaps because "in the pulpit he was eminently a teacher," it is not too surprising that he was also invited to become a member of the Madison faculty, teaching natural history (which then incorporated geology, zoology, biology, and botany). Natural science was as much a beloved pastime as a mental discipline to Dr. Brooks. His second wife, Abby Kinmouth, recalled his habit, even when still a pastor, of "dropping back in his chair with a book of science to rest himself after the labor of Sunday was over."

To a modern observer it would appear that Dr. Brooks was more amateur naturalist than rigorous scientist, "in love" as he was "with nature and full of its poetry and its life," often praying "in silent recesses of the wood" or meditating "amid the dewy dampness of the swampland, in the myriad companionship of the ferns and mosses, diatoms and amoebas."

Clearly, too, it was not the classroom—where he was reportedly an uninspired lecturer and abhorred giving tests— but the field that was Dr. Brooks's true métier (like the milliner Harriet Peebles, one of Walter's creations from a century later [see *Freddy and the Popinjay*]). His colleagues recalled his "enthusiastic conduct of field excursions" while a former student fondly remembered him as "an enthusiastic believer in field work" and extolled his "large-heartedness toward students who could not afford the extra expense of a (field trip) to Trenton Falls." Dr. Brooks routinely paid for their expenses himself, giving "many a tired student a much needed outing and starting him on a method of restful field work which has been a source of benefit and pleasure through years of hard professional labor." (Many have also noted that Dr. Brooks himself routinely paid for students' classroom materials when they couldn't afford them.)

This same enthusiasm enlivened Dr. Brooks's discussion of the flora and fauna of the field that he brought into the classroom. Years after his death, his Madison successor Professor Albert Perry Brigham recalled the power of imagination that led Dr. Brooks to "personify all plants and lowly animals and even fossils. As he handled them and showed them to his students, he felt the dignity of their life."

This sounds startlingly like his grandson Walter's own ability to anthropomorphize animals, as demonstrated in his famous Freddy the Pig books. Also like Walter, Dr. Brooks was a writer who was lauded for his "rare, pure use of simple English." The most personal of his four books, *God and Nature in Life,* was published posthumously in 1889 and was hailed as a book that "in warmth and vigor of thought, in beauty of expression, in devotional sweetness and strength is one of the most delightful that I know." Dr. Brooks's other three books were the more utilitarian texts: *Elements of Zoology, Invertebrate* (1886), *A Brief Treatise of Geology* (1884), and *Notes on Lectures in Zoology* (1881).

The distinguished theologian William Newton Clarke was always the most enthusiastic evaluator of Dr. Brooks as a teacher, claiming that just as he had revolutionized the thinking of the First Baptist Church, so "in six months he had revolutionized the thinking of Madison University and young minds were entering into deeper things than they had known before."

One of these "things," startlingly enough, was Darwinian evolution, which—according to Clarke—Dr. Brooks "fully accepted as the Divine method in creation." Clarke adds, "He was a scientist of the modern school who looked upon the world of nature in the light of recent discovery. He lived in two worlds: the world of nature and the world of Christ."

It was in the latter world where he was celebrated as a man of acute social sympathy. "He knew the common life and honored it," a colleague, Professor N. L. Andrews, asserted. "The humble, the poor, the neglected saw him in their homes more often than did the prosperous and the prominent." As would be the case with his grandson Walter two generations later, "This sympathy was rooted in his liking for the common man." And like Walter, Dr. Brooks "rejected sham and artificiality."

The Doctor seems to have been wonderfully sympathetic—perhaps because of his own personal sorrows and losses—and was "widely sought for visitation of the sick and burial of the dead." According to his step-grandson, Dr. Malcolm Kinmouth Smith, he had "a wonderfully kind and pleasing personality," and his generosity extended beyond students who could not afford that Trenton Falls field trip to the families of Civil War soldiers who were "often helped in their straits by his free-handed, unobtrusive benefactions."

"Unobtrusive" seems to be the operative word in this or any evaluation of Dr. Brooks's character, for all observers—no matter how much they disagreed about other aspects of his character—concurred about his extraordinary diffidence and modesty. "He was constitutionally unobtrusive," Andrews declared, "and declined prominence."

"His constant desire," Clarke concurred, "was that his own service should never be exaggerated or that of others overlooked. He was unspeakably happy in being able to give in the manner of the world's bounty for the relief of suffering and want without caring that they should know whence the bounty came. . . . The breath of praise disgusted him; compliments upon his preaching he utterly abhorred."

Was he really this saintly? Well, perhaps not altogether. Professor Andrews does admit, "He was not insensitive to appreciation *if delicately conveyed and expressed* [emphasis added], but all fulsome praise he disdained."

In fact, Andrews claims, "When the University in 1863 gave him (an honorary) doctorate, he was loath to wear the title."

In a letter to the Hamilton *Republic*, a local man named Orsino Beebee confirmed this: "He wouldn't accept the degree. As he said, 'He never practiced medicine.'"

There is probably more of Beebee than of Brooks in this claim, but it is an attractive anecdote about a man who was richly gifted in intellect, sensibility, and conscience—and in worldly goods, too, at least after he married Abby Kinmouth of Newton, Massachusetts. Twelve years his junior, she was already the widow of a wealthy Boston merchant and brought a dowry of some $500,000 (roughly $6,500,000 today) to her second marriage. The newlyweds bought an elegant two-story house on leafy Broad Street across from the Baptist Church and near the university campus. There, according to Beebee, "they kept a fine equipage and coachman and lived in style." Archivist Williams agrees that there was "considerable hospitality" at the Brooks house and that in terms of local aristocracy the Brookses occupied "pretty much the top level."

There is no extant record of their marriage date but it must have taken place sometime between the award of the doctorate in 1863 and 1868 when the newly expanded Brooks family traveled to Europe, Egypt, and Palestine. A deliberate as well as original thinker, Dr. Brooks is said to have studied his route so thoroughly beforehand "as to be often independent of the guide." (One

The Brooks home in Hamilton

wonders if this trip might have been the later inspiration for Walter's father's decision to study music in Germany, where he was a student at the University of Leipzig from 1870 to 1872. William's elegant, framed diploma hung for years in an upstairs bedroom in Walter's house in Roxbury, New York).

In the meantime the Civil War was raging and there was no question where Dr. Brooks's sympathies lay. An ardent Union sympathizer, his loyalty was tested when his oldest son, Arthur, went off to fight for the North. A boy of unusual intelligence and promise, Arthur had graduated from Madison University at the age of eighteen in August 1861. In October he enlisted in the 61st Regiment of the New York State Voluntary Infantry. He was appointed captain of Company G and on April 15, 1862, was promoted to major. Tragically, one month later, following the siege of Yorktown, the boy contracted typhoid fever and died on May 12, 1862. He was eighteen years and ten months old.

Three years later his younger brother Charles, then a sophomore at Madison University, died his own untimely death. He was twenty years and five months old.

Among Walter's papers is a two-page, handwritten manuscript recording many of these tragic passings in the shaky hand of an obviously elderly writer. Next to the death records of the two sons is written, in what seems to be singular understatement, "These are they that come out of great tribulation."

Despite these tribulations Dr. Brooks faithfully continued in the ministry for an additional eight years, until 1873 when he resigned as pastor of the Hamilton Baptist Church after fourteen years of service. Although he was reportedly a "sportsman, a crack shot on the wing, and a good fisherman," his health had never been robust and he was finding the demands of pastoral duties increasingly daunting. Since money was no longer a consideration thanks to his marriage, he began what one hopes was a pleasant semi-retirement.

Certainly he continued to find solace and inspiration in the beauty of the natural world. It may have been at this time that he wrote "An Act of Worship," one of his most moving short meditations (and one of his own personal favorites):

I thank Thee, O God, for all the silent, quiet places on the hills and in the fields and in the deeper haunts of silence in the woods—silent, quiet places where Thy Spirit broods and rests, ungrieved by the discords of human life, and where my spirit finds and feels Thy presence as I do not elsewhere; silent, quiet places, so like another world, and where the spirits of the dead gather on the outskirts of this world, and make their presence felt even to the spirit cumbered still with its clay.

I thank Thee, O Lord . . . for the sweet sense of a home in nature, begotten of these sympathies, even when the social home is desolate.

In 1882, after nine years of this quiet life of communing with nature, Dr. Brooks returned to the pulpit—not the highly visible one of Hamilton, where each Sunday was an occasion for critical public and collegial scrutiny, but the pulpit of a new church in rustic Randallsville, a village three to five miles south-southwest of Hamilton. It was "a snug little chapel, having a decent cupola, a spacious yard, and sheds for the accommodation of teams. The chapel had a tidy look, was convenient, and would seat two to three hundred people." In a sense this church, which had been dedicated on July 26, 1882, belonged to Dr. Brooks, since he and his wife had paid fully half the cost of its construction. But in a larger sense it was the man who belonged to the church, "for the labor of these years was just the kind that would most delight him, for he preached there in a quiet place, to a limited congregation, where he could simply be himself."

But even here there would be no sanctuary from sorrow.

In 1880 his youngest and only surviving son, William Walter, who was married by that time to the wealthy Fannie Stevens of Rome, New York, became ill with what was described as a "nervous disorder."

Despite the progressive nature of the disease, Willie, as he was known in Hamilton—or "Professor Brooks," as he was known in Rome, where he gave private music lessons—was able to continue working until early 1888 when he became so ill he had to abandon all of his professional duties.

The strain of the son's illness may have hastened Dr. Brooks's own death, which arrived in an almost theatrical fashion. On Sunday morning, February 19, 1888, Dr. Brooks was conducting the opening services at the Randallsville Chapel when he suddenly felt his left side becoming paralyzed. He was able to dismiss the congregation before collapsing from this stroke (or apoplexy, as it was called in those days). The congregants were afraid to move him and so he lingered, unconscious, for approximately forty-eight hours in the sanctuary of the chapel before dying there on Tuesday, February 21, at the age of sixty-six.

Fourteen years after his death, his widow Abby Kinmouth Brooks presented to Madison University the marble bust described earlier. It was placed in the library under the memorial tablet bearing the names of the men of the university who had fallen in the Civil War. Arthur Brooks's name was among them.

Four years after that, the friends of Dr. Brooks presented a memorial tablet designed by Tiffany & Company to the Hamilton Baptist Church. Placed on the eastern wall of the auditorium just north of the platform, it reads, simply, "Walter R. Brooks, D.D., Minister, January 1, 1859–October 1, 1873."

3

The Past Is Prologue, Part II

WHEN DR. BROOKS'S YOUNGEST SON, WILLIAM WALTER, wed Miss Fannie Stevens, "a lady of culture," on Wednesday, January 23, 1878, he married into one of the leading families of Rome, New York.

First settled by the British in approximately 1725, Rome is situated on the Mohawk River at the head of the Mohawk Valley, approximately thirty miles north of Hamilton and ninety miles northwest of Albany. Historians remember it as the site of the first flying in Revolutionary War battle of the newly designed American flag. According to local tradition, the flag was fashioned from a woman's red petticoat, a soldier's white shirt, and a captain's blue military cloak. One wonders if Walter had this in mind when, in *Wiggins for President*, he described the creation of another flag—that of the First Animal Republic: "With a pair of old blue overalls and an old white nightshirt and some old red flannel underwear of Mr. Bean's . . . she [Mrs. Wiggins] had laid out the flag and then Adoniram had stitched it up for her on the sewing-machine."

Rome is also remembered as the birthplace of the Erie Canal. Construction of the celebrated waterway began in 1817. A second canal, the Black River Canal, ran north from Rome and figured, many years later, in Walter's book *The Clockwork Twin*. (Speaking of books, Rome and the Erie Canal figure prominently in two once-celebrated historical novels by Walter D. Edmonds: *Drums Along the Mohawk* and *Rome Haul*.)

"Rome bustled with the surge of transportation," one early observer noted, "canal boats carried farm implements west and grain and potatoes east; lusty 'canawlers' crowded the dock-lined basin with their craft and taverns shook with their rough talk and loud laughter."

In 1826 Walter's maternal grandfather, Samuel Barron Stevens, then a twenty-one-year-old journeyman shoemaker, arrived in this raucous frontier town from Boston. A short, untidy-looking man with a perpetual scowl, Sam was the second Stevens son to be infected with pioneer fever. His older brother, John C., had already gone "to seek his fortune in the then far west" of Rochester, New York.

Little is known about John, but Sam is a different story. If Walter's paternal grandfather, Dr. Brooks, was a notable thinker, his maternal grandfather, Samuel Barron Stevens, was a notable doer, a veritable mover and shaker. In the best Horatio Alger tradition, Sam "married up." On October 22, 1827, a year after arriving in Rome, he wed Elizabeth Tibbits, daughter of one of Rome's leading citizens. Though she was born in a log cabin in 1812, Elizabeth's father, Henry Tibbits, who had originally come from Rhode Island, was a trustee of the village and a successful entrepreneur, owning a hotel, a concert hall, and considerable commercial real estate.

Samuel Barron Stevens and Elizabeth Tibbits Stevens,
Walter's maternal grandparents

In 1828, Sam, too, went into business, joining in partnership with Alva Whedon and Thomas Dugan to form Stevens, Dugan, and Company, purveyors of groceries and general merchandise. Three years later Sam—this time in partnership with John Whittmore—began a new business, selling leather and shoes (an appropriate choice for a former journeyman shoemaker). The two partners also acquired three tanneries in West Rome, North Bay, and Taberg (a hamlet that figures in Walter's book *The Clockwork Twin*).

In addition to his business activities, Sam—like his father-in-law—was occupied with public service, succeeding Henry as village trustee in 1834. Seven years later the voters elected Sam Justice of the Peace for a four-year term. "Squire," the title that accompanied the position, endured until Sam's death in 1884 and even longer—perhaps into the next century when his grandson Walter named his pet cocker spaniel "Squire." (Walter publicly claimed the name derived from a short story sale to *Esquire* magazine that provided enough money to buy the dog, but one wonders.)

Sam and Elizabeth had eight children. The first, Edward, was born in 1828; Henry followed in 1830, and a third son, William, was born in 1832. (Growing up to sport a bushy beard, the seemingly taciturn William may have been the inspiration for Freddy's owner, the farmer, William Bean.) In 1834 a first daughter, Lucy, was born, followed in 1836 by another son, Jim, and then Sarah in 1838. A third daughter, Rhoda, was born in 1844 and, finally, on April 13, 1848, the last Stevens child was born. It was Fannie who, thirty-eight years later, would become Walter's mother.

In 1851, three years after Fannie's birth, Sam's shoe and leather business failed, although the three tanneries remained in the Stevens family until his death in 1884. How to provide, now, for a wife and the six children still at home—"home" being a spacious new house of red brick on Court Street, just west of George, the construction of which had been completed that same year?

It would hardly have seemed reasonable for the then forty-six-year-old man to follow the example of his adventurous

third son William, who—five years earlier at the age of fourteen
—had shipped aboard a merchant vessel and was now nearing
the end of his third circumnavigation of the globe.

Sam's oldest son Edward provided a more reasonable
example. Demonstrating the same pioneer spirit that had animated his father's move from Boston to Rome, Edward had
left home in 1849 (also at the age of twenty-one) to pursue his
fortune in the California gold rush of that year. Edward found
success not in gold mining but in commerce, becoming general
superintendent of the Adams Express Company. This example,
along with the second gold rush of 1852, apparently convinced
Sam to become a pioneer again himself, for in September of
that year—along with his second son Henry—he set off for
California to remain in the Golden State for the next fifteen
years. The same year, 1852, William finally returned from sea
to join his father and brothers in California. This left only Jim,
then sixteen, at home in Rome.

Like his son Edward, Sam went to work for the Adams
Express Company, becoming an agent at Murphy's in
Calaveras County, the home of Mark Twain's celebrated frog.

Displaying his usual energy and ambition, Sam then
became, in short order, a district judge and a legislator, serving
one term from 1855 to 1856. A Democrat, he also was a delegate to the 1856 Democratic National Convention that nominated James Buchanan as its presidential candidate. In 1864
Sam was reelected as a delegate to the Democratic National
Convention to be held in Chicago in July.

The Civil War years, which claimed the life of Dr. Brooks's
oldest son, were kinder to Sam. Himself too old to fight (he was
fifty-six when the conflict started), he was now living in San
Francisco, where he had become engaged "very successfully"
in the banking business. Though they were young enough,
none of his four sons fought in the war, either. Jim, now in his
mid-twenties, was working for the Watertown Railroad, and
later, from 1863 to '66, was in charge of shipping for the
Western Transportation Company in New York, where he
doubtless met the woman, Sarah Sharpe, who would become
his wife.

Meanwhile, the oldest son Edward, who had been a superintendent for the Adams Express Company, had been hired to manage a mine in the Santa Rita Mountains south of Tucson, Arizona. Edward sailed from San Francisco to Guaymas, Mexico, accompanied by Samuel F. Butterworth, president of the Arizona Mining Company. Here is how the Rome *Sentinel* described what happened next:

> The two came from Guaymas to Tucson, where Stevens was met by J.B. Mills of the mining company. Mills and Stevens set out on horseback for the mine. They knew the Apaches often were about but went on into the mountains, where a narrow canyon gave a band of Apaches opportunity to ambush them. It is said that two Mexican boys tried to warn them with cries of "Los Apaches" but were not heard. Help came too late because only the mutilated bodies of the two men were found.

It was December 29, 1863. In the short space of a year and a half, both of Walter's grandfathers had lost their eldest sons.

Edward was buried temporarily in the small mine cemetery until his brother, the well-traveled William—now twenty-one and himself working as a miner in California—could arrive and undertake yet another arduous journey, transporting the body of his oldest brother across the continent and through the territories of nine different Indian nations en route, occasionally sleeping on the lead-lined coffin to guard it until they reached Rome and its cemetery, where the remains found permanent burial.

Such derring-do seems to have been routine for this apparently most adventurous Stevens who, having consigned Edward's remains to consecrated ground, returned to California. Altogether, William spent sixteen years in the West, where he worked as a miner, a stage

Walter's adventurous Uncle William Stevens

guard, a mine watch, and, in short, "encountered every phase of life which was common to those who lived on the western frontier in the early days of prospecting and settlement."

William spent 1867, his last year in the West, in Arizona, probably at Fort Yuma, where his older brother, Henry—who would have been thirty-eight that year—was a successful merchant, though he (Henry) later returned to San Francisco where he engaged in the commission business. As for William, he returned to Rome in 1868 when he was thirty-six.

Why? Perhaps he was simply weary of adventuring, but his return was probably more the result of his father's own return to the hometown the previous year (1867). Though he was now sixty-three, Sam was clearly not ready to retire. Gone for fifteen years, he had, nevertheless, maintained both his home on Court Street and ownership of the three tanneries. Having prospered as a banker in San Francisco, he quickly resumed an active commercial and political life in Rome. On May 1, 1869, he became president of the Oneida County Savings Bank and, the next year, was also named president of the Rome Merchant Iron Mill.

In 1875 Sam, then seventy, became the third mayor of Rome, the former village having been incorporated as a city in 1870. He was reportedly elected by an unprecedentedly large number of votes. Completing the term in 1877, he then became president of the Central National Bank of Rome.

The previous year, 1876, had been one of sorrow, not celebration; it was then that Henry, home from California to visit friends and recuperate from a lengthy illness, suddenly died on August 19 at the age of forty-six. His death was ascribed to apoplexy, which would subsequently be listed as the cause of the deaths of his father, his brothers William and Jim, his sisters Rhoda and Lucy, and of Dr. Brooks, as well.

Henry was the third of Sam's children to die. The rest of the family, however, seemed to be thriving. The daring William, now forty-two, had embraced domesticity on his return to Rome, marrying in 1869 and fathering two children—a son, William Henry, and a daughter, Blanche. Having worked as collector for the Erie Canal from 1868 to 1870,

William became a bookkeeper for the Washington Flouring Mills and then for his father's Central National Bank.

Lucy, now forty-two, and her sister Rhoda, thirty-two, were still living at home, spinsters who would years later be immortalized in their nephew Walter's Freddy books as the old maid ducks, Alice and Emma.

Fannie, the youngest child, was now twenty-eight and, like Lucy and Rhoda, still single, "a young woman of culture, highly esteemed in the society of Rome and a faithful member of the Zion Episcopal Church and of the Wednesday Morning Club."

This accounts for all of the Stevens family except for the fourth son, Jim, whose life would make an interesting book in itself, since he was surely, as historian Isaac F. Marcosson called him, "one of the most picturesque of all the Romans."

Jim's return to Rome from New York, where he had been working for the Western Transportation Company, seems to have preceded his father's by only a matter of months and was equally successful. Sam returned to take over the Oneida Savings Bank while Jim returned to take over the old hometown itself, being elected president of the village for the first of two terms in 1866. In 1868, while serving his second term, he was elected to the State Legislature and was reelected to a second term in 1869. In 1870 he was elected supervisor of the 4th Ward in the newly formed City of Rome, while in 1876 he was elected a delegate to the Democratic National Convention and, in 1879, was elected to the State Senate.

In 1872, in partnership with A. M. Jackson, Jim formed the A. M. Jackson Company, a dry goods purveyor, and became its principal shareholder, maintaining his interest until his death in 1912. In 1886 he also acquired the Rome Merchant Iron Mill and served as its sole owner and president until 1911. A year after acquiring the mill, Jim was elected to the first of two terms as Mayor of Rome and in 1889 he was reelected, serving until 1891. At the midterm of Jim's ownership of the mill in 1896 it was producing 12,000 tons annually and employing three hundred workers.

Jim's great success in politics and in business suggests that he was charismatic, larger-than-life, and every bit as ambitious and energetic as his father. Given these qualities of character, his stocky, thickset body, close-cropped hair, magnificent walrus mustache, and what Marcosson calls "his rough and ready manner," it is probably true that "he was always spoiling for a fight. He encouraged brawls in the mill, squared off opponents in a ring and watched the fun."

He was also in the habit of boarding the Ontario and Western train at the passenger station and riding the two blocks to his office. One can imagine the pleasure this gave to a man whose first job had been selling newspapers to passengers on the Watertown Railroad and the delight in the form of address he was accorded from the late 1860s until the end of his life: no longer just "Jim" or even "Mr. Stevens," he was now universally known as "The Honorable Jim" (not unlike the Bismuth children's "Honorable Pa" in Walter's book *Freddy and the Space Ship*).

Such honorifics seem to have been something of a small-town, nineteenth-century American tradition, and they were evenly divided between the Stevens and Brooks families, each getting two: "Squire" Stevens and "The Honorable Jim" Stevens being balanced by "Dr. Brooks" and, in the next generation, William Walter's "Professor Brooks."

Walter's uncle, the Hon. Jim Stevens

It was, as previously noted, the Professor who united these two remarkable families by marrying Fannie Stevens on Wednesday, January 23, 1878, at the Zion Episcopal Church in Rome. These youngest children of two of the leading families of Rome and Hamilton married relatively late in life. Fannie was thirty years old and Willie was twenty-nine. Having graduated from the University of Leipzig in 1872 with a degree in music, he was not only musical but was also, one old Hamiltonian recalled, "the best ballplayer I ever saw behind the bat." Football, not baseball, would be his

Walter's father, William Walter Brooks, and mother, Fannie Stevens Brooks

son Walter's sport, but baseball would have its innings, too, seventy-seven years later in Walter's book *Freddy and the Baseball Team from Mars*.

Home base for the young married couple was New York City, where Willie was associated with the New York Musical Institute. Their first child, a daughter, Elsie Curtice, was born there on November 5, 1878. Willie and Fannie remained in New York at 487 Fifth Avenue for three years, until 1881, when they returned to Rome, settling at 63 George Street. Then in 1884 they moved to a comfortably rambling two-story house with a wraparound porch at 218 George Street, diagonally across the street from the Stevens family home at 42 Court Street.

Willie was now self-employed as a teacher of music, giving private piano lessons in his home and directing concerts at the Rome Opera House. He was, one of his students recalled, "a music teacher of high order. I have never forgotten his insistence on the cultural details of piano playing. I have no doubt that his example has stayed with me unwittingly through the years."

Also marrying late was the Honorable Jim, who was thirty-five when he wed Sarah A. Sharpe of New York City in 1871.

218 N. George Street, Walter's boyhood home

Like his older brother William, Jim would also father two children, a boy and a girl, Samuel B. II and Lucy K.

This family pattern of two children, a boy and a girl, was continued by Fannie and Willie when, on January 9, 1886, a baby boy, Walter Rollin, joined his older sister as the newest member of the household.

Losses

WALTER WOULD BE THE LAST OF THE STEVENS/BROOKS grandchildren who, in 1886, ranged in age from infancy to sixteen. Though new life flourished in the 1880s, it was also the decade of the death of both grandfathers. Dr. Brooks lived long enough to see both of his grandchildren, though Walter was only two and Elsie ten when he died on February 21, 1888.

Squire Stevens, however, dying at the age of seventy-eight after an eleven-week illness on May 4, 1884, did not live to see Fannie's second child. The Rome *Sentinel*'s headlines reported the "Death of Squire Stevens" and "The Eventful Life of a Boston Boy Who Came to Rome Over Half a Century Ago." The lengthy obituary that followed concluded, rather flatly, with the simple declaration, "Mr. Stevens had been a useful man."

Indeed. How successful he had also been, at least materially, is suggested by his will, in which he left his widow Elizabeth—in addition to "his house and lot no. 42 Court Street, household furniture and all personal property in and about the family residence"—the then very considerable sum of $25,000 (equivalent to roughly $530,000 today). To his surviving children William, Jim, Lucy, Rhoda, and Fannie he bequeathed "all the rest, residue and remainder of his real estate" plus "all money, papers representing money, bank stock and railroad stock . . . share and share alike."

The value of these individual shares is impossible to calculate now, but it is probably no coincidence that William, then fifty-two, "retired" and that two years later Jim pur-

chased the Rome Merchant Iron Mill, which had been founded in 1868 and which his father had served as both trustee
and president.

Sam's will was written in October 1876. Three years
later, on May 30, 1879, he added an interesting codicil
directed at Fannie, who, by that time, had been married for
seventeen months. Essentially it stipulated that Jim should
act as executor of Fannie's share of their father's estate, pay-
ing to her semi-annually the "full interest and income there-
of and no more . . . and no part of said principal sum shall
ever be paid" to Fannie, though on her death her share
would go to her children "and heirs of her body" to be
divided equally "when they shall respectively arrive at the
age of twenty-one."

This, of course, promised a substantial inheritance for
Walter and Elsie, but one can only speculate what it meant
in terms of Sam's feelings for Fannie and her marriage. Why
didn't he trust her to manage her own affairs? After all, he
made no such provision to protect the principal share of his
other daughters. But, of course, they were unmarried. Did the
codicil reflect some animosity between Sam and Willie? True,
it might have reflected Sam's concern about providing for
Fannie after her husband's death, but the latter's terminal illness didn't manifest itself until two years after the codicil was
added.

We will probably never know the answer to these tantalizing questions. But one thing we do know: the Honorable Jim
was clearly viewed as the next head of the family, a position he
assumed on the death of his father and the retirement of his
older brother, William.

With Sam's death, Jim became his successor as president
of the Central National Bank, a position he held for four
years, resigning, then, to give greater attention to his new
enterprise, the Rome Merchant Iron Mill. In 1894 the Central
Bank re-entered Jim's life when he was appointed its receiver
"at the personal request of President Grover Cleveland. He
settled up the affairs of the Bank to the satisfaction of the
depositors and with highest credit to all concerned."

Uncle Jim Stevens's mansion

This effort seems to have marked the end of Jim's extremely active civic life, since he retired from public affairs and thereafter found, according to a local newspaper account, "his greatest happiness in his home at 315 N. Washington Street." And why not? For Jim appeared to have built his dream house. Described as "the most attractive residence in the City," the three-story Potsdam red sandstone mansion took two years (1890–'92) to construct at a cost of $100,000 (roughly $2,000,000 today). Measuring 65 by 90 feet (exclusive of verandas and porticoes) and of Romanesque architecture, it was furnished with Long Meadow Kidby brown sandstone and boasted base trimmings of white Massachusetts granite.

Though not a member of any clubs or secret societies, Jim must have entertained on a fairly large scale, since his dining room table could seat thirty and the entire third floor was devoted to a splendid ballroom. "There were beautiful parties in that ballroom," one observer recalled. "The Stevens always had a special cotillion at Christmas. Mrs. Stevens was very musical and enjoyed giving concerts and parties."

The mansion itself was lavishly appointed and furnished with hand-carved ceilings, frescoed walls, Japanese silks, Persian rugs, imported tapestries, and more. The house still stands but has not been a private residence for many years. Acquired for $15,000 in 1946 by the Veterans of Foreign Wars, it is now home to Post 2246.

The same decade that saw Jim's retirement from public life was ushered in by the death of Walter's father, William Walter, on February 16, 1890. He was forty-one years old and his death was attributed to "cerebral effusion. For several months previous to his death he endured great suffering," according to the *Sentinel*. He left a widow, Fannie, who was then forty-two, and two small children, Elsie, ten, and Walter, four.

Six years later, on July 7, 1896, Sam's widow, Elizabeth, died at the age of eighty-six. "She had no particular disease," the local newspaper reported, "her death being due to a general breaking down brought on by old age."

Five years would pass before another death occurred but this one would change Walter's life dramatically. On Tuesday, May 21, 1901, Fannie was standing on her front porch saying good-bye to her sister Rhoda, who had been visiting. Turning, she entered the house and was immediately "seized with a feeling of faintness and called to Miss Margaret Roberts, a friend and employee of the household. Before Miss Roberts reached her, Mrs. Brooks fell to the floor, expiring instantly."

Fannie had had a heart attack though, the *Sentinel* stated, "There had been nothing to suggest any symptoms of heart disease." At age fifty-three, the paper effused, "her life had been one of unceasing activity in many lines and by reason of it she had formed many warm friendships. She was always ready to aid anyone in need of assistance and was the possessor of many capabilities which she used to every advantage of her many deeds of kindness. In her family circle she was the best of mothers and a very devoted wife."

A memorial resolution of the Wednesday Morning Club, which was devoted to self-improvement through the study of current events and literature, noted that Fannie's "greatest love since girlhood of the master poets of English literature and her keen appreciation of the true and beautiful in art made her influence as a club member invaluable and inspiring."

Five months to the day later, in a kind of cruel coda, William Stevens died. "He had been in poor health all the summer but his condition was not considered at all serious until about two weeks ago. His death was caused by a stroke of paralysis." William was sixty-nine and his life, the *Sentinel* reminded its readers, "had been one of varied experiences. In conversation he was modest and unassuming and not given to relating his stories except to intimate friends. He was alike to all men at all times and was everybody's friend."

Even given a certain large latitude for hyperbole, these two newspaper accounts and their reports of the "unreality of Fannie's unexpected death," her readiness in life to assist others, and her brother William's capacity for friendship oddly foreshadowed two important themes in Walter's writing: first, a retreat into unreality (fantasy) and, second, the overwhelming importance and enduring value, in the real world, of friendship and the expression of that friendship through helping others.

But all of that was still in the future. For the present moment in 1901 Walter, only fifteen years old, was orphaned; his mother, father, grandparents, and six of his ten uncles and aunts were all dead.

5

Second Chance

"I T OCCURRED TO ME," WALTER WOULD WRITE FORTY-SEVEN years later, "that a man's evidence about his childhood would be as incorrect and as slanted by his ambitions and vanity and so on, as much of the evidence given in court."

True as this may be, there seems little reason to impeach Walter's own later testimony that his was a nice childhood, or that his hometown, Rome, was a pleasant place. For while it is true that his father died scarcely a month and a half after his fourth birthday, Fannie, the "best of mothers," lived on. Two doting aunts resided less than a block away and there were uncles and cousins close at hand as well—an extended family that provided the security, comfort, and prestige of belonging to one of Rome's leading families.

Beyond that, life was full of the kind of pleasures that a small town provided before the turn of the century (Rome's population in 1892, when Walter was six, was 13,638.) They were the kind of pleasures that Walter remembered in a sweetly autobiographical story he wrote for the *Saturday Evening Post* in 1948. Titled "Second Chance," it offers a day in the life of Thomas H. Brewer, "chairman of the board of a small corporation," who gets caught in a "time kink" and, for twelve hours, is transported back to his childhood.

While it is the fictional Mr. Brewer who gets transported, it is pretty obviously Walter's childhood he visits and the discoveries he makes are the kinds of modest but universal childhood experiences that are lost in the process of growing up:

First he discovered that it was fun to run upstairs. He ran up and down one step at a time and then two steps at a time, and he was just starting down three at a time when his father began to roar, so he slid down the banister the rest of the way and went outdoors.

The next thing that struck him was the pleasure of wasting time. For the past thirty years there had never been a wasted minute. [*Not* like Walter, whom his friend Frank Bellamy once called "the laziest man in America."] Now, as a boy of twelve with neither business nor social obligations to fit into the long afternoon hours, he rediscovered the delight of just looking at things. He spent fifteen minutes watching two small clouds creep slowly up the western sky and another ten staring at the sunlit grass and letting the green soak into him. For a long time he watched a spider spinning a web; he didn't try to understand the creature's engineering problem but watched her movements without thinking about them.

Since Walter's own mother died when he was fifteen, the most touching discovery Mr. Brewer makes (at least for the reader) regards his mother:

Now Mr. Brewer's mother had died when he was twenty, so he remembered her perfectly. He had loved her very much. He still loved her very much but now he was looking at his real mother and not at his remembrance of her, and this remembrance became all at once very remote and a little ridiculous. For she was not slim and lovely as he had always remembered her but plump and rather homely.

Walter overstates the mother's appearance for dramatic effect. As a few surviving photos show, Fannie was not homely, but she was plump! "At the same time," the story continues, "she was much more

Fannie and Walter, mother and son.
"She was not slim and lovely . . ."

wonderful, much more—he couldn't define it. But he saw that the remembrance he had kept for nearly forty years was a very thin and cheaply prettied-up facsimile."

Having made this point, Walter returns Mr. Brewer to the present where "what astonished and confused him was not the miracle of having relived twelve hours of his boyhood but the realization that in growing up, he had lost his past. That gradually he had re-arranged his memories to be more in keeping with his growing importance until the picture of the past he carried with him was completely unrecognizable to the boy he had been."

There is no knowing how recognizable to the boy Walter's adult picture would have been, for—being a private person— he shared tantalizingly few written memories of his childhood.

He did remember for the record, "There were no movies or radios in those days, and we had to organize our own entertainment." And we may surmise that reading was probably the chief form this took, for Walter also acknowledged that "I had always read a good deal more than anybody but my mother had thought was good for me." In "Second Chance" Mr. Brewer's mother gives him a copy of *The Merry Adventures of Robin Hood*, which was one of Freddy the Pig's favorite books, too (see *Freddy the Pilot*), and Walter's personal library was sprinkled with books *his* mother had given him, including— yes—*The Merry Adventures of Robin Hood* (the wonderful Howard Pyle edition).

For another form of juvenile entertainment, Walter recalled, "We wrote and put on plays up in our barn. The audience had to shut their eyes while the scenes were being shifted between the acts. The audience was mostly aunts and they got tired of shutting their eyes after a while and made us a curtain. The first writing I ever did was part of an act in one of these plays."

Unfortunately, none of those plays survives, but Walter used the experience to good effect in *Freddy's Cousin Weedly*, when the animals put on a play for the benefit of Mr. Bean's Aunt Effie and Uncle Lucius Snedeker (Walter himself had a paternal great-uncle named Lucius, by the way).

One wonders if Walter's own six aunts (four in Rome and two in Rochester) were as "difficult" as the aunts—like Effie—

Walter's Aunt Rhoda and his sister Elsie

in his fiction. For in addition to that independent and sharp-tongued one, there are the equally difficult aunts Minerva and Elmira of Freddy's friend, Mr. Camphor (Walter also had a great-Aunt Elmira).

> "I didn't know you had an aunt," Freddy said.
> "Goodness [Mr. Camphor replied]. Everybody has aunts. I've got two; I've made quite a study of aunts. There's two kinds: there's the regular kind, and then there's the other kind. Mine are the other kind. . . ." (*Freddy Goes Camping*, p. 5)

It seems likely that Walter's maiden aunts, Lucy and Rhoda, at least, were the regular kind. One photograph of Rhoda survives showing her, plump, shiny-cheeked, and smiling as she sits at the Thanksgiving table with Walter's sister, Elsie.

Aunt Lucy, ten years older than Rhoda, remembered Elsie and Walter in her will. To Elsie she bequeathed "a shawl, a three stone diamond ring and a point lace handkerchief" and to Elsie and Walter, along with her sister Rhoda and all of her other nieces and nephews, "an equal share of all the rest, residue, and remainder of my estate." Lucy died on January 12, 1911, ten years after her sister Fannie and her brother William. Rhoda—though ten years younger—died on February 13, 1911, one month and one day after her older sister with whom she had lived her entire life.

As previously noted, their nephew Walter memorialized Rhoda and Lucy as the spinster sister ducks, Alice and Emma. "Emma didn't care for jewelry and never wore any but Alice occasionally put on a string of pearls when she went calling. She would have liked to wear some of the diamonds, but Emma did not think that diamonds were refined." (*Wiggins for President*)

One supposes that ducks and aunts alike would have been scandalized by one bit of light-hearted childhood larceny that Walter recalled:

> As children we seemed to have gone in for a good deal of amateur burglary. It was a specialized form, church burglary. The Presbyterian had the steeple; the Baptist had a sort of tower, but there were bells you could ring if you wanted to stir things up a little. Also, after ice cream socials, the Baptists left the freezers behind. There was once, I remember, something like four gallons for five of us. I remember the occasion well. The Methodist was a hard nut to crack; the Episcopalian was easy but not very interesting as I saw plenty of that on Sunday.

All of these churches were within easy walking distance of Walter's home on George Street and could have been handily accessed, like Mr. Brewer's church in "Second Chance," via "the jungle trails that led through backyards and down alleys and only crossed thoroughfares in the darkest places where there were no arc lights."

Walter's childhood lasted for barely fifteen years. It was "a nice and pleasant" place for a boy to be. But one wonders, these many decades later, if Walter were ever really a boy. Did a child ever look at a camera with such a look of bemused and ironic detachment as Walter did in the few photos that survive from his early childhood?

> "This is Mr. Bean when he was three," Mrs. Bean said.
> "The picture showed a chubby little boy in a plaid dress. He had a frightened look, and his hair was cut in a sort of bang low on his forehead." (*Freddy and the Space Ship*)

There is a picture of Walter when he was three (or thereabouts), a chubby little boy in a dress with his hair cut in a sort of bang, low on his forehead. But the look on his face is not fearful. It is detached, contemplative, emotionless. He looks out at the camera from somewhere behind his eyes, from the same ironic remove from which he stared at the camera when he was only five months old and from which he would stare in a formal adult portrait years later.

Walter at three. "His hair was cut in a sort of bang . . ."

Mr. Bean, Walter's creation, hid his expression and thus his emotions from his wife and the world behind his bushy whiskers. Meanwhile, Walter hid his behind the ironic detachment that, if this were a fairy-tale, would be a cloak of invisibility. Consider that when he wrote, years later, about his fifteenth year, he did not write, "My mother, whom I loved very much, died when I was fifteen." Instead he wrote, in flat, emotionless understatement, "When I was fifteen, our home was broken up."

Clearly Walter's boyhood ended the day Fannie died. Is that why, as an adult, he recreated an idealized childhood in the Freddy books, a place loosely rooted in Rome just before the turn of the twentieth century, yet set outside of time so that it would always be there for a visit—a refuge for both its creator and for children whose own childhoods might not have been so nice and pleasant as his? And what of his adulthood? Why did he write so many short stories about unhappy men who learn, to their sorrow, that there is no second chance, no escape from reality into the tantalizingly adjacent but ultimately inaccessible worlds of the past or the equally magical worlds of Pan, unicorns, and fairies at the bottom of the garden?

We will find out.

6

The Moheganite

At fifteen my entire future was planned and mapped out and much more definitively than it has ever been since. I was to go through college, through medical school, graduating magna cum laud. I was then to return to my hometown and successfully practice my profession. The plan suited me. I didn't know anything about medicine. My hometown, Rome, New York, was a pleasant place. I was very fond of books and would have plenty of time for them while I was waiting for patients. This plan worked well until I got to medical school. I did not graduate magna cum laud. I did not graduate at all. At the beginning of my third year, I suddenly decided I was not cut to the medical pattern. I forsook medicine and took up advertising. —*Walter R. Brooks*

THOUGH WALTER DOESN'T ACKNOWLEDGE IT, THE "CAREful mapper and planner" of his future was probably his brother-in-law, Dr. William Perrin, a prominent homeopathic doctor in Rochester, New York. He and Walter's older sister, Elsie, had been married on August 14, 1901, scarcely three months after Fannie's death, "at the home of the bride's aunt, Miss Rhoda H. Stevens, in the presence of only the immediate relatives of the contracting parties."

If 1901 were a year of deaths (Fannie and William's) it was also a year of marriages, for Walter's cousin Lucy, daughter of the Honorable Jim, married, too, only a week before Elsie. Lucy would ultimately marry three times: her first husband died young; her second husband committed suicide; and— after a number of years of widowhood—she married Alexander H. Rutherford, who had been, according to her nephew Sam, "an early and unsuccessful suitor."

Walter and the wealthy Lucy remained friendly until his

death in 1958. In fact, she offered him the use of "La Bellucia," her fabulous Palm Beach, Florida, estate, for a honeymoon following his second marriage to Dorothy Collins in 1953. Walter declined, grumbling privately to Dorothy that he had no desire "to go down there and have to talk to all those society people."

Lucy's brother, Samuel B. II, twelve years older than Walter, was apparently less interested in society than in automobiles. "Maintaining a fleet of the best cars," he became a nationally known amateur racing driver. The editor of *Automobile Magazine* wrote in the early 1900s, "Stevens, Barney Oldfield, and William K. Vanderbilt are the greatest automobile drivers in the United States." The second Sam raced at Daytona, Ormond Beach, Old Orchard Beach, and elsewhere—and "with two assistants crossed the U.S. in five days, eighteen hours, and thirty minutes for a record at that time." Typically referred to in the press as "a well known sportsman," Samuel B. II was among the first Americans (if not *the* first) to own a Rolls Royce, a 1907 Silver Ghost.

The Honorable Jim and his son Sam, "the well known sportsman,"
in the famous Rolls

Sam had attended a private school, the Mohegan Lake Military Academy, near Peekskill, and it was there that Walter was sent following Fannie's death. Founded ca. 1866, the Mohegan Lake Academy was a small, private boy's school (enrollment was limited to forty-two students) that promised "a thorough Christian preparatory education in an atmosphere free from the distracting and pernicious influences of large towns and railroad centers." Among its alumni were the diverse likes of legendary choreographer Busby Berkeley and New York City planner Robert Moses.

While there, Walter became an assistant editor of the school newspaper, *The Moheganite*, and played left end for the scrub football team, scoring two touchdowns in a 1902 game against Mt. Pleasant. Being a scrub must not have been much fun ("If the scrub had not gone out regularly every afternoon and been pounded around the campus by the first team, we would have had a very different season," *The Moheganite* noted) but, nevertheless, the experience stood Walter in good creative stead when he came to write *Freddy Plays Football* in 1949.

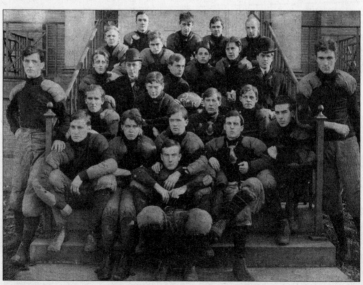

The Mohegan Lake football team. Walter is front and center.

Wea. _____ WED. JAN. 1, 1902 _____ Ther.

The first page of Walter's boyhood journal

Freddy would be a better player than Walter, however, making the first team and carrying the field against archrival Tushville. Freddy also bettered Walter in the editorial way, becoming editor-in-chief of *The Bean Home News*, while Walter settled for remaining only the assistant editor of *The Moheganite* and he had mixed feelings about even that: "Worked like hell all the afternoon to get all my stuff into *The Moheganite* . . . I hate so much work and may resign," he confided to his boyhood journal, adding "but it is an honor & places me well up in the school."

Walter recorded these thoughts in an often sketchy journal during his first two years at school, when he was sixteen and seventeen, and it gives us a look at the type of boy he was, while also offering one of the few places where he actually revealed his feelings.

The entries begin on January 1, 1902. They find him in Rochester, visiting his sister Elsie and brother-in-law, Dr. William Perrin, while on holiday break. "Will's birthday," fifteen-year-old Walter notes. "I smoke in the house now. Great fun to watch Will sometimes." Walter seems to have enjoyed annoying Dr. Perrin, not only by smoking but also by trying to spoil the older man's billiard games, moving suddenly when the doctor was lining up his shots.

From the journal we also learn that Walter's school vacations were divided between Rochester and Rome, for on Saturday, January 4, he boards a train in Rochester ("Dear old Elsie saw me off"), arriving in Rome four and a half hours later. There he visits friends, calls on his cousin Blanche Dyett (the daughter of his late Uncle William), who had moved into his childhood home with her husband Herbert T., who was secretary-treasurer of the Wire and Telegraph Company of America, and, he notes, "She has our old house fixed up fine."

After supper he goes with a friend to the Methodist Church ("No girls d___ it!").[2] Afterward he sees a Mr. Barringer and "gets him laughing." Later he composes a note to Winnie Howlett, a girl he had spoken to after church. Monday morning he goes to Rome High School for an hour to visit friends and then boards the train to Peekskill, noting, "Rather sorry to go this time. Train slow as hell. Late but excused myself fairly well. Study hour in evening as usual." And then, poignantly, he writes, "D____ it all till next vacation. I'm homesick." The next morning he writes again, "I'm homesick as ____. Sometimes you like to cry but being homesick is different. It's a sort of combination. It sort of hurts to cry then." And the next day he continues, "Tomorrow is my birthday. First one away from Rome, home, and Mama. That combination is enough to make anyone homesick. Gee." And then, on January 9: "Today is my [sixteenth] birthday and the least like a birthday I ever hope to spend."

Walter gradually got over his homesickness, though, and by Valentine's Day he is hoping that Aunt Rhoda—"with persuasion"—will let him stay in Peekskill for the Easter holiday (she won't!).

Walter's free time seems to have been evenly divided between physical activity—running, rowing, swimming, ice skating, and (like the Bean Farm animals) playing duck on a rock—and quiet reading. Some of this was presumably school related: *The Faerie Queen*, *Vanity Fair*, and—in Latin—work by Caesar and Cicero. The latter, he notes, "was not so terribly hard." No surprise there, since learning foreign languages

---

2. Walter's habit of not spelling out imprecations was probably more Edwardian convention than adolescent discretion.

later became one of his hobbies. Much of his reading, though, was for pleasure, and he records enjoying such then popular novels as *The Virginian, Hearts Courageous* (by Hallie Erminie Rives), *The Lady Paramount* (Henry Harland), and multiple works by George DuMaurier and F. Marion Crawford.

He also read literary magazines, looking for books he wanted to buy and mentions having ordered works by Francis Parkman and Edmund Gosse, and *Hours with German Classics* by Frederic Henry Hedge. While his family had given him books as gifts since before he was old enough to read, this is his first recorded experience of buying them for himself, a habit that would last a lifetime as he grew into being both a book collector and part-time book dealer.

Ironically, given his obvious love for books and reading, English seems to have been one of his worst school subjects, which may explain the gentle war on punctuation and paragraphs that, as we will learn, he affected in so many of his adult short stories. And despite his adult disclaimers, he routinely excelled in mathematics.

Walter also excelled in misbehaving—"raising hell" as he usually put it. His journal entries are filled with references to the number of demerits he has received and the number of times he is confined to quarters (oddly, he also faithfully records every shower bath he takes!). Often his punishment was the result of being caught smoking or being disobedient to authority (his general contempt for those in charge later found expression in his satirical treatment of authority figures in the Freddy books). Sometimes, though, his infractions were rooted in, well, simple indolence. In March 1903 he notes having received a "Hell of a letter from Will. Long lecture." And a year later, in February 1904, he received a blistering letter from Aunt Rhoda, who wrote:

Dear Walter,

Yesterday morning I received a letter from Will, telling me what Mr. Bradstreet had said concerning your conduct with regard to your school matters. I cannot say that I am surprised, for I saw some time ago how things were tending, only it has come a little sooner than I had expected &

I am mortified, ashamed, and indignant. You have had love, affection, and all kinds of favors poured out on you, and this is the way that you repay them all—nothing but an indolent desire to have a "good time." If kindness and persuasion are to none effect, then it will be necessary to resort to stronger measures. Your Uncle Jim is in Florida but when he returns, I shall tell him all about it, and I know what he will say and that is that you had better go to work. Idling away one's time is not getting an education, and not one penny of my means will I give to encourage it. When people do good honest work, they then understand not only the value of money but of time, too, and when they rest, it's not from a mere love of ease, but from necessity. I cannot see why you choose your associates as a general thing from among the careless and the insubordinate, instead of those who honor and respect right government and proper authority and have a suitable regard for the approval and esteem of their teachers.

Your mother had said to me more than once, "What I want most of all for Walter is that he should be a *good* man," and what are you doing in that direction? Education itself is but a poor thing if not upheld by truth and honor and unswerving integrity. The manliest man is one who can be firm in the face of temptation, and true courage is steadfastness in the things that are right and true.

If you are expelled from school as you undoubtedly will be if you continue in your present course, you have yourself alone to answer for it, and such things have more of an affect on young peoples [sic] future than they imagine, and may be a cup of bitterness to them in time to come.

Your affectionate
Aunt Rhoda

Walter was not expelled, of course, but following his graduation from the academy in 1904 he did not return to Rome, but instead went to Rochester to live with his sister Elsie and her husband William, or "Brother Bill," as the adult Walter would wryly refer to him.

Dr. Perrin had graduated from the University of Rochester in 1898 and it was there that Walter was sent next, though he had wanted, instead, to attend Hobart College in New York's Finger Lakes country. Walter had also toyed with the idea of attending Colgate, noting, "Wrote to Registrar of Colgate University. Signed my name in full. Bet it will surprise some of them if they notice, as Grandfather's bust is set up in the University." Nothing came of it, however. While at the University of Rochester, Walter pledged a fraternity, Delta Kappa Epsilon, and his pin remained among the personal effects he left at his death fifty-four years later. In 1906—after two years at the university—Walter was sent to the New York Homeopathic Medical College in New York City (Perrin had interned at the Rochester Homeopathic Hospital).

As he had in military school, Walter kept a desultory journal of his first year, 1907, in New York City. More of an appointment book than a journal, most of the entries record his winnings at poker or evenings at the theater where he saw *Peter Pan*, *Squaw Man* (later turned into a movie by Cecil B. DeMille), and such now forgotten plays as *Great Divide*, *Student King*, *Man of the House*, and others. He also records having seen such still cele-brated performers as Ethel Barrymore, Nazimova, and Grace George but unfortunately offers no reactions to the experience.

As for books, he notes having bought O. Henry's *The Four Million*, Barrie's *Sentimental Tommy*, Paul Leicester Ford's *Story of Untold Love*, A. E. W. Mason's *Miranda of the Balcony*, and others.

Beyond this, there is little of biographical interest except for the entry of May 10, 1907: "Took Empire to Rochester. Will has a Cadillac."

Walter survived only two years of medical school, since going there was apparently not his idea in the first place. As he later wrote, "My family [Dr. Perrin?] had somehow taken it for granted I should become a doctor, but I was interested in a lot of other things, too. Maybe I would have kept on with medi-cine but I was particularly interested in a girl in Rochester, which was a long way from New York. So I abandoned medi-cine and Anne Shepard and I were married the next year."

Anne Mary Shepard had been born in Rochester on December 30, 1885. Her parents were Alice Judson and Frank E. Shepard, who had worked as a clerk, cashier, and salesman until he went to work for the Rochester Lead Works in 1892. Anne herself was a teacher, "a very strict one," Walter's second wife Dorothy Brooks recalled tartly, though it appears that Anne stopped working following her marriage to Walter on January 22, 1909, in Buffalo. The newlyweds were both twenty-three years of age. At five feet, five inches, Anne was an inch shorter than Walter. She had brown eyes and brown hair, while Walter had blue eyes and (according to his passport) "fair hair." The couple settled at 303 Kenwood Avenue in Rochester. They lived there for no more than a year, however, since Walter took a job—his first—with the Frank Du Noyer Advertising Agency in Utica, where the couple lived at 84 Howard Avenue.

Writing advertising and publicity copy became Walter's first career and provided a profession, as well, for many of the protagonists of his short stories, the most famous of these being Wilbur Pope, the owner of Ed, the talking horse.

Walter kept a file of his work for DuNoyer, including ads and fliers for the local distributor of Elmore automobiles ("Advantages Enjoyed by Elmore Owners Which Are Denied to You"), the Curtis School for Dancing ("A School Rich in Sweet Memories"), E. M. Spieler ("Artistic Ladies' Tailor"), and— most notably—Oneida Ale for which he created a baseball-themed series of rhyming newspaper ads featuring such participants as The Umpire, The Pitcher, The Second Baseman, etc. These offer the first surviving examples of his poetry, including "After the Game": "After the game / When the setting sun / Darkens the field / Where the game was won / The players hasten / To hit the trail / For the nearest bar / and Oneida Ale." Another is "The Short Stop": "When the husky short stop comes to bat / He will clout the ball a mile / And you'll see the grandstand settle down / With an optimistic smile. / Not a sizzling, red hot liner / Not a whistling, whirling fly / Not a swift, erratic grounder / Has ever passed him by. / To see the reason you cannot fail / For he always drinks Oneida Ale."

"I don't suppose I was ever very ambitious," Walter wrote some years later, "At least I had never decided I wanted to be anything special." Perhaps this is the reason that, a year later, he and Anne were back in Rochester, living this time at 76 Rugby Avenue. As for working, Walter had "retired" and would remain so for several years, though "I don't know quite why," he commented many years later.

This may have been disingenuous, for we may infer that— aside from not being overly fond of work—he retired because, like his Uncle William, he could suddenly afford to. Of course, he would have inherited his share of his mother's estate in 1907 when he turned twenty-one, but this was now augmented by his share of the estates of his aunts Lucy and Rhoda, both of whom died in 1911, leaving between them estates totaling $276,834.00 (Lucy's was slightly the larger at $145,794, while Rhoda's was valued at $131,040). The aunts' wills divided their holdings equally among their nieces and nephews, Walter inheriting $22,876.50 from Lucy and $21,840 from Rhoda. These were, for the time, considerable amounts of money (the total inheritance of $44,716 would equal more than $900,000 today!), meaning Walter

Anne Shepard Brooks's passport photo for the 1913 trip to Europe, the first of many such travels she and Walter would enjoy

was certainly situated well enough financially in these years not only to retire but also to travel abroad to Europe in 1913.

His newfound leisure turned out to be a godsend for his literary career, since it was during this period of early retirement (roughly 1911 to 1917 when he was twenty-five to thirty-one years old) that Walter began writing seriously, though how seriously is open to interpretation. Walter himself observed, "I think a great many people write stories because they like the clean click of the keys and the long straight lines of type. Some of my friends said they couldn't see any other reason for my writing them. They said my stories were not good stories. I pointed out that my typewriter was not a good typewriter. It was not until I bought a brand new machine that my stories began to sell!"

Published!

N O MATTER HOW GOOD OR NEW THE TYPEWRITER, IT WAS not a short story but a sonnet titled "Haunted" that would be Walter's first published work. It appeared in the celebrated literary magazine *Century* for April 1915. And here it is:

> Without the window lies the rain-streaked night;
> Without, the wet, black pavement shines like glass,
> Mirroring in long, wavering lines of bright
> Pure gold the haloed street lamps. Figures pass
> Like wind-blown wraiths across the dripping pane,
> And, passing, turn a moment toward the light
> Pale faces, dumbly questioning. The rain,
> Blurring the window, blots them from my sight.
> Within is warmth and comfort that derides
> Their wistful eyes. I turn away. And still
> Those faces haunt me; one thin pane divides
> My life from their life, my good from their ill.
> What must I do, then? How act? Undismayed,
> Throw up the window, or draw down the shade?

Perhaps *this* is when he bought a new typewriter, for later that same year, 1915, his first short story, "Harden's Chance," was published in the December issue of *Forum* magazine. According to historian Frank Luther Mott, this distinguished monthly had a well-deserved "reputation for excellence in the field of the short story," publishing early work by Sherwood Anderson, H. L. Mencken, Joseph Hergesheimer, and others. Though in excellent company, Walter's first story is slight—in both length (less than a thousand words) and substance. It's the sketchy story of a man named Harden, who returns to the rural scene where he had murdered a hated enemy named Farley. Improbably, Harden—who is on the run from the law—discovers that the murder weapon (an axe) he had abandoned is still at the scene of the crime. No sooner has he discovered this than Farley shows up. Yes, Farley! "A great scar seamed Farley's face from his ear to the roots of his hair, and Harden knew that he was alive—and that he had not killed him." Initially Harden feels "the sudden weakness of great relief," but then "the hate surged back into his heart . . . and before the other could fling up a hand to break the force of the blow, he [Harden] swung the axe high in the air and brought it down upon the head of his enemy." The End.

So it's not Chekov, but at least it's a start—and, for its time, maybe not such a bad effort. Walter told an interviewer many years later, it was about this time (i.e., 1915) that "he and a friend were discussing stories in current magazines and decided they could do as well as some of those writers. They collaborated on a short story for which they were paid $15.00."

The story, Walter's second, was written under the pseudonym "Aeneas B. Hooker," and was titled "The Elopement." It appeared in the January 1916 issue of a pulp magazine called *Breezy Stories*, which also published the early work of Erle Stanley Gardner, the creator of Perry Mason. A more substantial effort than "Harden's Chance"—at least in length and plot development—its protagonist is also a man named Harden. Walter Harden is devastated to discover a letter to his wife, suggesting she is about to run off with a secret lover whom she is to meet that evening at a costume party. The lover will be clad in a harlequin costume. Harden decides that he will rent a similar costume and surprise his wife in the act of assignation. He is the one who will be surprised, however, when he discovers that the "suitor" is his wife's ne'er-do-well brother, who is wanted by the law. Far from planning to run off with him, the wife is hoping to spirit him aboard an ocean liner bound for parts unknown.

"God forgive me!" muttered Harden strangely. "I have made a mistake—a mistake because I loved you so."

Behind him as he ran up the corridor sounded the swifter footsteps of his wife.

"Oh, Walter," she was calling, "wait for me!"

"The Elopement" is a predictable bit of pulp melodrama and not much better than the four other stories Walter and his collaborator would subsequently produce.

Who was the collaborator? He was Walter's best friend for more than fifty years, Francis Rufus Bellamy. (We can presume the "B." in "Aeneas B. Hooker" stood for Bellamy, while the "Hooker" was a nod to Barrie's Captain Hook, since Bellamy claimed a pirate among his ancestors.) Unlike Walter, Bellamy actually came from a family of writers, including an uncle, Edward Bellamy, author of *Looking Backward*, and a cousin, Francis Julius Bellamy, who wrote the Pledge of Allegiance to the Flag and later served as an editor of *Youth's Companion* magazine (and who, it being a small world, is buried adjacent to the Stevens family plot in Rome). In due course, Bellamy also became a professional magazine editor and the author of eight published books, the first of which, a novel titled *The Balance*, appeared in 1917.

There is no firm evidence of when or how Bellamy and Brooks first met. It may have been when they were children, since a branch of the Bellamy family lived in Rome, where an uncle, David Bellamy, was pastor of the First Baptist Church (he being also the father of the Francis Bellamy who wrote the Pledge of Allegiance). It's more likely, however, that they met in Rochester, where Bellamy (who was born in New Rochelle, New York) lived from the age of two and where, as a child, Walter often visited members of his extended Stevens family. His Uncle John C. had five children and his Aunt Sarah had six. And, of course, Walter himself began residing in Rochester in 1904, when both he and Bellamy would have been eighteen. At any rate, Walter's first recorded mention of Bellamy is in his appointment book for January 1, 1907, where he notes, "Frank and Estelle to dinner." (Estelle was Estelle Zimmer, whom Bellamy married in 1914.)

Wherever and whenever they actually *first* met, it's no surprise that they became fast friends, since they had so much in common. Consider: both were born in 1886 (Walter on January 9 and Frank on December 24); both had family who were Baptist ministers; both lost their fathers at an early age (Bellamy's father, Rufus W., died when Frank was two; Walter's father died when he was four); both had musical parents: Walter's father was a music teacher as was Bellamy's mother. Even their initials were almost identical (WRB and FRB).

There were differences, of course. For one thing, Bellamy seems to have been the more outgoing personality. In "Remember Tomorrow," another of Walter's autobiographical stories, another middle-aged protagonist—Dr. Henry Pryde in this case—is sent back into the past. This time it's to Rochester, New York, in the year 1907, where Dr. Pryde encounters Jed Straker. "[He] had been his best friend for thirty years. They had played golf together yesterday. But it was not the hard-bitten and cynical Jed of yesterday but a grinning hobbledehoy with a large nose who rushed at him and seized him by the seat of the pants and frog-walked him into the house yelling 'Hey everybody!'"

There is little doubt that Pryde is Walter's conception of himself, while Straker is a stand-in for Bellamy, who did have

Left, Francis Rufus Bellamy, ca. 1917
Above, Bellamy in 1951

a rather large nose, though as a young man he was strikingly handsome with dark hair and strong, regular features. Unfortunately, those same features began to droop as he grew older so that, by middle age, he bore a closer resemblance to a basset hound than to the "grinning hobbledehoy" of his youth.

The young men's common interest in books and writing clearly overrode any differences, though, and they ultimately collaborated on five stories, only two of which—"The Elopement" and a trifle called "Cicero Betts' Best Bet" were ever published. "Cicero Betts" is the story of an elderly miner who strikes it rich and sets off to tour Europe, with comical results. Published in *World Traveler* magazine for August 1921, it's the first of a series of stories that Walter would write throughout his career in which salt-of-the-earth, rustic types encounter—and best—snooty urbanites, who are often Europeans. It is doubtless inspired by another series of nine travel pieces Walter did for the same magazine from May 1920 through December 1921. Though its editor stated, "We try to have our travel stories be records of personal experience and adventure," Walter's pieces are almost wholly fiction—though they are, for the most part, set in countries that he and Anne visited when they traveled abroad in 1913, i.e., Greece, Montenegro, Egypt and North Africa, Malta, Romania, and Italy.

As for the three Brooks/Bellamy stories that remained unpublished, one—"Mr. Peddick"—is a slight effort about a young man who is sitting pretty financially but whom the ladies refuse to take seriously, since he is the manufacturer of the Solid Comfort Toilet Seat. The story is absolutely forgettable except for its inclusion of Walter's first sly put-down of his own career in advertising: "The seat was just a seat but it sold because the advertising said it was more comfortable. And after all if the customers believed that it was more comfortable, then it was. That is why all advertising is true."

The other two collaborations, "The Road to Nyon" and "The Prosaic Professor and the Diviner of Dreams," are labored melodramas; the former is a World War I spy story and the latter is a wannabe thriller in which an unscrupulous suitor is unmasked.

Walter and Frank seem, from the first, to have had a kind of symbiotic—some might even say codependent—relationship. Bellamy appears to have been chronically short of ready cash and repeatedly turned for relief to Walter, who seldom seemed to say no. As early as January 1907, the month Walter would turn twenty-one and receive his half of his mother's estate, Bellamy was asking him for a loan of $2,500 to buy a farm near Rochester. Walter was willing but Uncle Jim refused to let him endorse the note. Walter may have found another way to get Bellamy the money, however, since Frank listed his profession, from 1907–1911, as "dairy farmer."

Frank remained a farmer for only four years, going to work in 1912 as a salesman for the publisher Grosset & Dunlap. Bellamy seldom lasted more than three or four years at a job and, by early 1916, he was listing his profession as "author"—and justifiably so, since his first novel, *The Balance*, was published the next year by Doubleday & Page.

A year later, Bellamy had another new job—as Washington editor of *The Red Cross Magazine*—and a new residence at 2904 P Street N.W. in the nation's capital. And, more importantly, Walter had left his "retirement" to go to DC himself to work for his friend (and now boss) as a staff writer, establishing a pattern of working relationships that would be repeated at least five times over the course of the next twenty-three years.

Speaking of patterns, Bellamy remained only a year in Washington, for by 1918–1919 he had become a European correspondent for the magazine (this was during World War I, after all). In 1920 Bellamy was back in the United States, but living in New York City at 106 W. 75th Street, where he was listed in the city directory as "Mgr. Editor American Red Cross." A year later, however, he had moved to Holliston, MA, and presumably had left the organization.

Walter demonstrated greater longevity, remaining with the Red Cross through 1926. During that time he seems to have lived periodically in Washington (where he wrote *To and Again*) while keeping the Rochester residence until he and Anne moved to New York City sometime in 1919, settling in at 135 W. 12th Street. Two years later they bought a handsome four-

Walter's house at 27 Bank Street in Greenwich Village

story, red brick townhouse at 27 Bank Street in Greenwich Village, where they would live until 1948.

Meanwhile, between 1922 and 1926, Bellamy published three more novels: *A Flash of Gold*, (1922), *March Winds* (1924), and *Spanish Faith* (1926). Walter was comparatively less productive during this period—he kept his day job after all—but in addition to the stories already mentioned, he published eight others and one poem between 1916 and 1926 (see annotated list at end of the book). He also published fifteen articles and stories that were clearly related to his work with the Red Cross (e.g., "Trouble? Red Cross," published in *The Red Cross Magazine* for November 1918).

Arguably more interesting than any of the published pieces is one unpublished manuscript that survives. Titled "The Toll of the Island," it is a horror story about two friends who go camping on an island that is haunted by terrific natural powers. The island is, in short, alive and violently resents the intrusion by these two puny human beings. Twenty or more years later Walter would recapture something of the spirit and mood of this story in *Freddy Goes Camping*. A related story, "Beyond the Border," was published in the May 1916 issue of *People's Home Journal*; based on Native American legends, which Walter may have read in a volume titled *Myths and Legends of Our Own Land* (a Christmas gift from Aunt Lucy in 1896), it tells of mysterious Floating Islands in the Great Lakes that are actually "a sort of select happy hunting grounds peopled by chiefs and sons of chiefs."

Altogether, six of the eight stories Walter published during these years could be described as "speculative fiction" and reflected the influence of some of his favorite authors, including Lord Dunsany, A. E. Coppard, M. R. James, Lafcadio Hearne, Algernon Blackwood, and others.

Undoubtedly the most ambitious of Walter's published work prior to 1927 was a six-part novel titled *The Romantic Liars* that was serialized in *Country Gentleman* magazine from July 25 to September 1925. Never published in book form, it is the intermittently entertaining story of two friends, Kent (a seldom successful writer) and Bingham. The self-styled "romantic liars" of the title, these two enjoy fabricating elaborate whoppers that they loudly swap in public, hoping to be overheard and thereby "help their fellow men." Walter writes:

> It was the latter's [Kent's] belief that the entire human race is possessed of an insatiable thirst for romance, for adventure. "It's my duty to do something for the race," he explained; "and being prevented by circumstances from founding charities or helping in a pecuniary way, I try to make their lives brighter by injecting a little romance into them." And as the romances he so assiduously wrote only infrequently found a publisher, and thus failed to add in any degree to the happiness of the public, he chose this way, he said, to help his fellow men.

The liars get a bit more than they bargained for when—for the benefit of the stranger who has joined their table at a nightclub—Kent spins an especially elaborate yarn about undiscovered treasure buried by Captain Kidd on an island off the coast of Maine and the stranger, a Mr. Smith, then offers to finance an expedition to search for the pirate's trove.[3] It turns out that Smith has recently come into an unexpected fortune and can finally indulge his middle-aged passion for romance and adventure (apparently Kent was right!). Only momentarily taken aback, the two liars decide to go along for the ride, fabricating a phony map that leads the expedition to an island where Kent had spent summers as a boy. To their (and the reader's) astonishment, they actually discover buried treasure there that, in short order, is stolen from them by Smith's nephew and niece who have witlessly become involved with modern-day pirates (i.e., bootleggers).

---

3. Walter had already published a short story, "Spanish Doubloons," about lost pirate treasure that might have inspired this plot point.

The plot then turns into an increasingly improbable quest to recover the treasure. Meanwhile, Kent is also busily trying to win another treasure: the heart of Smith's niece who wants nothing to do with him and is not at all shy about letting him know this. The often hot-tempered exchanges between the two are, no doubt, designed to sound sophisticated and brittle but, frankly, just seem tiresome, as increasingly does the stretched-thin plot.

Perhaps sensing this, Walter, midway through the novel, introduces an abandoned (but still furnished) hotel that boasts a secret room and two of "the most fantastic personages" Kent has ever seen. One is Adolphus Featherbone and the other, his friend, Mr. Dodds. Featherbone is a Falstaffian figure and Dodds is distinguished by his contrastingly dry and dour demeanor. The two are apparently vagrants who are squatting in the abandoned "hostelry" (Walter's word). Stereotypical comic types that can be traced back to the King and the Duke in *Huckleberry Finn*,[4] they add almost nothing to the plot (including humor, alas) but they do presage the arch, even twee treatment of the sailor characters in Walter's second Freddy title, *More To and Again*. They also evidence Walter's interest in pirates, and at one point are even described as "comic opera pirates" (part 4, p. 48).

Several years after the publication of *The Romantic Liars*, Walter wrote in a press release for his agents Brandt & Brandt:

> It might be of interest to know that a part of *The Romantic Liars* was founded unconsciously on fact. There's very good evidence that Captain Kidd actually did hide the bulk of his treasure on an island off the Maine coast. The Astor fortune is said to have been founded on it. The owner of the island, a Boston architect, as a result of discoveries made on the island and among jewelers' records sued the Astor Estate to recover the treasure, but the case was settled out of court. At the time of writing the story I knew nothing of this but it seemed the sort of course a sensible pirate would pursue.

---

4. Walter might have read this as a boy, since his father owned a first edition copy, which remained in Walter's personal collection.

Freddy fans will recall that the character of Captain Kidd reappears in *Freddy's Cousin Weedly* when Hank, the old white horse, plays that part in the play that Freddy writes for the animals to perform for Mr. Bean's visiting relatives, the Snedekers.

Walter's interest in piracy—and, indeed, the inspiration for this novel—may well have derived from the fact that his friend Bellamy claimed a pirate ancestor. *The Pirates' Who's Who* by Philip Gosse lists a Captain Samuel Bellamy ("Black Bellamy") whose career lasted from 1717 to 1727. According to Francis Julius Bellamy, "Gosse tells us that Bellamy had a considerable gift for public speaking and seldom missed an opportunity of addressing the assembled officers and crew of the ships he took." (This, of course, sounds more like the Freddy books' Charles the Rooster than Captain Kidd!)

There are several other aspects of the novel that seem to be Walter winking conspiratorially at Bellamy. The most significant of these is the rather shaky motivation of Mr. Smith's niece and nephew for their initial theft of the treasure. It is, apparently, designed to persuade the uncle to cough up the money the nephew needs to maintain ownership of an apple farm he has bought. The romantic Mr. Smith disapproves of this prosaic choice of profession, desiring instead that his nephew should become a poet (shades of Freddy!). The niece, meanwhile, is unable to help her brother financially, since her uncle has control of her estate. This, of course, echoes Walter's inability to loan Bellamy funding for the purchase of the (dairy) farm he desired, since Uncle Jim refused to authorize the loan.

Even more fundamentally, the very premise of "romantic lying" seems to have been borrowed from real life. Walter grew up reading the romantic adventures of the likes of Robin Hood, Chevalier Bayard, King Arthur and his Knights of the Round Table, the hero stories of Howard Pyle, and more—all of which were in his personal library. Accordingly, the lion's share of stories he wrote and/or published prior to 1927 either can be classed as "romantic adventure" or involved travel to exotic—sometimes imaginary—foreign lands. In Bellamy, Walter seems to have found someone who enjoyed this "lying" as much as he did. The two enjoyed peppering their later correspondence with references to fictitious figures of their own devising (a Cap'n Hooker—compare to "Aeneas B. Hooker"—being a recurring favorite) and they routinely couched their letters to each other in a kind of inflated pirate argot. One example speaks for the rest: in an undated note to Bellamy, Walter writes, "Waaaal, here I be to Cazenovia—th' old Hooker homestead. I write to inform my deeeear friend, haw, haw, that after some correspondence wi papa Scheitlin, he havin took 3 days to answer each time, I ha' refused the kind offer of 250 monthly and no expenses. . . ."

Another offer—one that Walter did *not* refuse—came once again from Bellamy who, in 1926, had become the executive director of the Woodrow Wilson Foundation. Very soon thereafter we find Walter "associated with the Foundation," though in precisely what capacity is not known. In Walter's *New York Times* obituary it is simply noted that he "worked with the Woodrow Wilson foundation." Judging from the files he kept, however, it appears that he worked principally on the Woodrow Wilson Prize Essay Awards, a national contest aiming, according to the foundation brochure, "to bring Woodrow Wilson's ideals before the young people of America." To that end, essays of no more than 2,500 words on the theme "What Woodrow Wilson Means to Me" were invited from young people aged twenty to thirty-five and prizes totaling $50,000 were offered. The funding came from a cadre of distinguished donors, including Bernard Baruch, Cyrus McCormick, Henry Morgenthau, and others.

Considering the size of the financial inducement (two awards of $25,000 each were promised), it is no surprise that more than 10,000 entries were received. By all accounts—and judging from the sample of entries Walter kept in his files—the submissions were uniformly awful and not all of them complimentary. One of these, for example, states that Wilson "tried to wear the shoes of Jefferson, Lincoln, Roosevelt, Washington but which pinched his feet causing corns, bunions, blisters, chafing and ended in sciatia [sic.] rheumatism."

Several years later Walter wrote, "Personally we don't approve of prize contests. Perhaps because we once read some

2,000 short MSS., and after the first dozen they all looked so much alike that we were totally incapable of deciding which was the best—or even which was the worst. Next time we shan't read any of them but shall pick one blindfold, because you can only satisfy one contestant anyway, and it doesn't make much difference which one." ("Behind the Blurbs," 12/18/29)

Only forty-four of these essays actually made it through a screening process to the judges, Professor Mark Van Doren of Columbia University and the then young poet Alan Tate (who, at the time, was also working as the live-in custodian of Walter's house at 27 Bank Street!). None was chosen for the top two prizes, though fourteen ultimately received "third prize of $100 each and thirty others were awarded honorable mention, which carries with it a $20 award."

As if this weren't bad enough, the cost of conducting this contest totaled $55,027.57! As a result, the whole effort was regarded as a fiasco, the *New York Herald Tribune* editorializing, "A more completely bungled episode . . . has rarely been exposed to public gaze." A foundation associate sent Walter a newspaper account on which he wrote, "We have had many letters today from the amateur and the immature. We all wear false whiskers when we emerge on 42nd Street" (the Foundation office was at 17 East 42nd Street). Soon thereafter neither Bellamy nor Brooks was any longer "associated with" the Woodrow Wilson Foundation.

This might have been more devastating if it were not for the fact that the year was now 1927. In June of that year, *To and Again,* the first of what would come to be known as the "Freddy books," was published, an event that—as we have seen— changed both Walter's life and the evolution of American children's literature.

8

The Outlook *Years*

THOUGH THERE WAS NO FREDDY BOOK IN *HIS* FUTURE, Bellamy also survived the fiasco of the Wilson Foundation. The same year that *To and Again* was published, Walter's friend somehow secured sufficient funding to acquire a controlling interest in the highly regarded magazine *The Outlook*.

First published in 1867, *The Outlook* had its beginnings as a Baptist paper called the *Church Union*. Under the editorship of Henry Ward Beecher, though, it gradually changed into a family magazine while still retaining a religious emphasis. In 1893 it changed both its name and editorial emphasis, becoming a regular and influential journal of opinion.

Bellamy's name first appeared on the magazine's masthead in the issue of October 12, 1927, where he was listed as "General Manager." Within two weeks, in the issue of October 26, the title changed to "Publisher." One of his first acts was to publish an unsigned editorial defending the Wilson Prize Essay Contest. It begins, "In declining to make an award of either first or second prize in the contest . . . the Jury of Award . . . acted in accord with good sense, with courage, with self-respect and, most important of all, with respect to the memory of the man whom the offer of the prize was designed to honor."

To Bellamy's credit, he himself acted with courage at least once during his tenure as publisher of what soon became *The Outlook and Independent* when he acquired a second venerable journal of opinion—*The Independent*—in 1928 and merged it with the first. In the fall of that year the new magazine attracted considerable attention when it published a series of articles in defense of Sacco and Vanzetti, the Italian immigrant anarchists whose trial for murder became a cause célèbre of the 1920s.

"The magazine under Bellamy was bright and interesting," Frank Luther Mott wrote, "but it lacked the old 'feel' of strong personalities." Brooks fans would dispute this, of course, since one of the strong personalities whose work was a regular feature of the magazine was Walter himself, whom Bellamy employed in 1927 first as a columnist and book reviewer, and then in 1928 as an associate editor.

Walter's first weekly column debuted in the issue of October 26, 1927. Titled "Ivory, Apes, and Peacocks,"[5] it is a "New Yorkerish" exercise in window-shopping, containing, as its prospectus promised, "notes on the newest contributions of American genius and inventiveness to the art of living." In other words, Walter would be writing about consumer goods, about gadgets, gimcracks, games, and geegaws. The prospectus also promised, "These notes will represent the buyer's [point of view]. And they will not confine themselves to articles advertised in these columns."

The first column was devoted to the prosaic subjects of radiators and lamps but began on a rather philosophical note:

> American designers have frequently overstepped the bounds of good taste in trying to make some of our common household objects aesthetically pleasing. In making a silk purse out of a sow's ear, they want to make the article look like a silk purse, and yet to retain all the homely uses—whatever those may be— which the sow's ear possesses. The telephones, for instance, which masquerade as dolls in crinoline. Hasn't the telephone enough personality to be just frankly itself? And if it hasn't, wouldn't it be more sensible to manufacture better-looking telephones than to make such pathetic and unfortunate efforts to have them socially presentable?

---

5. This quotation is from the Biblical First Book of Kings but it's more likely that Walter borrowed it from John Masefield's once-famous poem, "Cargoes." Masefield was a particular favorite with Walter, who owned more than a dozen volumes of the poet's work.

After then acknowledging that "nobody has a kind word for the radiator," Walter proceeds to extol the aesthetic virtues of Slyker Radiator Furniture, "which has the virtue of not attempting to make it look like something entirely different." Walter also had good words for lamps he had seen at Altman's and at Yamanaka's. At the latter store, Walter noted, "We were also impressed with the fact that the title of this department is not entirely symbolical. For we saw ivory, and we saw apes and peacocks—in ivory—along with a multitude of other creatures, real and mythological." (Was Freddy among them, one wonders?)

For the first three months of its life the column was signed only with Walter's initials ("W.R.B.") and his name did not appear in the magazine's table of contents. In the issue of January 4, 1928, Bellamy—in acknowledging several newcomers to his editorial staff—mentioned Walter R. Brooks of "Ivory, Apes, and Peacocks" and a month later, in the February 1st issue, Walter's name appeared in full.

Though for the most part dated and of interest today principally to students of American commercial culture and history, the column does contain some nice examples of Walter's sprightly style: in his column of 12/28/27, for example, he describes modernistic furniture as looking like "nothing so much as the relics of an explosion in a trigonometry factory." The column also conveys a sense of his own personal style, aesthetic, and interests. Despite the fact that it was written during Prohibition, for example, much attention is given to cocktail shakers (and even more to cigarette boxes: Walter was an inveterate smoker until he was laid low by a serious heart attack in 1949). And it becomes increasingly clear, as the columns accumulate, that Walter detested artifice, for among his "pet animosities" were "the things that look like what they aren't"—e.g., a loudspeaker that looks like a lamp, a fire-screen which turns out to be a bridge table, book ends that are pipe racks, etc. This dislike found its way into at least one of Walter's short stories, "To Break the Monogamy" (*Liberty*, 4/22/39), which features Mr. and Mrs. Seymour Cluett, who "were pretty comfortable on the money Mr. Cluett made out of a terrible-looking combination piano and oil heater for rural homes which he had invented."

The radio also incurred his wrath, even when it looked like a radio:

> The entrance of the radio into American homes has spoiled the appearance of more than one living room. [They] squat like obscene beasts at our firesides." [11/9/27]). "To us, the important point about any make of radio [is] the ease with which it can be turned off. We have a radio, and we use it, but we have to admit that while we sometimes get pleasure from turning it on, we always get pleasure from turning it off. Lots of times we just turn it on to have the fun of turning it off—of choking off the Blattworthy Sisters in mid-caterwaul—of hearing the blessed silence rush back into a room that has been clamorous with the warbling of sopranos of the hot potato school, with the rantings of eighth-rate actors and the wisecracks of twentieth-rate humorists. Perhaps the chief benefit that the radio has brought most of us is an appreciation of the value of silence. Just as the automobile, and probably the airplane, will eventually teach us the value of staying in one place. But the radio we are looking for now is the one that will allow us to turn our neighbor's radio off. (9/2/31)

The true delight of reading these columns eighty years after they were written is coming across a casual nugget of autobiographical information. In his third column (11/16/27), for example, he writes:

> When we were in our teens we spent a summer at a seaside hotel [perhaps the inspiration for the hotel in *The Romantic Liars?*] with our aunt. Every evening after dinner we had to play a game of backgammon with our aunt before we were free to follow our own devices. Although our aunt invariably won, we still think that our play showed a superior brilliancy and *finesse*, since our endeavor was to lose as speedily as was consistent with an appearance of good faith. And our aunt never suspected us. (11/16/27)

In the next column he mentions "some small nieces" who must have been the children of Anne's brother, since Walter's sister Elsie was childless. In the column of 12/21, he writes about a toy theater: "When we were a child, we would probably have gone mad with joy if any one had given us a toy theater. We, personally, like these things better than the highly specialized mechanical toys, which seem to us to give little scope to the child's imagination."

Here is a sampling of other insights worth recording:

1/18/28: "In our early youth we used to slide down the front stairs on an enormous tea tray, which had as a decoration a Biblical scene in brilliant colors, with palm trees and camels and patriarchs in gay robes. Once we tried the back stairs, which were uncarpeted, but met with noisy disaster on the hairpin turn halfway down."

11/28/28: Writing about a new children's book titled *Secret Messages: How To Read and Write Them,* Walter notes, "We remember that quite a lot of our own childhood and that of our friends was spent in making up ciphers in which we communicated with each other."

6/11/30: "We are fond of Nature; we like to rest our eyes on green pastures and clouds, and blue hills; we yearn over wild flowers and listen rapt to the tootlings of the birds, our little feathered friends, as we like to call them. But no summer landscape is complete for us that does not contain somewhere in the immediate foreground a deep and comfortable chair. We yearn and listen most effectively, we find, in a semi-recumbent position."

In other columns we learn—or have confirmed for us— that Walter played golf (as did Bellamy); that he spoke Swedish, French, and German; that he traveled by subway but also owned a Ford; that he had an office at the magazine (at 120 E. 16th Street); that he enjoyed long baths ("There's no place like a bathtub for reading philosophy or modern poetry, because you're practically outside of space and time. Callers and telephones can't get at you. There are no interruptions") (4/4/28); that he had "no more mechanical ability than an aardvark"; that he was terrible at math; that he was a serious "re-gifter" at Christmastime; that he disliked having to scrub out the bathtub at prep school; that he had no confidence in collapsible boats, having sunk in one on the Erie canal as a boy; that he once took banjo lessons; that—"short and fair"—he would rather have leisure than beauty (though he confessed to an interest "alas in incipient baldness"); and that he enjoyed painting in pastels, though elsewhere he professes a "lack of knowledge in matters artistic" (5/2/28) and features a running gag about his editor's failure to appreciate the drawings that he wanted to use to illustrate his column. We also learn that he played chess, spent a month in Germany in the summer of 1930, once smoked "denicotinized cigarettes," and enjoyed poking fun at Bellamy—who was his best friend, yes, but also that authority figure, the editor.

Closer to home, we also learn from his column for January 27, 1932, that he knows "a portrait painter who makes portraits from daguerreotypes, life size and at a reasonable price, too." This is a bit of shameless self-interest, since the painter in question is his own wife, Anne, whose portraits of Walter's uncles Edward Stevens and Charles Brooks hung on his living room walls. "The likenesses are excellent," he concludes. Whether this sparked any sales for Anne is unknowable but it is interesting in this context that Walter's column occasionally contained a firm disclaimer, stating "emphatically" that "not a line of what appears in this department is advertising, either paid or unpaid."

Nevertheless, a November 7, 1929, memorandum to Walter from "Eliott D. Odell" notes, "Mr. Stone [the Chicago advertising manager] is very anxious indeed to pass along possible leads to you for comment from time to time, and I have assured him that you are always in the receptive mood for honest-to-God novelties. It is not news, of course, but some comment on the new Chrysler equipped with a radio—and Packard likewise—might be looked into

Anne's portrait of Walter's Uncle Edward

at the local dealers. Both of these contracts are warm on the griddle." (Walter later owned a Packard, which, years after, he gave to Bellamy, who was in sore need of a means of transportation.)

The equation between potential sales and a favorable mention of novelties in Walter's column is inescapable, of course, as is the corollary incentive for manufacturers to advertise in the magazine. Perhaps for these reasons, "Ivory, Apes, and Peacocks" was Walter's most sustained contribution to the magazine, surviving from 1927 through April of 1932 when, thanks to declining sales and the economic depredations of the Great Depression, *The Outlook and Independent*—in severe financial extremis—finally went into receivership, was re-organized, and sold.

"Ivory, Apes," and "Worse"

WHILE CONTINUING TO WRITE HIS WEEKLY "IVORY, APES, and Peacocks" column, Walter, beginning in the spring of 1928, also contributed three different book-related columns: "Picked at Random" ran from 5/2/28 through 9/11/29; "Behind the Blurbs" from 10/23/29 through 11/18/31, and "The Week's Reading" from January 1–April 1932. (The magazine became a monthly for its last two issues, March and April 1932.)

What Walter wrote about reviewing in general applies well to his own work in this department: "Book reviews today are, as a rule, pretty well written. The general run of reviewers are fluent, entertaining, and able to give you some idea of what a book is about. This is about all the reader can expect. One reviewer, no matter how erudite, can scarcely be expected to give on successive days really expert judgment on a book about Africa, a translation of a novel by Gide, a life of Robert E. Lee and a history of philosophy. But he can be expected to think clearly as far as he goes, and to express himself in English." ("Prose and Worse," 6/10/31)

Walter treated this subject more satirically in an essay for *Bookman* magazine, in which he lamented that "the great trouble with book reviewing is that you have to read the books." One sympathizes with him. As he noted in an unpublished (and undated) essay on the same subject, "For several years I have read at least one book a day for review." And received scant respect for his efforts, apparently, for in the same article he called the book reviewer "the stepchild of the literary family" and "the clown in the literary circus."

For the most part, Walter's reviews were informative, sprightly, and brief (seldom running longer than 150 words). Typically reviewing as many as five books in each weekly issue, Walter did manage to cover a surprising variety of literary forms and subjects. Nevertheless, he specialized in mysteries, adventure stories like his own serialized novel *The Romantic Liars*, and books about nature and natural history. In keeping with *The Outlook*'s editorial policy, he focused on "only the most interesting of those books which people everywhere are buying and reading" ("Speaking of Books," 10/19/27). In other words, he focused on popular literature and, as a result, many of the books he reviewed are forgotten today. But by no means all.

When it comes to authors and titles that *are* remembered, Walter nearly always showed discerning taste. Among humorists, for example, he gave special praise to Robert Benchley, Wolcott Gibbs, Franklin Pierce Adams (FPA), Anita Loos, Thorne Smith, and Don Marquis. He gave poets Dorothy Parker and Ogden Nash positive attention, while in the realm of nonfiction, he praised Margaret Mead's *Coming of Age in Samoa*, noting, "The unusual feature for a book on psychological subjects is that it is exceedingly well written and possesses charm." And he showed courage and a salutary sophistication in also noting, "It seems a shame that the necessary prominence of sex in the treatment of the subject may prove a bar to the enjoyment by the general reading public of the absorbing recital of the intimate details of Samoan everyday life." On a less lofty note he also lavished praise on *The Savoy Cocktail Book,* which he called "A very joyous book in appearance, intent, and effect."

As might be expected, he enjoyed deflating self-importance and exaggerated reputations and styles. For example, of Gertrude Stein he wrote, "We have always been a great admirer of Gertrude Stein. Give her one small idea that another writer would be able to make only a 7-word sentence of, and she'll spread it over 50 cents' worth of paper. Cheap paper at that.

And even then the reader doesn't get it until it's explained by a third party. With her gift we could fill our column with a review of the first verse of Little Miss Muffet and have enough left over for next week." (11/20/29)

And in a review of a new edition of *The Time Machine* by H. G. Wells (whose work he collected), Walter wrote, "This reviewer wouldn't trade it for all the heavy and frequently tiresome volumes Mr. Wells has written since he gave up story writing and took to saving the world."

Similarly, he was dispassionate enough to note deficiencies in a later title by another early favorite, Lord Dunsany. In a review of *Seven Modern Comedies*, he writes, "Seven times in this volume Lord Dunsany draws the magic circle and lights the mysterious powder and mutters the magic words but only twice does the incantation work. Are the spirits growing weary of being summoned?"

Acknowledging Jeffrey Farnol's knowledge of boxing, Walter nevertheless can't resist criticizing—in Farnol's own style—his accounts of *Famous Prize Fights*, noting, "We liked not the manner of the telling. 'Twas vastly annoying to us—the continued intrusion of the author's personality, his literary mannerisms, his "egads" and "verilys." Yet now and again he forgets these sentimental trappings and the fight becomes a fight vividly realized. But not for long. For soon again the tale is smothered in 'tushery.' Why, odd rabbit us, we're beginning to write that way ourself!"

His shrewdest judgments were often reserved for genre fiction. "We have read mystery and horror for years," he writes, "and the faint air of apology with which people show the title of a detective story when asked what they are reading seems to us an affectation, and a confession of the most poisonous form of pseudo-intellectual snobbism." ("The Week's Reading," 9/11/29) His discerning fondness for the form is evidenced in his appreciative reviews of work by Agatha Christie, R. Austin Freeman, Edgar Wallace, and Dorothy L. Sayers, among others.

This does not mean that he gave a free pass to the mysteries that came to his attention. On the contrary—and despite his disclaimer that "Long practice enables us to skip like a young lamb through detective stories" ("Random," 1/30/29)—Walter reserved some of his most thoughtful criticism for this form. He actively disliked the once popular Philo Vance mysteries of S. S. Van Dine, for example, stating—a bit acidly—"Philo Vance is to us a long-winded pedantic bore. We embark happily upon this story [*The Bishop Murder Case*], assured of a pleasant voyage by the testimonials from various critics printed upon the jacket only to have it sink slowly beneath our feet until we are wallowing in a sea of verbiage. There is a Jonah aboard, and that Jonah is made of lead, and that Jonah's name is Philo Vance."

If Vance were lead to Walter, another detective—Sam Spade—was pure gold. And Walter's finest hour as a reviewer was, arguably, to be among the very first to recognize the genius of Dashiell Hammett. Of *The Maltese Falcon*, for example, Walter wrote, "This is not only probably the best detective story we have ever read, it is an exceedingly well written novel. There are few of Mr. Hammett's contemporaries who can write prose as clean-cut, vivid, and realistic."

By this time, of course, Hammett's reputation was made but Walter had recognized his potential in his very first novel, *Red Harvest*. "A thriller that lives up to the blurb on the jacket is unusual enough to command respect," Walter wrote. "When, in addition, it is written by a man who plainly knows his underworld and can make it come alive for his readers, when the action is exciting and the conversation racy and amusing—well, you'll want to read it. . . . We recommend this one without reservation. We gave it an A plus before we'd finished the first chapter." Walter's early praise did not go unnoticed. "Many thanks for your kindness to *Red Harvest*," Hammett wrote Walter, signing this laconic note, "Gratefully yours."

Walter's good opinion of Hammett's work and the fact that the two shared a publisher—Alfred A. Knopf—led, several years later, to one of the saddest might-have-beens in literary history. As one of Hammett's biographers Diane Johnson writes, "Like everybody else he needed money, and he contracted desultorily to do little tasks."

One of these was to write an introduction for the then forthcoming *Freddy the Detective*. Hammett seems to have undertaken
this task with a good will, writing to Walter on January 12, 1931:

Dear Mr. Brooks,

I've tried several times without luck to get you on the phone
since Mrs. Knopf spoke to me about the forward [sic.] to *Freddy the
Detective*. Will you give me a ring?

Sincerely,
Dashiell Hammett
Hotel Elysee
60 East 54th St.
NY

Perhaps Walter failed to reach him or perhaps Hammett
was a procrastinator worthy of Freddy himself, for he failed to
deliver the foreword, despite increasingly impatient
reminders from Knopf who wrote, on April 2, 1932, "We have
to have that introduction of yours immediately . . . do you
think you can manage this?" And again on April 5: "Just to
remind you again that I need the introduction to *Freddy the
Detective* badly." And, lastly, on April 12, "I have been trying to
get you on the telephone as you had promised me the introduction to *Freddy the Detective* last week. Do you think you
could manage it for me?"

The third time was not a charm, alas, for—since no introduction was ever forthcoming—the answer, apparently, was "no."

Of the thousands and thousands of words that Walter
wrote for *The Outlook* between 1927 and 1932, it is his reviews
that contain his best writing. Some of his worst are to be found
in yet another column, which he conducted between January
1931 and March 1932. Titled "Prose and Worse," this column
suffered from a lack of focus that was foreshadowed in its very
first appearance in the issue of 1/28/31. It starts, "'You write
well on nothing in particular,' said the editor grimly, 'so it's

really up your street to conduct a column on that subject.' The implication was, we suppose, that we write well enough as long as we don't get out of our depth, and that our depth is in with the eight-year-olds, about a tenth of the way out to the raft."

Unfortunately, it turned out that Walter *didn't* write very well about nothing, and the result was an often tedious exercise in heavy-handed whimsicality. A recurring character, for example, was a talking mouse named Mr. Meadowcraft, who was accustomed to leaving Walter notes (shades of *Archie and Mehitabel* by Don Marquis, one of Walter's heroes). The trouble was that the notes were never very funny, though Freddy fans would be intrigued by the mouse's early mention of "Mr. Bean the farmer." Turns out the rodent hailed from a farm in upstate New York and had come to Manhattan in an effort to find his sister, who had run away with a traveling salesman. In due course, Meadowcraft found work with a bootlegger and, after a flurry of unanswered notes, finally paid Walter a personal call, demanding to know why his contributions were no longer being published in "Prose and Worse."

Walter explained that his stuff had gotten "too advanced. As long as you stuck to your own experiences on the farm, and in New York, it was fine. But when you started that stream-of-consciousness stuff, The Odyssey of a Mouse—well, of course you've been reading Joyce, and it's a very creditable addition to that type of literature. But good heavens, I had no idea mice had such thoughts as that." It's hard to tell if Walter were copying himself here or Don Marquis.

As far as the column itself was concerned, the model must have been Franklin P. Adams's celebrated column "The Conning Tower," which contained not only FPA's own witty observations (he was a member in good standing of the celebrated group of wits called the Algonquin Round Table) but also, and more importantly, unpaid contributions from other writers, some of the younger of whom—like Dorothy Parker and James Thurber—launched their careers with their offerings.

Consider that in his very first "Prose and Worse" column, Walter wrote, "We have no intention of filling all this space all by ourselves every week. You've got to do your share, and in

order not to change our percentages in the middle of a column, we'll put your share at nine tenths. Let us have your
views. If we agree with them, we'll print them. If they're in
verse, we'll probably print them whether we like them or not."
(Many of the free will offerings to the "Conning Tower," of
course, were in the form of light verse.)

Despite repeated entreaties in future columns, Walter
received precious few submissions and those he did receive
were of a caliber to suggest why he called his column "Prose
and *Worse!*" The best submission came from Walter himself.
One of them, "The Red Gods Call," reappeared some years
later, in slightly modified form, in a Freddy book:

> Hooray for the printemps! Hooray for
> the Fruhling!
> All the little lambs on the hillsides
> squealing!
> Tighten up your braces! Tuck in your
> shirt!
> All the little green things growing in
> the dirt!

Another, longer effort comprised the entire column for July
29, 1931. Titled "Showers and Cooler," it's one of Walter's most
ambitious—and best—poems. Here are the first two verses:

> In a sultry summer swoon
> Dreams the golden afternoon.
> Quiet rings the world around
> In a drowsy haze. No sound—
> Song of bird or sigh of breeze—
> In the windless air;

> Only the hum of slumberous bees
> Everywhere.
> Talking to each other slow
> Thunder voices mutter low,
> Grumble-growl in undertones,

Every leaf the linden owns
Shudders, listening, while the air,
Hushed and breathless, watches where
Slow the thunderers lift their heads
  Up above the rim
Of the earth their bulk o'erspreads,
  Dark and grim.

In due course, the lack of outside submissions led Walter to invent a character whose verse submissions—and later whose person—would become semi-regular fixtures of the column. The first two submissions, both untitled, appeared in the columns of 6/17 and 7/8/31, respectively, and went unnoticed. The third, however, which appeared on August 12, 1931, stirred the pot of controversy. Also untitled, it began with the lines:

Breathes there a man with soul so dead
Who never to himself hath said
This is my own, my native land . . .

As a number of outraged readers were quick to point out, this was written not by Walter's correspondent, but instead by Sir Walter Scott. As one outraged lady from Mississippi wrote, "Every fifth grade child in my state has learned to recite it and knows that it was written by Sir Walter Scott. I am shocked that Outlook is so careless as to have allowed such a mistake to be printed."

Walter must have been shocked that any reader could have thought this was a serious attempt to plagiarize, especially since he had identified the correspondent who "submitted" it as "Mr. Aeneas B. Hooker," which was, of course, the pseudonym he and Bellamy had used for their youthful collaborations. Even those who didn't recognize the name should have been tipped off by the paragraph Walter wrote to introduce the verse:

We are pleased to print another contribution from Mr. Aeneas B. Hooker. "This verse I am sending is not new," writes Mr. Hooker. "I wrote it a number of years ago, and came across it when looking through several trunksfull of old manuscripts in the attic. I was really surprised to find how good it was. I shall be much pleased if you find it worthy of being presented to your readers."

To those who wrote to complain, Walter sent the following reply:

Thank you for your recent letter regarding Scott's verses from The Lay of the Last Minstrel, which I printed under Prose and Worse in the August 12 issue of The Outlook. It has been a source of satisfaction to me that I have received so many letters regarding them, since one purpose in running them was to endeavor to ascertain to what extent Outlook readers were still familiar with the classics, which seem today to be undeservedly neglected. The other purpose, I may add, was to introduce the fictitious character, Hooker, whose opinions and adventures will, I hope, furnish some entertainment in future issues.

Indeed, Hooker would appear sporadically in seven later columns, the first being that of August 26 in which Walter printed Hooker's reply to the charge of plagiarism. It read, in part, as follows:

Sir: I seldom reply to letters criticizing or condemning my conduct, inspired as they invariably are, by envy, or by the hope to shine in some reflected glow of fame. . . . You state that the authorship of this poem is claimed by one "Sir" Walter Scott. Who is this Scott? I never heard of him. I do not find him in Debrett, and can only conclude that his title is, like his authorship, a fiction of his own imagination. And speaking of titles, I am *Captain*, not *Mister* Hooker, and I will thank you to remember it. I earned that title first at sea, and though I later won many others, in a dozen campaigns both at sea and on land, I wish to be known only as Captain. As for honorary titles, I care little for them. Dozens have been offered me, but I have always refused them. As the late Kaiser said to me when I paid him a short visit at Potsdam in 1912 . . .

And on it goes from there. Hooker quickly emerged as a kind of blowhard pirate-type who, though claiming to be "living in retirement down here in quiet old Wophasset," bragged windily of his continued prowess with pistol, rapier, cavalry saber, broadsword, and Krummsaebel and promised to challenge "this man Scott" to a duel.

If such a duel ever took place, Walter failed to record it and, besides, Scott was long dead—though that might not have been enough to stop Hooker. In his January 13, 1932, column Walter did share a very long account from the bombastic captain of his visit to heaven, where he plotted (unsuccessfully) to become commander-in-chief of the celestial armies (are there echoes here of Mark Twain's story "Captain Stormfield's Visit to Heaven?").

Most readers seemed to feel that a little Hooker went a very long way . . . too long for some. "I note with pleasure," one reader wrote, "that your 'Prose and Worse' article is omitted from the Sept. 2 issue. I do hope you have decided to discontinue it. It was awful!"

Others, however, entered into the spirit of things, writing to Walter in the imagined persons of Hooker's relatives Hester, Sapphira, and William. Like the Captain, they all claimed to be the true authors of poems previously ascribed to others—such as Edgar Allan Poe, Thomas Hood, and even William Shakespeare. Walter gleefully published them all, noting, with tongue firmly in cheek, "It is surprising how many poets there are in the family!"

As for Sir Walter Scott, Walter wasn't quite finished with him. Some years later, Walter's alter ego Freddy the Pig would write a poem that began, "Breathes there a pig with soul so dead. . . ." (For the complete effort see *Freddy and the Bean Home News*.)

But that wouldn't be for another ten years. For the moment Walter's work seemed to be increasingly labored and his humor, more and more forced. It was time for a change, which circumstances provided when declining circulation resulted in the suspension of *The Outlook's* publication in the spring of 1932; four months later the magazine was sold to new owners who installed former New York Governor Alfred E. Smith as editor. But not to worry, for Brooks and Bellamy were about to begin a new chapter in their continuing adventures in collaboration.

The Manhattanite

WITH THE DEMISE OF *THE OUTLOOK AND INDEPENDENT*, Bellamy—and, inevitably, Walter—moved on to a new adventure. *New Yorker* founding editor Harold Ross had installed Bellamy as his managing editor and, as a result, Walter had begun writing pieces for "The Talk of the Town" column. True to past patterns, Bellamy lasted in his new job "only a few months. 'He smoked cigars,' was Ross's only explanation for firing him"—and, no doubt accordingly, Walter's memories of the *New Yorker* days (however few they were) were not happy ones.

In fact, in an interview five years later, he described the magazine as a place "where no one speaks to anyone else and the men sit at their desks looking serious as they can be." However disagreeable Walter found the atmosphere there, he did manage to produce more than two dozen pieces for "The Talk of the Town" on topics ranging from Sears Roebuck to Campbell's Soup and from hurdy-gurdies (a piece that would inspire a later story, "Organgrinder's Swing") to a store that sold snakes. At least one of these pieces elicited favorable comment from Ross himself, who wrote, to Bellamy, "I thought Brooks's re-write of the squash revenge story a very good job on a difficult piece. A very hard story to tell so short. I did a little tinkering with it which I hope he won't mind. I did only a little."

Many of these pieces are so much of their time (the early 1930s) and place (New York City) that they are all but inexplicable to contemporary readers. A number of them—like Walter's pieces in *The Outlook*—deal with the privations

Prohibition visited on the drinking class; several betray other personal interests. A longish piece on *Uncle Tom's Cabin*, for example, certainly reflects Walter's interest in publishing, bookselling, and book collecting. Another—a whimsical mini-profile of the president of the American Association for the Advancement of Atheism—is not only newly timely, thanks to the recent popularity of such atheist authors as Sam Harris, David Dunnett, and Christopher Hitchens—but also contains a perhaps unconscious nod to Walter's family's history: Walter describes a leaflet the atheist presses on him "containing rather fanciful portraits of Bible patriarchs, with an interpretive description of each: Noah, the first drunkard; Joshua, a cold-blooded butcher *with no more mercy in his nature than an Apache Indian*"—shades of Walter's murdered Uncle Edward!

The greatest value of these pieces probably lies in their confirmation that Walter—after a decade of living in Manhattan—was now a confirmed New Yorker.

Having moved to Manhattan in 1920, Walter and Anne first lived at 135 West 12th Street until 1922 when they bought a four-story townhouse at 27 Bank Street in Greenwich Village. Built in 1856–57, the red-brick residence had most recently been a rooming house and required extensive remodeling—no mean feat since the former owners refused to move out. "So we moved in on top of them and started alterations," Walter wrote to a correspondent. "After several months of daily quarrels, and efforts on their part to stop the work—during one of which they locked me in a room where I stayed for half an afternoon before I could get out—they left."

Alas, it seems they left behind an "insane" cat and an equally insane former tenant, of whom Walter wrote:

The crazy woman . . . had lived in the house for a number of years, and we found later that she had paid no rent, but had intimidated the landlady by threatening to steal her husband. We thought she had gone but found her rolled up in a grimy old quilt under the eaves. She explained in a cultured voice, when I turned the flashlight on her, that she had not been able to look for a room that day because she had had to take a man to dinner at the Waldorf. Finally, however, she too was persuaded to go.

(One wonders if this were the "tenant" who, it was said, was a friend of Patrick Dennis's aunt, Marion Tanner, who claimed to be the inspiration for his famous creation Auntie Mame and who owned a red-brick house of her own at 72 Bank Street.)

As for the cat, according to Walter, "it yowled all night in the lower halls, then unoccupied. There were so many holes for steampipes in plumbing that we could not catch it . . . so we organized nightly cat hunts. The housekeeper started in the attic, and I in the cellar, and we worked toward the middle, each carrying an old quilt. Finally we managed to drive the cat out of doors."

Not that Walter necessarily disliked cats. He and Anne had one of their own, which they named "Bitte Schoen," and one of the most charming pieces Walter wrote for *The Outlook* was an account of the "cat elevator" that he and Anne contrived to convey the cat outside when it wished to have some fresh air:

> The window of our apartment being some fifteen feet above the level of the back yard our cat was forced to stay indoors . . . until it occurred to our brighter half to tie a cord to a bushel basket and lower him to the yard. The basket has become an institution. Several times a day he climbs into it, and sits there patiently yowling until somebody notices him and lets him down. When he becomes bored with Nature, he gets in again and howls to be pulled up." (7/1/31 "Prose and Worse")

Given Walter's problems with tenants, it is a bit surprising that he then became a landlord himself, renting the upper floors of his house to tenants. Little about this experience— except, perhaps, the revenue it produced—was particularly salutary. In fact, it seemed to have brought nothing but trouble. But Walter was a writer and he recognized opportunity in annoyance. The result was a spate of stories and articles about the exigencies and aggravations of being a landlord. In one of these, "The Mossgrip Arms," a story he wrote for *Esquire,* a landlord surprises a thief in his building and quickly decides to join the felon in robbing his tenants, most of whom are in arrears on their rent.

Fortunately, not all of Walter's tenants were a nuisance. The poet Allen Tate and his writer wife Caroline Gordon lived at Bank Street for a time, exchanging their services as live-in custodians for rent. In a letter to her friend Sally Wood, Gordon explained, "Have I written you since we became janitors? We have an apartment, half of which we rent, for our services. It's rather hectic at times but better than having a steady job."

And it clearly left them time for their writing. Walter expanded on this:

> My janitor has become a fairly well known critic. He is invited frequently to teas where budding women poets submit their verse to him, and he usually charges them a nice penny for his opinion. At present he is doing a book on Stonewall Jackson [which would be published in 1928]. When he sells an article—or his wife, who is a writer also, sells one—there is occasion for a great celebration in the basement apartment, and often the guests include men and women who are quite prominent in the literary world. It is a funny arrangement, and the janitor and his wife are a very amusing couple. They don't have much money but they appear to have an awful lot of fun.[6]

Walter's interest in the city and its attractions and oddments had been further demonstrated by the publication, in 1931, of his first book for adults (*The Romantic Liars,* remember, was never published in book form). Titled *New York: An Intimate Guide,* it was published—like the Freddy books—by Alfred A. Knopf and offered a diverting, opinionated, and lively intro-

---

6. This quote comes from a newspaper clipping in Walter's scrapbook. Like many others, it gives no date or source, though internal evidence suggests it was published in the Rochester newspaper in 1927 when Walter was doing a great deal of publicity on the publication of *To and Again.*

duction to the city for both the visitor *and* resident. Served up in nineteen topically arranged chapters, it contains all that Walter knows about New York. (He's quick to offer a disclaimer in his foreword, however: "But no one ever Tells All. He merely Tells All He Knows.")

In Walter's case that was quite a lot. In fact, he claims, "I have kept nothing back." That said, much of the content of this now nearly eighty-year-old book is dated and of little interest to any but Brooks aficionados and perhaps to economic historians (quite a lot of the book is devoted to shopping and clearly grew out of Walter's "Ivory, Apes, and Peacocks" column). Recent visitors to New York will find it wryly amusing to read that single rooms at the then newly opened Waldorf-Astoria Hotel—and at the longer established Plaza—could then be had for $8.00 a night. As for tipping, it's certainly useful to know that "if a luncheon check for two is $1.70, you will tip 20 or 25 cents."

Walter wasn't always so generous. (This is a man, after all, who made his second wife, Dorothy, darn the darns on his socks.) Consider his advice on shoeshines: "If you insist on sticking to the rule that a dime is the smallest possible tip, go ahead and tip a hundred percent for your ten-cent shine, but you're doing it without our approval. A nickel is certainly enough." He was even more ferocious on the subject of hat-checks: "The hat-check system, by which you pay out in one year to brigands who lurk just inside the doors of restaurants ten times the original cost of the hat, can't be beaten unless you are willing to go bareheaded or wear a cap that can be stuffed into a pocket."

Careful though he may have been about money, Walter clearly valued less tangible things as well, for one of the longest chapters in the book is titled "Improving the Mind" and is devoted to lectures, courses, and special schools. Ever a realist, Walter is quick to acknowledge that many people will find this sort of stuff dull. "Even New Yorkers fail to grasp how New York's enormous educational opportunities can enlarge their lives," he writes. "Which is not their fault. 'Educational' is a dull word that may well scare off anybody who doesn't realize that the theater is educational, that life itself is at its dullest only when it is not being educational."

Such nuggets of timeless truth are strewn about the pages of a book that is otherwise a celebration of the long-gone. In this *plus ca change* regard, consider what Walter says of driving in the city:

> To attempt to do any sightseeing in your own car is rather foolish. You will see only the long lines of vehicles on either side of you, and, in front, a kaleidoscope of skipping pedestrians, gesticulating cops, and red and green lights. The New York pedestrian will make no appeal to you as a man and brother, for he will pay no attention to your horn and in order to get across the street he will do everything but dive between your front and rear wheels. And it's when you want to stop driving that you have trouble, for parking space is seldom where you want to find it.

Plus ca change, indeed!

Though much of the text is focused on useful information presented in a brisk, no-nonsense style, Walter's obvious love for the city occasionally finds expression in a more—well— *rhapsodic* voice:

> New York differs from most foreign cities in that it is the newest things that the visitor wants to see, not the oldest. . . . But if there is no Old World glamour to enchant the visitor, there is a New World glamour which will delight if it does not overpower him, and to which only the most accustomed eyes can be immune. It is in the crowds, in the motion, hanging about the glittering pinnacles and jumbled cliffs of the enormous buildings, most of all perhaps in the effects of light, reflected by day from thousands of facets of stone and glass and steel, sparkling and glaring by night from millions of electric bulbs. It is the thing that keeps many New Yorkers in New York—happy to be boxed up in their stone cells in the clamor and dirt of a stone city, willing to forego cleanliness and quiet and green trees and spacious rooms to live in.

Walter continues to celebrate the city in this sensitive style for another long paragraph before—seemingly embarrassed by having, himself, fallen under New York's "tremendous spell"

—he verbally shakes himself and becomes once again his normally wry self, addressing the reader directly: "Good heavens!"
you exclaim, "Is the man going to burst into song? Get on with
your guidebook."

And so he does, though continuing to enliven the pages
with witty asides and injunctions. For smokers he notes that
Dunhill makes up pipe mixtures practically like a prescription,
only with much more ceremony and a larger overhead. Of the
new House of Detention for Women, "the snappiest thing in
women's prisons you're likely to see," he observes, is that it's
"so attractive that many apartment-hunting women have
stopped in to enquire about rentals . . . to be met with the
information that the only way they can become tenants is to
shoot their husbands or something like that."

For the biographer, though, the most interesting few paragraphs in the book are those Walter devotes to his own neighborhood, Greenwich Village, where he and his wife Anne had
been living since 1922. In them he displays his signature impatience with pretense:

> The Village, once an inexpensive refuge for impecunious artists
> and writers, was never, after it became self-conscious, particularly
> convincing. It drew the near artists, the imitators. Some were
> sincere but the sincere artist seldom has time to grow a beard or
> follow the rigid rules of the unconventional. The desire for self-
> expression which drew so many inexperienced boys and girls to
> the Village was a form of exhibitionism. The desire to do some
> work may have been behind it but in general the wish was father
> to the talk—and the deed got left out in the cold.

There is no hard evidence of it, but one supposes that it
was the inexpensive nature of the neighborhood and not any
desire to live *la vie boheme* that drew Walter to Bank Street,
where he would remain until 1948, when he and Anne moved,
year-round, to the Catskills village of Roxbury, where they had
been summering since the mid-1930s. Like many other good
New Yorkers of reasonable means, the Brookses routinely
deserted the city in the summertime—in the 1920s it was for

their log cabin in the Adirondacks. Walter never stated precisely where the cabin was located but in his 1948 story "George's Magic Carpet," one of the characters has a camp at Two Fawn Lake in the Adirondacks. While there is no *Two* Fawn Lake, there is, indeed, a Fawn Lake near the village of Lake Pleasant, just sixty miles northeast of Utica (which is also mentioned in the story). It's highly likely that Walter's own cabin would have been there or at least in the vicinity. Of it, Walter observed, "We have traveled a good deal, but we have never found anyplace we liked better. From September 1 to October we'd rather be there than in heaven."

In the early 1930s, however, Walter and Anne went looking for heaven elsewhere and apparently found it in Higganum, Connecticut, on the banks of the Connecticut River. They summered there until 1937 when, as noted above, they discovered Roxbury.

Meanwhile, Walter's intimate guide was well reviewed. Creighton Peet of *The Outlook* (for which Walter was still writing) said, "Even if you were born and bred in New York, Mr. Brooks' engagingly written little manual will be able to tell you things about the city which will make you a happier and more contented citizen," while the literary magazine *Books* cheered, "Mr. Brooks has outdone himself to make his collection of data efficient." Nevertheless, Walter's memories of the project were not terribly happy ones, since, as he told a newspaper reporter many years later, the book required an enormous amount of research and proved less profitable than his fiction.

And speaking of fiction, the year before *New York: An Intimate Guide* appeared, Walter's second Freddy book, *More To and Again*, was published. Walter slyly managed to slip a review of sorts into his "Behind the Blurbs" column in *The Outlook:*

We had an odd experience yesterday. We picked a book from a pile on our desk. There were a lot of animals on the cover. We started to read, and found that it dealt with the adventures of a group of farm animals. "Fairly well written," we thought, "though he didn't make the most of his situation here. And that last chapter was sort of pointless." But the farther we went the better we liked it, although a strange sense of familiarity began to creep over us. "Good stuff," we thought, "but this man must have stolen it all somewhere. I have a distinct recollection of having read this before." But in spite of the taint of plagiarism, our enthusiasm grew and at last we shouted: "This fellow is good!" Our shout aroused the editor from his afternoon nap. He came to the door. "What's this?" he growled in his morose way. "Can't have this, you know." We explained. He glanced at the book. "Why, for heaven's sake, man!" he exclaimed. "It's your own book." We looked at it. "By Walter R. Brooks," it said. It was indeed a book for children that we had dashed off one lunch hour and forgotten all about. But it's darn good, at that. We never change our decision once we have rendered it. (August 27, 1930)

Other reviewers were not as kind. The *New York Times*, for example, while acknowledging that "the popularity of *To and Again* will find readers for this second book," went on to say, "But it bears the unmistakable marks of a sequel." On the other hand, the *Boston Globe* called it "a delightful and original nonsense story, with Freddy the pig for a hero," while May Lamberton Becker, who would become literary editor of the *New York Herald Tribune* and was always favorably disposed to Walter's work, said, "The story . . . is told with a humor that will tickle both children and grown-ups."

Certainly it *is* delightful, in parts, but it lacks the originality of *To and Again*, the central premise of which it simply recycles, though sending the animals north this time, instead of south. The introduction of Santa Claus as a character seems to be a more self-conscious effort by Brooks to appeal to a juvenile audience. On the other hand, his inclusion of a clutch of sailors, the crew of a whaling ship called *The Mary Ann* captained by a very piratical-appearing Mr. Hooker, is not so much self-conscious as self-indulgent. Here is the captain: "A man came into the room—a tall, thin man with drooping black moustaches and hard, sharp black eyes. He had sea boots on, and a red sash about his waist, in which a pistol was stuck."

Though Mr. Hooker's first name is not given in *More To and Again*, it's obvious that, once again, Walter is winking at

Bellamy in resurrecting this character based on his friend's pirate ancestor Samuel Bellamy, aka "Black Bellamy," whose first ship was indeed called *The Mary Anne*.

Walter also borrows a plot point from *The Romantic Liars* when—to get rid of the increasingly tiresome sailors—he has the animals fabricate a phony map to Captain Kidd's treasure. Though this map locates the swag off the coast of Florida instead of Maine, it is actually truer to the personal history of Black Bellamy, who did, indeed, sail in search of lost treasure off the coast of Florida.

Walter and Bellamy were so taken with the character of Aeneas B. Hooker that they continued to mention his name in their correspondence for years while also affecting a Robert Newtonesque pirate argot. And often—for their amusement and that of others—they would slip into character as crew of *The Mary Ann* and improvise situations and dialogue for hours. Seeing them in action was, Dorothy Brooks recalled years later, "worth the price of admission."

The end of Walter's association with *The Outlook* also marked the end of his full-time editorial employment, though Bellamy's misadventures in magazine publishing continued to provide part-time editorial employment for Walter. Following his brief interlude at the *New Yorker,* Bellamy returned to publishing by starting yet another magazine, *Fiction Parade*—a kind of literary *Reader's Digest*—and immediately added Walter to its staff as a contributing editor. Walter doesn't seem to have contributed much, though several of his previously published stories were reissued and he also wrote at least two essay reviews. One of the latter, in which he took on the critics of British suspense novelist Geoffrey Household's first novel, *The Third Hour*, elicited a two-page letter of thanks from the author and a brief mention in Walter Winchell's famous syndicated column "On Broadway."

Merging with the decade-old *Golden Book* in 1936, *Fiction Parade* lasted until early 1938 before the publishing parade passed it by. Later that same year Bellamy became editor of *Commentator* magazine—which had been founded in 1936—and again brought Walter aboard, this time to write a column called "Once Over Lightly," which was billed as "a page of hasty notes sent to us at the last minute by Our Official Philosophical Observer." Its first appearance was pseudonymously signed "Bertram Bashwater," which was, of course, the name of one of the sailors in *More To and Again*. The column continued when *Commentator* was merged with the venerable *Scribner's* magazine in 1939, by which time the column was signed, more soberly, "Walter Brooks." This enterprise lasted until mid-1940 when Bellamy was let go, though this time to his credit, since the magazine had taken an editorial hard right turn to become a leading advocate of isolationism and a fawning admirer of the then arch-conservative Charles Lindbergh.

Though Walter and Bellamy would remain fast friends until the former's death in 1958, their longstanding editorial association ended with Bellamy's departure from *Scribner's Commentator*.

Lifelong friends Walter and Frank in later years

This had little, if any, professional impact on Walter's career, however, since by this time he was clearly established as not only an increasingly popular children's book author, but also as a noted author of fiction for adult readers. Indeed, the six years from 1934 through 1939 would, as we will see in the next chapter, prove to be the most remarkably productive of Walter's entire writing life.

Ernestine and Others

To GET SOME SENSE OF HOW VERY PRODUCTIVE—AND successful—Walter was in the decade of the 1930s, consider his previous levels of output: in the teens he published one poem and six stories; during the 1920s he published another poem, seven stories, nine (lightly fictionalized) travel articles, one serialized novel for adults and, most importantly, the first Freddy book. In the 1930s, however, he published two articles (both in *Bookman* magazine); two books for adults—*New York: An Intimate Guide* and the novel *Ernestine Takes Over* [1935]; five Freddy books: *More To and Again, Freddy the Detective, The Story of Freginald, The Clockwork Twin,* and *Wiggins for President*; and sixty-six short stories for adults. The fact that the first of these stories did not appear until 1934 meant that he was publishing at a blistering average rate of eleven stories per year!

His success can be measured in more than numbers, however. Eighteen of his stories appeared in two of America's most distinguished publishers of short fiction: editor Arnold Gingrich's sensationally successful new magazine *Esquire,* which had debuted in 1933, and the much more venerable *Atlantic Monthly,* helmed by another legendary editor, Edward Weeks, who expressed his high opinion of Walter's work in a letter dated February 23, 1940: "I hope you appreciate how much we have come to depend upon the refreshing qualities of your mind. Your native blend of sagacity and humor was never more needed than in a grim time like the present."

Another thirteen stories appeared in the less lofty but nevertheless widely popular pages of *Liberty,* a general interest magazine that, for a time, approached the stature of *The Saturday Evening Post* (where Walter would also publish, but not until the 1940s).

The income Walter derived from his adult writing of the 1920s and '30s varied. For his serialized novel *The Romantic Liars*, for example, he received $2,500. For a 1932 *Bookman* article, he earned $60. For his 1930s *Esquire* short stories, he typically earned $100 (which went up to $112.50 by the middle of the decade). The *Atlantic Monthly* paid $135, and *Liberty* offered from $270 to $360. As for the Freddy books, the records are fragmentary, though we know he received a $250 advance for *Detective* (and a royalty of ten percent) and—seven years later—a $350 advance for *Wiggins for President*.

Most of the work Walter produced in this new decade differed significantly from his stories of the teens and twenties, so many of which had been slightly ponderous romantic fantasies, lacking humor and tending to be very British in tone and lofty inflection. The new work, on the other hand, was *sprightly*—sophisticated, witty, self-assured, and told in the same kind of easy, conversational American voice that Walter had introduced in *To and Again*. Perhaps the most striking thing about these stories, for the first-time reader at any rate, was their purposeful lack of punctuation. Here is a sample (from "A Bare Possibility," *Esquire*, May 1936):

> This Ed Wagstaff was a member of the publishing firm of Samphire & Mellow but he had a laboratory fitted up in his attic because he liked to dabble in science and one day when he was dabbling he got something pretty good. He had been fiddling around trying to get a ray that would make whatever you turned it on disappear because he had figured that such a thing would be pretty useful to doctors and in gold mines and such places but he hadn't been successful. And then this day he made a few changes in his machine and what a surprise. He focused it on a cracker box and the box disappeared. But there was a fly walking across the box and the funny thing about it was that the fly didn't disappear at all.
>
> He stayed right in plain sight.

Aside from novelty, was there a serious purpose to this device? Here's what Walter had to say in the "Contributor's Column" of the August 1937 *Atlantic Monthly*:

> I can't seem to think of anything else except perhaps to defend the lack of punctuation in my stories which bothers some people. It seems to me to give the effect of a story told as if to children and made up as you go along—as it is—and to gain speed and interest and occasional non-sequiturs not otherwise obtainable. I think people will read them through without stopping, partly from the feeling that it would be impolite to interrupt the speaker.

In an editorial note accompanying one of Walter's stories in the August 1937 issue of *Scribner's*, his friend Bellamy had something similar to say: "Mr. Brooks has often been criticized because he writes these stories without punctuation and paragraphing. He says it makes for speed and directness. 'As you tell a story to a child,' he writes, 'the child says, 'What happens next?' and he doesn't even pause for a comma before finding out.'"

Another striking thing about so many of these stories is their inclusion of some element of the fantastic in their characters' otherwise-routine daily lives. But not the same sort of lofty—and sometimes dark—high fantasy of his early stories. Instead this is the kind of cheerful, practical magic that also informed the work of one of Walter's favorite children's fantasists, E. Nesbit, whose work he collected.

"There can be magic in everything," Walter wrote. "But the point is that you have to believe in it and then it's there. It can't be proved. But if you believe anything hard enough it comes true." Characteristically, Walter never strives to explain this magic. It's just there—like the invisibility ray in the passage quoted above. What interests Walter the storyteller is not the cause but the effect.

The method he used to get the effect was, he claimed, "the same as in telling stories to children. They are yarns rather than stories, without any special purpose and with sometimes an idea, but not always. It's the difference between telling a yarn and writing a story."

All of these elements—the easy, conversational tone, the everyday magic, the lack of punctuation, the breezy, sprightly style, the sophisticated subjects and settings—are present in Walter's very first story to be published in the 1930s, "Imagine That," which appeared in the April 1934 issue of the celebrated *Vanity Fair* and for which he earned fifty dollars. Actually more sketch than story (it occupies only half a page), it tells the abbreviated tale of an insurance man named George Thompson who—bored silly by parties—amuses himself by imagining that "he was sitting beside a swell beautiful girl who talked to him about all the things he was interested in and said all the things he liked to hear and that nobody else said."

As time goes by and these imaginary encounters become increasingly vivid, Mr. Thompson actually begins looking forward to parties because "he would see Ernestine" (the name he's given her). To his surprise, other people—including Mrs. Thompson—begin seeing Ernestine, too. Things might have gotten out of hand were it not for the fact that one of the other people who sees the girl, Mr. Fred Washburn, has, Ernestine tells our Mr. Thompson, "a nicer imagination than you." Accordingly, the two go off together and Mr. Thompson "never saw Ernestine again."

Ernestine Takes Over,
published February 1935

Readers did see her again, however, since this story would serve as the inspiration for Walter's only published adult novel, *Ernestine Takes Over* (Morrow 1935). In it Walter starts with the same premise but treats it a good deal more expansively. This time Mr. Thompson (whose first name is now Fred) is an executive in charge of advertising for a glass company, which is owned by his wife Ethel's father. His attitude toward parties, however, remains unchanged:

Parties! There seemed to be a party of some kind nearly every night; if he didn't go to someone else's party he stayed home at a party of his own. Or of Ethel's. She loved them. Gave very nice ones, too, he admitted to himself as he rapped out his pipe [yes, Walter himself occasionally smoked a pipe] and went for his hat. Only—why were they so alike, and all so dull?

Given his druthers, Fred would rather stay home, "mooning"—as Ethel puts it—"over a lot of words" or, he being a nature lover, going for long cross-country walks.

Fred, with some justification, regards his wife as being "like two persons. One of them warm and companionable, the other cool and sarcastic. And he never knew which one he was dealing with. They'd done such nice silly things together, too." Since it is the cool, sarcastic, and endlessly party-loving Ethel who is most often on display, it is no surprise that Fred turns, as in "Imagine That," to a chimerical companion for company. Again it is a lovely, vivacious young woman whom he names "Ernestine." And again she comes to life, just as he imagines her. Which is fine until she becomes such a vivid presence that other men begin seeing her and, well, imagining things about her, too. Though it sounds a bit eyebrow-raising, none of this is really salacious, only slightly bawdy. A reviewer of the British edition of the novel is spot-on in calling it "this harmlessly naughty farce from America."

But the book is not terribly original, either, being fairly derivative in subject and style of the slightly racier work of Thorne Smith, who is best remembered as the creator of Topper, the banker who is bedeviled by the ghosts of the dipsomaniacal George and Marian Kirby. *Ernestine's* publisher, William Morrow, obviously hoped to capitalize on the similarities, even commissioning illustrations by Herbert Roese, who had provided the saucy pictures for Smith's books as well.[7]

For a biographer, however, the more interesting similarities are those to be found between Walter's characters and his

---

7. Speaking of similarities, Smith, like Walter, lost a parent—his mother—at age four, and grew up to live in Greenwich Village, work in advertising, and even, for a time, write for the *New Yorker*.

own life—and wife! Like Walter, Fred Thompson loves words, puzzles, books, and nature. He is professionally engaged in advertising, works in New York City (unlike Walter he lives in Connecticut, but Walter did summer there and set a number of his early 1930s stories there as well), and has both a lively imagination and "a relish for the odd and grotesque." The profession he imagines for Ernestine is that of portrait painter, à la his own wife Anne. And speaking of wives, one wonders whether Walter has Anne in mind when he has Fred's wife Ethel sniff with mild distaste, "What it is to have a clever husband."

Walter's depiction of the Thompsons' strained relationship invites speculation, of course, about the nature of the Brookses' real-life relationship—especially since (as we will see) marital turbulence is a leitmotif of many of the stories that Walter published, not only in the 1930s but also in the 1940s. Whether Walter—like Fred Thompson—found extramarital companionship in his imagination or in something more rooted in the real world is a moot question, but both Dorothy Brooks, Walter's second wife, and her good friend Pauline Hopkins were convinced Walter had had what they called a "girl friend."[8]

Of course, "girl friend" is the term Ethel Thompson applies, sniffingly (she sniffs a lot!), to Ernestine, which causes Fred to retaliate in kind, by referring to the hapless and married Henry Platt as his wife's "boy friend." Clearly Walter intends to suggest a special relationship between Ethel and Henry that antedates the emergence of Ernestine, but whether any physical intimacy is intended remains unclear. The reader does know, however, that there is nothing particularly physical about Fred's friendship with Ernestine— though she becomes so vividly imagined that there *could* have been, and he does, at one point, kiss her. In due course Fred will learn that both of Ethel's parents have had, well, *adventures* themselves and Fred will find himself the object of the would-be amorous attentions of Betty, another married member of the Thompson's social set.

---

8. A recently unearthed correspondence from Bellamy reveals that they were right. The woman—whose name is unimportant—had been a Bank Street neighbor of Walter's.

All of this is presented more or less humorously, though Ethel's planned pursuit of a divorce will cause Fred real pain.

Interestingly, in Walter's copy of his early story "The Elopement" someone (Walter?) has underlined, in pencil, the following passage: "they had promised each other complete freedom of action and perfect liberty in their own respective affairs." As Walter seems to suggest in *Ernestine*, this idea may be fine in theory but the real emotions of real life tend to compromise the intention.

Ultimately, Walter seems to suggest, the problem with the Thompsons' marriage has less to do with the partners' respective extracurricular interests than with Fred himself—his personality and his attitude toward the partnership aspects of marriage. At one point, for example, Fred thinks "he was too soft, too unsure of himself." At another, he deplores his "innate tendency to think of people as preferring almost anyone's conversation and society but his own." "Good Lord," he thinks later, "he's got to stop this meekness." For, as the conniving Betty puts it, "Who wants a scared husband?"

How Walter will resolve this is suggested fairly early in the novel. On page forty-six Fred suddenly realizes that Ernestine has brown eyes and asks:

> "Why are they that color? I never imagined—"
> "You never imagined any special color for them," [Ernestine explains] "it was your friend Mr. Smith that thought they were brown."

Realizing that she has been seeing that roué Smith, Fred flies into a rage and he catches her arms "in a grip that made her cry out."

> "You little devil," he said in a low angry voice, "if you ever see him again. . . ." He stopped abruptly, for she was looking him full and fearlessly in the face and he realized all at once that her eyes were not brown any more; they were a deep and intense blue.
> "You see?" she murmured. "Oh, I love you when you're angry like that, Freddy."

So is Walter suggesting that the answer to marital problems is temper? Well, yes and no. It turns out that Ethel's eyes
are also blue, and that, like Ernestine, she is a blonde.
Indeed, the more Fred comes to know Ernestine, the more
like Ethel she becomes—but an idealized Ethel, the Ethel that
Fred wishes he had married.[9]

Ultimately, Walter seems to imply, it is through learning to
"manage" Ernestine that Fred ultimately learns to "manage"
Ethel. And how is that? Alas, by treating her roughly. At one
point an exasperated Fred says to Ernestine,

> "I ought to beat you black and blue."
> She snuggled against him. There was an excited gleam in
> her blue eyes.
> "Oh, would you Freddy?"
> "I don't go around slapping girls."

A disappointed Ernestine continues to goad him and finally
slaps him three times in succession. That does it. He retaliates
"with a stinging open-hander."

The result is, apparently, designed to be instructive for the
reader: "Her arms clasped convulsively around his neck. 'Oh,
Freddy!'

"'I did that because I wanted to,' he said and twisting her
face up, pressed his mouth harshly against hers. Her eyes
blazed blue into his, then the lids dropped."

Uh-oh, the reader thinks. And, sure enough, a later, similar
slapfest engenders a similar response, but this time from Ethel,
leaving Fred to think, "Ethel's behavior had followed his imagination perfectly when he had slapped her. He wasn't afraid of
her any more."

In the final scene a now dominant Fred says, to his newly
submissive wife,

> "Tell you what we might do. Take a good long cross-country
> walk. Like we used to."

---

9. It would be a lovely thing if there were any evidence that the creators of "I
Love Lucy" had borrowed the names of Lucy and Rickie's neighbors, the
Mertzes, from Walter; but, alas, there is none.

"I'd love it. [Ethel answers] You mean instead of playing contract?"

"Yes. [Fred replies] To hell with the McLeods. Go get your walking shoes on."

She rose obediently. In the doorway she turned and smiled back at him. "Darling Fred," she said softly.

Mr. Thompson smiled back indulgently. "Go on, get ready," he said.

She vanished.

Mr. Thompson looked after her thoughtfully. "My God, it was as easy as that all the time!" he said to himself.

Fade to black and, presumably, blue.

For the modern reader who believes in the equality of the sexes, this is all rather horrifying, but for Walter's contemporaries it was, presumably, *de rigueur*. Certainly the reviews of the novel were universally favorable. The *New York Times* called it "gay, slightly mad, and plausibly fantastic. The Thorne Smith school of fans should find the book thoroughly entertaining."

While also acknowledging the Smith connection, *Books* magazine gave Walter his due: "Ernestine . . . naturally reminds one of the writings of Thorne Smith," Lisle Bell wrote, "but Mr. Brooks displays a talent which is genuine and not imitative. If 'Ernestine Takes Over' doesn't leave you chuckling, your chuckler needs overhauling."

Once established, the theme of the sometimes physical war between the sexes becomes a recurring one in Walter's short fiction, for—as he wrote in his story "Everything Is Nothing," "when normal people marry they either fight and separate or fight and stay together." Unfortunately, the fighting often manifests itself as a bout of slapping, scratching, clawing, and even—occasionally—spanking.

In light of all this is it possible that Walter was a misogynist? Well, he did write an unpublished satirical essay titled "Why Men Hate Women," which starts "I hate women because they want to eat their man and have him, too." While he makes a halfhearted effort to develop this theme, it quickly becomes obvious that what the thrifty Walter really hates is not women but their spending habits. "I hate women," he admits, "because their chief interests are interests that involve spending. With men spending is incidental, and even an unlucky poker player won't lose as much in a year as his wife spends on clothes. He has nothing to show for it? Well, what have women to show? Look at their hats. . . ."

When all is said and done, though, Walter's conclusion is that the thing he really hates about women is that they are . . . necessary. They certainly were to him. After all, he remained married to the same woman for forty-two years, and that relationship ended only because of her death. And within four months of that unfortunate event, he remarried. Complain though he might about their spending habits, their tendency to dominate their husbands, their over-emotionality, their inconsistency, their lack of humor, their passion for security, and so on, Walter couldn't seem to get along without them.

12

The Thirties: Chucklesome Romances and Roxbury

I F WALTER COULDN'T GET ALONG WITHOUT WOMEN, THERE were many other things that he would have liked to do without, among them lawyers. And he brought a good deal more genuine passion to another unpublished essay, "Why I Hate Lawyers," than he had to the piece about women. Bellamy also disliked attorneys and wrote a companion piece to Walter's. It's not clear if they intended to write a collaborative essay but Walter's finished piece does incorporate much of what Bellamy had written.

Together, these two essays suggest that, though Walter may not have been a misogynist, he may have had an inclination to misanthropy. Certainly his one published essay on this general theme had the much more ambitious title, "Why I Hate Everybody."

Odd, then, that so many other of Walter's stories from the thirties were what *Liberty* magazine routinely billed as "chucklesome love stories." Chucklesome? Well, why not? For Walter, the pursuit of romance was almost always risible. It was only when it was won that love seemed to become *serious*—and even rather tiresome—for both the marriage partners *and* the reader; for example: "He showed his love for her by always giving in to her and she showed hers by bossing him around." ("The Worm Returns," *Woman's Journal*, 1937)

The dramatic device Walter typically employs to restore a stale marriage to its pre-wedding piquancy is to introduce some element of novelty, whether it's as elaborate as bringing an imaginary Ernestine to life, taking up amateur burglary, or becoming a hermit, or as simple as a wife losing a tooth: "Wh-what is it? she stammered. Your lisp! he said. Why it's charming. And that funny little tooth out. You look so young and so sort of silly! Darling you're lovely! O gosh said Mrs. Cluett and fell into his arms."

The willingness to be—or at least appear to be—silly is as important as novelty in Walter's stories. In *Ernestine*, remember, Fred recalls wistfully all the "silly" things that he and Ethel used to do. Happily, for Walter's characters at least, silliness is seldom absent for long, since they generally have little practical need for seriousness—or sobriety. How so? Well, consider Watson Pryor, a typical protagonist: "After college with the large quarterly income payments made him by the trustees of his father's estate, neither interest nor necessity counseled work." ("What the Doctor Ordered," *Atlantic Monthly*, May 1939)

Or Herbert Petheridge: "As his parents were wealthy he decided that happiness and ambition could never occupy the same bosom and so he renounced ambition and never let it get a grip on him again." ("The Worm Returns." *Woman's Journal*, 1937)

Where do such people live? Well, typically on the east side of Manhattan or in pricey areas of nearby Long Island or Connecticut. Here, from "Ghost, My Eye," is an example of the latter: "There was a big house on a hill overlooking the Connecticut River not far from Middletown and in it were Mr. Bailey Harper the artist and his widowed mother Mrs. Gilbert Harper and a cook and three maids and a ghost." (*Scribner's*, August 1937)

To these palatial, servant-staffed houses come hordes of guests who are "all frivolous and smart and country-house-broken and they [are] merry and full of cocktails from morning to night." ("One Does What One Can," *Liberty*, December 1936) Though they're never so merry that they forget that "the unwritten law of country houses is never to recognize anybody you meet in the hall after midnight." ("Ghost, My Eye!")

Whether the tone of these stories is whimsical, farcical, madcap, or even slightly satirical, they are, in form, virtually all romantic comedies, even when they incorporate another genre like the ghost story, as in the case of "Ghost, My Eye!" For even there the ghost is only a device to help the protagonist, Mr. Harper, win back his former fiancée, Miss Galt, "a handsome, dark girl with a sultry look [who] loved to quarrel passionately about unimportant things."

That so many of these stories feature rather silly characters of substantial means is, at least in part, a reflection of the Depression era in which they were written; it was a time when the foibles of the wealthy routinely provided a nice escape from the dreary realities of life, not only in stories like Walter's but also in motion picture comedies such as *My Man Godfrey, The Lady Eve,* and *It Happened One Night,* among others.

The stories' verisimilitude, however, is surely due to the fact that this was a stratum of society that Walter knew well. He grew up in a wealthy family, of course. And, thanks to his extremely wealthy cousin, Lucy Stevens Kingsley Rutherford, who had lavish homes in Cape Vincent, New York, and Palm Beach, Florida, the adult Walter was no stranger to the lifestyles of the rich. These paragraphs from "In the Garden" are clearly borrowed from his personal experience:

> We sat that evening as was the custom in that great house on the Sound, among the neat lawns and decorous borders and hedges of the garden.
>
> "I love Nature," Mrs. Mallison Murchard was wont to assert simply.
>
> As I had been asked because I was Mrs. Mallison Murchard's cousin, it was unnecessary for me to attend to the conversation. Besides, Mr. Bashwater (the artist and conversationalist) was attending to it.

Lucy was a fixture of Palm Beach society. She and her husband "often hosted Northern and foreign friends, entertaining them with forays to the Everglades Club and, to the benefit of the whole winter colony, with the various musical celebrities they were instrumental in bringing to Palm Beach." Their mansion, La Bellucia, was designed by celebrity architect Addison Mizner. Built in 1920, the 12,000-square-foot house sat on four acres of oceanfront property and clearly provides the setting for still another story, "Neck's Appeal," in which Mr. Flint, "a young man with a small income and no ambition," is invited to visit the Van Sickert Waynes in Palm Beach. "Oh, what the hell," he thinks after a moment's hesitation, "it will be interesting to see how the rich live."

It doesn't take him long to find out. After only four days he has seen enough of how the rich live and now wants nothing more than "to get back to civilization."

Though Walter clearly loved to poke fun at the rich, he was just as clearly fascinated by money and, at one time, even hoped to write an entire book on the subject, covering such topics as the history of money and banking, the romance of coins, credit systems, the difference between money and wealth, and more. He wrote a sample chapter and outline, which his agent, Carl Brandt, shopped around, but it appears there was not enough interest in the project for Walter to pursue it any further. Perhaps that was because he seemed to be more interested in factual presentation than in conveying to readers his own interest in and feeling for his subject.

This same problem visits many of these stories about the idle and silly rich. Amusing though they might be, the reader —and perhaps even Walter—cares nothing for the characters, because they are too often little more than exercises in superficial sophistication. As a result, the stories they populate seem somewhat facile and even formulaic. Clearly there was a market for this kind of material, but one wishes that Walter had allowed himself to write with personal feeling more often, for on the rare occasions when he did, the results were deeply engaging and satisfying.

One such effort is titled "Believing's Seeing" (*Esquire*, June 1938), a story about Risley Dill and his wife Ricky. Mr. Dill is a romantic who believes there's magic in everything, especially in the fairytales he enjoys telling his two small daughters. Mrs. Dill is a realist, however, who "thought it was too bad to fill children's heads with silly notions which would just make them fanciful." Her opinion is confirmed by her "friend," Mr. Whiffly, a publisher "who knew all about children's books [and] said that children did not like those absurd old-fashioned tales any more."

It's clear from the outset whose corner Walter is in, and throughout this simple but cleverly conceived story he treats his characters with sympathy and affection instead of his usual ironic remove. Without resorting to slapping or scratching, he manages—by invoking some transformative magic—a satisfying comeuppance for Mr. Whiffly and a happy rapprochement for the Dills, involving a thoroughgoing change of heart on the part of Mrs. Dill who, when last seen, is actually telling her daughters a fairytale!

Another deeply felt story—though one with a less happy ending—is "Life Is Too Short for Unicorns" (*Commentator*, October 1939). For Walter, this is a rare coming-of-age story. Its protagonist, John Rider, a junior in college, is walking in the woods behind his house one day when he discovers a unicorn and casually takes it home with him. To his surprise no one else seems to value his discovery; indeed, most of his friends even refuse to believe him when he tells them about the unicorn, and when he continues to talk about it they raise their eyebrows and gradually begin to drift away. John is dismayed by this but, continuing to think the unicorn miraculous, he refuses to give it up. And who can blame him? For, as Walter writes,

John took long walks with it and although it was not companionable or affectionate like a dog it led him places that he had never seen before although he knew the countryside well. It would be a cave high in a hill or maybe a bank of mountain laurel glimmering along the slant of a ravine or they would come out of the high woods at a point from which everything below in the valley looked strange and almost unrecognizable although each grove and spire and hill was familiar enough. It was always like seeing it for the first time.

John never tires of the unicorn; he builds a hut for it in the woods where he can visit it, but all the while he is growing increasingly unhappy about being shunned by his friends. Even his girlfriend has begun seeing another boy and finally John makes his decision:

> The next morning John went up to the unicorn's hut and tore it down while the creature lay among the ferns and watched him. When he had about half-finished the job John stopped and said angrily to it if you'd only act a little sorry—or upset—or something—But the unicorn merely blinked its green inhuman eyes at him and after a minute John went on working.

When he has finished he sits with the unicorn looking out over the valley with the river winding through it. "He knew he would never see it just like that again. When he looked at these things now there would be recognition only—never again would there be wonder."

And with that, the unicorn gets up and walks away.

"And after a while John got up and went home."

Many readers may find this ending a heartbreaking one, for unlike Mr. Dill, John has chosen reality over wonder, and it is clear that Walter feels the boy's life will be the poorer for it.

There seems to be little doubt that this is offered as a cautionary tale and that, in his own heart, Walter wished to believe in the reality of this alternative world, which surely *must* exist in some kind of uneasy juxtaposition with the one we generally regard as being the "real" one. To access it one need, simply, believe in it. Unfortunately, the typical price of growing up is giving up that capacity for belief. As for Walter, however, no matter how many brittle, sophisticated, urban stories he might have written, he seems never to have lost that simple gift, which he generously shares in his finest work, the Freddy books.

For an author who was making a name for himself by writing for children about talking animals, Walter produced surprisingly few adult stories about animals, loquacious or dumb. Only nine of Walter's sixty-nine adult stories from the thirties feature animals. Among these are a homesick, middle-aged goldfish named Elbridge; a sparrow couple named Hubert and Enid who leave their tony Manhattan nest to move upstate to a bucolic village and a humbling encounter with "unsophisticated" locals; and a country mouse named George who finds, in a barrel of booze, the courage to stand up to his controlling city in-laws.

Four of the remaining stories are about animals that can—and choose to—talk to humans, the first being "Major," a whimsical farce about a plumber, a mortician, and a milliner, the last of whom owns a cat that speaks up long enough to play cupid. It was published in 1934, anticipating by two years *The Story of Freginald*, the first Freddy book in which animals communicate with humans. Another of these stories with a more substantial connection to a later Freddy book is "Till the Cows Come Home," a story published in the July 1939 *Atlantic Monthly* that charts a revolution of farm animals and is clearly the inspiration for the much later *Freddy and Simon the Dictator*.

The most important of these stories, however—indeed, the most important story Walter would write in the 1930s—introduced another animal that could talk to humans: a horse named Ed, who debuted in the aptly titled story "The Talking Horse," published in *Liberty* for 9/18/1937. This was, indeed, the same Ed who would subsequently inspire twenty-four more stories *and* the 1960s television series *Mr. Ed*, which, in the years since it debuted, has become a cult classic.

Coincidentally, Walter "discovered" the character of Ed in the same year, 1937, that he and Anne also discovered the Catskills village of Roxbury, New York, where they would spend their next eleven summers, staying "above" town in a rough wood cabin that Walter had built on a rural hillside lot leased from a nearby farmer, Irvin Mead.

Filled with trees and charming nineteenth-century (and earlier) wooden homes, Roxbury—with good reason—is described in the American Guide Series as being "one of the most charming villages in the Catskills." Its pride of historic houses and its artist's palette of crisp fall colors now prove an attraction for

The cabin in Roxbury with Walter's dog, Squire, standing guard

Walter's view from the Roxbury cabin

tourists, but it was also once celebrated as the birthplace of both the railroad baron Jay Gould and the naturalist John Burroughs, who were improbable childhood friends in the early nineteenth century. Gould's daughter later built a spacious summer home there and the family, still later, endowed the handsome Jay Gould Memorial Reformed Church on Main Street, where Walter and Anne were congregants.

Walter and Anne first came to Roxbury in the summer of 1937 to be near an art school at the Burro Ranch, which was operated by Elizabeth Hunt. Mrs. Hunt was the sister of Samuel Hopkins Hadley who, with his wife, operated the parent School of Related Arts and Sciences in New York City, where both Anne and Walter had studied painting earlier. For Walter this had an unusual but salutary effect. "I found that after I began painting for some unknown reason that I cannot explain it was easier for me to write," he told a reporter, "and while I used to be slow in getting started, now I go right to work almost without thinking. A children's book used to take me four months. Now I can finish one in six weeks."

Of the two, Anne was clearly the more serious artist, having studied at the Art Students League as well as the School of Related Arts and occasionally selling her work. She also had at least one showing of her oil paintings at the Lakeland Inn in Cazenovia, New York, in the summer of 1932. As for Walter, only two examples of his work survive. Both are oil paintings; the larger—copied from the endpapers of a book—is called "Aden" and offers an illustrated map view of an imaginary country. The second is smaller and more whimsical; it shows a figure—intended to be his brother-in-law Dr. Perrin—on horseback against the backdrop of a woods. Titled "La Perrine Goeth Down to Ye Black Water," it is signed "Watteau" Brooks and mock-dated 1642.

Walter and Anne became friendly with Mrs. Hunt and her husband Charles and in the winter of 1938, two years after the Hunts opened a branch of the School of Related Arts and Sciences in Utica, where Walter taught a course in creative writing.

The Hunts' daughter, Elizabeth Starks, recalls having had lunch with Walter and her parents one hot summer's day at an elegant outdoor restaurant atop the Beekman Tower in New York. Walter amused himself, while waiting for service, by modeling figures out of the tar he tweaked from the rooftop.

He must have been in a particularly antic mood that day, since for his entree he then ordered frogs' legs, "so that when they arrived," Mrs. Starks recalls, "he could pick them up and make them dance all over the tabletop."

Walter maintained a similarly tongue-in-cheek correspondence with Mr. Hunt. In a 1939 letter, for example, he writes,

> I must apologize for the way in which my new sec'y has taken down this letter. She is a little unaccustomed to this work, having previously only held a job as student in the N. Y. school writing class. Her style, I think, is excellent—short, sharp, concrete and to the point. Anyhow, I have had to let it go thru as is, because of press of social engagements here in Roxbury, and also high and getting higher cost of stationery.

Walter is referring to an enclosed mock bill for several books he had bought for Hunt. Here it is:

School of Related Things
Utica. N.Y.

C. M. Hunt (holds some office, I forget what)
2 books (cant remember titles), one at 75 cents and one at 1.25, plus ad for them, 50 cents

PAST DUE!   COME, COME, PAY UP!

FOR CRISSAKE REMIT!

Walter's concern about the cost of stationery—and other paper, for that matter—was expressed only partly tongue-in-cheek, since Elizabeth Starks recalls that he was in the habit of buying used stationery on lower Broadway in New York. Indeed, many of his manuscripts are typed on the verso of such stationery from organizations like Mercy Ships for Children, the Brown-White Company of Philadelphia (an engineering firm), as well as on publishers' press releases. A follow-up "bill" to Hunt is even typed on old stationery from *The Outlook* magazine. Walter acknowledges this as follows,

Mr. Charles M. Hunt, delinquent debtor of Utica, N.Y.

Sir:

The magazine on whose letter head I write is defunct. But I am not. Late last July I ordered for you a BOOK. It cost $1.75. I wrote you to that effect. No reply. I wrote you again. No reply. I wrote you again. No reply. I then addressed myself to your conscience. A forlorn hope, true; but I thought perhaps—well, no matter. No reply from your conscience. I now therefore resort frankly to blackmail. Unless I receive a check in full payment VERY SHORTLY, I shall tell ALL. Useless for you to cower behind the pretence that you don't know what I am talking about. YOU KNOW WHO I mean, and what occurred YOU KNOW WHEN and YOU KNOW WHERE. God knows why, but that is his affair. I deal with FACTS. I have PROOF. Those letters signed 'oo's little moon pie,'—eh, that makes you jump, I guess. You didn't know I had those—all 14 of them. Well, I have said enough to show you what you may expect. Awaiting your early and terrified reply, I am, sir,

Determinedly,
W. Brooks

In a letter dated January 7, 1940, Hunt replied:

Dear Wallie:

I wouldn't have thought it of you! For you to take after your namesake! I simpsonly can't understand it! After all our years of friendship and you know what. . . . If you have kept the letters it must mean you still care and that you are using this method to get us together again. It can't be that you would stoop so low for $1.75.

oo's little moon pie

In another letter to Hunt, on another subject, Walter assumes the fictitious persona of J. J. Witherspoon, President of the Personal Finance Company. The letter reads, in part,

Referring to your letter of the 24th, there seems to be some confusion in the minds of our directors as to just which of your breach of promise suits is the one which you wish to settle at this time. You cannot of course fail to realize that through the unfortunate newspaper publicity we have learned not only of the unhappy Mamie Gubbins case, but also of the suits brought by Miss Hedwig Glub, Miss Katie Mulligan, and the little girl in the Oswego cheese factory. And while our deepest sympathy goes out to these victims of your unfortunate promissory mania, we hardly feel that our company, strong as it financially is, (Resources $7,000,000.56) would be adequate to settle all these claims. Particularly as we understand there are several other cases developing.

However, if you will kindly indicate to us which of the claims you wish to settle, we will be glad to consider the proposition. We should of course require you to have two sponsors on your note—preferably someone like W. R. Brooks or J. P. Morgan—and would further stipulate that all future proposals of marriage or of whatever nature shall be put into writing, properly attested and mailed to us for our OK before being submitted to the lady or ladies in whom you are currently interested.

Walter made a hobby of writing such tongue-in-cheek correspondence, especially after he and Anne had become so taken with the village of Roxbury that in 1948 they bought a house on Main Street and moved there year-round, though they kept their cabin and rented it in the summertime to Bellamy and his wife, Ruth.

Since 1941 Bellamy had been writing books and working as a special Washington correspondent for *The Reader's Digest*, a position he would hold until 1955 when he became director of the Association of College Presses, remaining there until 1958 when he became president of University Publishers.

13

Ed

THE ED STORIES BRIDGE THE DECADES OF THE 1930s
and '40s, the equine character making his first
appearance in 1937 and his last in 1945. There
were ultimately twenty-five stories about the chatty quad-
ruped. That there were also twenty-five Freddy novels is
surely a coincidence, though—in Walter's own mind—there
were similarities between the two series. "I try to write the
same for children and grown-ups," he observed in 1948, "or
rather, it is the only way I can write. The talking horse and
magic stories in the [*Saturday Evening*] *Post* were just children's stories for grown-ups, and I find that many grown-ups
read my kid stories. I don't plan them ahead, though; I have
never learned how, though I've tried." Apparently Walter—
like another great children's author, Sid Fleischman—sat
down each day to write, looked at his typewriter and ordered
it to "Surprise me."

The other area of commonality between the Ed and
Freddy stories is, of course, the presence of talking animals,
though Ed—unlike Freddy—resolutely spoke to only one
human, his owner Wilbur Pope. Ed explained this by saying,
"Look Wilb. You know what will happen [if I talk]? Reporters
and Hollywood scouts and these candid camera lunkheads and
people with babies and their lunch in a bag—that's what will
happen by the million. And all peeking and snooping. Except
for your wife's friends we have a nice quiet life up here in Mt.
Kisco. Why spoil it?"

Why, indeed? Besides, Ed's self-imposed silence offered
Walter all sorts of comedic opportunities, for when Ed actually

did say something in the presence of other humans, it was usually something outrageous and people naturally thought Wilbur was the one who had spoken.

As for himself, Walter dryly observed, "None of the animals I have ever known could talk, which seems a pity, since I have had to make up a lot of things that I could otherwise simply have taken down from their dictation." Walter may have had the sometimes perverse and always ornery Ed in mind when he went on to observe, "It is true that animals that can talk are probably a lot more fun to read and write about than they would be to have around. Your dog would give you an argument every time you told him to lie down, and your cat would criticize everything you did in an unpleasant voice."

Like Walter, Mr. Pope was also fascinated by talking animals. "When he was a boy, he had had a dog named Horace who could almost talk. But Horace had died without saying a word. Mrs. Pope wouldn't let Mr. Pope have a dog but she thought it would be nice if he had a horse so he bought a horse named Ed. It was just a horse."

Well, Mr. Pope enjoys riding Ed around the countryside on weekends as he looks for a magic leaf he has read about that, when eaten, is supposed to give you the ability to understand the speech of animals. One Sunday, Walter continues, Mr. Pope, after having downed a number of highballs, takes Ed out for a ride and—feeling unusually merry—starts to sing.

Ed looked around at him a couple of times but Mr. Pope just smiled and patted his neck and said You're a good scout Ed and if you die I promise I'll have you stuffed and stuck up whole over the mantelpiece. And he went on singing.

And then it happens:

Ed turned around again and said O for Pete's sake Wilb shut up.

Well Mr. Pope's seat almost failed him and he grabbed at Ed's mane and held on and said in a shaky voice Ed why I must have found that magic leaf and eaten it without knowing it! O can that magic stuff said Ed and don't be such a sap! Judas you'd believe anything!

This is made even funnier because Walter has already mockingly established that because Wilbur is an advertising man, "he had immense powers of belief."

As he has in previous stories, Walter treats this element of magic as matter-of-factly as Ed does, simply having the horse explain to Wilbur that, of course, all animals can talk, "only they almost never let humans know it because they'd just get a lot of extra work shoved on them. And anyway what does talk get you? Just trouble that's all."

Naturally, Wilbur wants to know why Ed has chosen to speak to *him*. Ed's answer is characteristic: "Because I couldn't stand any more of that singing." And with that Walter is off to the races with a new talking animal character and a premise that would prove enormously popular and successful. In fact, once Walter hit his stride, twenty-two of the twenty-nine stories that he published between 1940 and 1945 featured Ed and Wilbur.

Their characters and circumstances were already fully developed in the very first Ed story, "The Talking Horse," which appeared in *Liberty* magazine for 9/18/1937.

As noted, Wilbur Pope is an advertising account executive (the name of his firm established a bit later as Weatherbee, Overstreet & Ochiltree). He and his wife live comfortably in Mt. Kisco, New York, and Wilbur, like many another suburban-ite, commutes by train to his work in the city each morning and routinely returns home on the 5:28 train.

And like so many of Walter's other husband characters, Wilbur has a, well, *difficult* wife. Her name is Carlotta and she is "part Spanish and part bad temper. Most of the neighbors were in love with her because she was beautiful all right and as seductive as all get-out. But when she was in high spirits she didn't pay any attention to her husband and when she was low and cranky she didn't pay attention to any one else."

Mrs. Pope's penchant for holding noisy cocktail parties every Saturday and Sunday is the principal reason Mr. Pope gets a horse, so that he can ride away from the noise—and all the neighborhood men making eyes at his wife (and her making eyes right back at them).

From the first, Ed regards himself as "just folks" or, as Walter puts it, "once you'd said he was a horse you'd said everything. I don't know but maybe you'd said a little too much. But he was better company than most horses because he could talk. It's true his conversation was a little vulgar at times, but Mr. Pope was broad-minded and made allowances. After all, Ed had been brought up in a stable."

Somewhere between the stable and the saloon Ed has also developed quite a thirst; indeed, it seems that the favorite parts of his vocabulary are those three little words, "Pass the bottle." Accordingly, the rides that he and Wilbur enjoy assume a sort of soft focus: "He and Ed ambled over the countryside stopping at wayside taverns for beer and lolling and arguing about life under roadside trees."

Walter, astride

When Wilbur decides to teach Ed to read, he goes to the stable with a bottle and a primer that starts with "A is for Aardvark."

What the hell is an aardvark? Said Ed. Why not teach me words I know? Like A stands for Ale. B stands for Beer. And what's this? C said Mr. Pope. C stands for Scotch said Ed. No no Ed said Mr. Pope. C stands for—let me see—Cognac.

Well this didn't make sense to Ed and Mr. Pope tried to explain and they got into an argument that lasted until it was so dark they couldn't see the letters any more. The bottle was empty too.

While the two friends were getting into an argument, Walter was busy getting into the pages of the *Saturday Evening Post*. By the time he had published a dozen Ed stories (eleven in *Liberty* and one in *Esquire*), the series had become so popular that the *Post* began buying them, publishing four during the eleven months from July 1942 through June 1943.

The first of these, "Mr. Pope Rides Again," (July 4, 1942) is a prime example of an Ed story (it was later anthologized in *The Saturday Evening Post Carnival of Humor,* Prentice Hall, 1958) and, as such, is worth a closer look.

It opens with Ed and Wilbur on one of their weekend rides. Having had enough exercise and beer, they're headed toward an abandoned orchard where they like to go to take a nap in the shade. This time, though, they find another rider there, Mrs. Niles, who explains that she has taken up horseback riding since, now that tires are so scarce (it being wartime), her husband won't any longer let her use the car on Sundays when he plays golf. It's quickly established, by way of foreshadowing, that he is on the tire-rationing board and, accordingly, has "six brand-new tires in his garage."

Mr. Pope and Mrs. Niles ("My friends call me Nita") enjoy a brief conversation and when Mr. Pope says he must head for home, Nita says she'll ride back with him. And so she does, displaying a nice talent for "turning everything he said into a compliment to herself and that was a kind of back-handed flattery that made him feel how clever and fascinating he could be even when he didn't try."

"Ed," Walter tells us, "was pretty bored though." And when Nita leaves them, the horse, disgustedly snorts, "Pah."

> "Pah yourself," said Mr. Pope. "What's the matter, Ed?"
>
> "Oh, you make me sick," said Ed, "sitting up there gloating over your conquest."
>
> "What conquest?" said Mr. Pope self-consciously.
>
> But Ed just shrugged his shoulders so Mr. Pope's hat fell over his eyes, and then they were home.

Well, to Ed's disgust and Wilbur's bemusement, Nita manages to encounter them every Sunday thereafter until, one Sunday, a "worried-looking" Mrs. Niles tells a startled Wilbur that her husband "has found out about us and he's frightfully angry." To make matters worse, he's called Mrs. Pope about it. Nita begins to cry and Wilbur awkwardly pats her shoulder. She continues crying and he continues patting as he reflects that "it was rather pleasant to comfort a girl who was crying. For Mrs. Pope only cried when she was mad, and if you tried to comfort her then, you would probably lose an eye."

Of course, Mr. Niles shows up at just this moment, unpleasantness ensues, and Mr. Pope and Mr. Niles part on less than amicable terms. To make things worse, Mr. Pope arrives home to discover that his car has two flat tires, Mrs. Pope having run off the road and into a barbed-wire fence:

> Mr. Pope asked how it had happened.
>
> "Well, I had Jed Witherspoon with me," said Mrs. Pope.
>
> "Ah," said Mr. Pope "and were you driving with one hand or something?"
>
> "Well, in a way," said Mrs. Pope, "because I had to slap his face and we were on a curve and I sort of lost control."
>
> "Couldn't you have waited until pulling up before slapping him?" said Mr. Pope.
>
> "No," said Mrs. Pope, "because he would have misunderstood if I had stopped the car."

The conversation goes downhill from this point and it, too, ends on less than amicable terms. Then Ed gets huffy when Mr. Pope tells him that since his car is out of commission and he can't possibly apply to Mr. Niles's rationing board for new tires, he's going to have to ride Ed to the train station every morning, which means the horse will have to spend every day at Duffy's garage.

Everybody goes to bed unhappy. The next morning when Wilbur goes out to the stable to saddle Ed, he discovers two brand new tires in the middle of the floor. Yes, Ed has swiped them from Mr. Niles during the night. From this point on things quickly get complicated. Mr. Niles shows up, gets locked by Ed in the stable closet, the police arrive and discover that Mr. Niles is hoarding tires. He is then forced to sell Wilbur the two tires that Ed has "borrowed." The two friends celebrate in typical style and then, wouldn't you know it, Mrs. Niles shows up. Wilbur, who has had just about enough of this, finds courage and inspiration in the whiskey he's consumed and with an implied wink at Ed proposes to Mrs. Niles that they run off together.

> "What on earth are you talking about?" an alarmed Mrs. Niles demands.
>
> "Talking about us," said Mr. Pope. "Two loving hearts serrated by a few words mimbled by a minister—I mean mumbled by a minister. Nice word 'mimbled.' I remimber—I mean I remember when we were married, the minister—" He stopped as Ed gave a loud snort.

Terrified by the prospect that Wilbur might be serious, Nita heads for the hills at full gallop. And that's the end of their "friendship." Fortunately the friendship that matters—that of Wilbur and Ed—survives. The last the reader sees of the two, they're sitting, once again, in the orchard and Ed is saying, "Yeah, some folks take women for their inspiration but me, I take whiskey. Pass the bottle, Wilb."

According to Dorothy Brooks, the editors of the *Post* (a family magazine, after all) soon began complaining that there was too much drinking in the stories and Ed and Wilbur would have to take the pledge. Walter refused, adamantly, and took the franchise to *Argosy*, which published the final eight titles in the series. This sounds like one of those stories that's too good to be true and it may be; however, consider that the second story *Argosy* published was a satire on temperance, tellingly titled "Ed Signs the Pledge." One can almost hear Walter saying, "Take *that*, *Saturday Evening Post*."

Though the *Post* objected to Wilbur's drinking, Mrs. Pope never seems to mind. One is not sure if the same could be said for Mrs. Brooks about her own husband, however. Alcohol flows freely in almost every story that Walter wrote and it's obvious that he enjoyed its company as much as Ed and Wilbur (Scotch—spelled with an "S"—was his drink of choice). Though far from the best, one of the most interesting stories Walter published in the 1930s appeared in *Collier's* and was titled "Another Little Drink" (8/12/1939). It is the tale of "a Miss Mary Wayne who married a man to reform him in the fall of 1935." The man is named Mr. Duncan Crocker (as in "drunken" and "crocked," perhaps?) and, Walter writes:

> He was pretty depraved all right. He tried to plan on going to bed drunk about three nights a week. When he was sober he wrote adventure stories for children, which were popular and really very charming and nicely supplemented a moderate inherited income. When he was drunk he was charming too, though hardly in a vein suitable for children. I won't go so far as to say that he was always a gentleman in his cups but he was always entertaining. And though sometimes vulgar, he was never common.

One can almost hear Walter saying, "Take *that*, Anne Brooks."

In retrospect it's a pity that Walter and the *Post* parted company, since the four Ed stories he published there are among the best of the series, perhaps because they were the most carefully edited or perhaps because Walter gave greater care to their composition. Certainly they were the most carefully plotted and contained some of the series' best writing. The *Post* showcased them nicely, too, hiring the great *New Yorker* cartoonist Peter Arno to illustrate them. The eight *Argosy* stories that followed, on the other hand, are easily the weakest in the series, seeming, too often, to be tossed off and perfunctory.

This is probably due to Walter's fading interest in Ed and not to any diminution of his talent, since the same month (September 1945) that the final Ed episode, "With Teeth and Tale," appeared, one of Walter's finest non-Ed stories, "Miss Emmeline Takes Off," also appeared, to be followed three months later by another standout, "Mr. Whitcomb's Genie." That both of these stories appeared in the *Saturday Evening Post* suggests there were no lingering hard feelings about Ed's earlier "eviction" from its pages. And Walter earned more for them, too—$675 each, compared with $450 for Ed.

Both of these excellent tales are about elderly people who encounter life-changing magic. "Miss Emmeline" stars the titular Miss Emmeline Valiant, who loses her ancestral home and most of its contents to the wealthy and grasping Mr. Maule. What particularly pains Miss Emmeline is her discovery that when she had to vacate the property, she forgot to take her prize possession with her. That would be the "queer little flat trunk which was said to have belonged to an ancestress who had figured in one of the New England witch trials."

The elderly ladies in Walter's stories are always ingenious, and though Mr. Maule refuses to either give or sell her the trunk, Miss Emmeline does manage to get it back and discovers inside it a jar of ointment that, when applied, enables her to fly—with the aid of an antique broom that is conveniently stored nearby.

Well, what with one thing and another, Miss Emmeline will recover her property, Mr. Maule will get his, and Miss Emmeline's best friend Mrs. Bishop, who has taken to flying with her of an evening, apparently begins—with no seeming ill effects—to consort with a dark power. "But," Walter concludes, "you must draw your own conclusions. I feel, with Miss Emmeline, that the matter is now out of our hands."

"Miss Emmeline" closely resembles an earlier story Walter wrote in the 1930s. Titled "Plant Early Two Feet Apart," it was published in the *Atlantic Monthly* for January 1938. It, too, features an elderly protagonist, Miss Harriet Pretty, who has fallen on hard times and nearly loses her ancestral property to a greedy neighbor. When some "funny seeds that Sister Lucy got in Greece" sprout and grow into a legion of ancient Greek soldiers, Miss Pretty is saved—not by battle, but by the ballot box! The soldiers, you see, were "born" in Miss Pretty's small community and thus are eligible to vote in a local election that will turn the rascals who threaten her property out of office.

Like "Miss Emmeline," "Mr. Whitcomb's Genie" has a simple premise: an old couple named Mr. and Mrs. Jethro Whitcomb discover an ancient brass lamp on their small farm "up back in the hills" and, trying to clean it up ("It would look real pretty on the parlor mantle," Mrs. W. observes), unwittingly conjure up the genie of the lamp.

> He was just a trifle over eight feet from the soles of his sandals to the top of his turban and all he had on between was a white loincloth.
>
> Mr. Whitcomb was not scared of much but Mrs. Whitcomb was not scared of anything and she stopped rocking and said severely, "You ought to be ashamed of yourself going around like that! Go put some clothes on!"
>
> "To hear is to obey," said the man in a voice that rumbled like thunder under the porch roof, and he turned and vanished. But in no time at all he was back and now he had on a loose white robe belted with a green sash through which was thrust a huge scimitar.

A simple premise, yes, but the execution of this story is more complicated than that of "Miss Emmeline" and, if anything, even more entertaining. As the Whitcombs gradually come to understand the powers of the genie, they begin wishing for things, simple ones at first (six new aprons and a damask table cloth), but then as they begin to wish for more complicated things like a new barn and a new tractor, their unpleasant neighbor begins to take notice and, before you know it, has reported them to the local OPA Board. The

Whitcombs may be old and unsophisticated but they're no fools and they manage to turn the tables on the neighbor. In the process, however, they begin to question the wisdom of keeping the genie. As Mr. Whitcomb says, "'Tain't natural the way we've been living. And what ain't natural ain't right."

Mrs. Whitcomb agrees, adding, "Enough's enough. And someday if we keep on we'll find ourselves in a fix we can't get out of. Things you don't pay for don't do you much good."

How the Whitcombs resolve their dilemma is heartwarming, a word one uses advisedly, since what makes both of these charming stories so successful is that Walter obviously cares for these characters. And because he admires them and enjoys their company, so do his readers. Perhaps that is also why both of these stories were among Walter's most widely anthologized; Walter's thoughtful introduction to the inclusion of "Mr. Whitcomb" in Scott Foresman's *Wide Wide World* is worth quoting:

> In writing this story I followed a practice which I have used in all my short stories. I take quite ordinary people and face them with something incredible: a ghost or a piece of magic. Treated matter of factly such things as a hat that makes you disappear or an Aladdin's lamp become if not entirely credible, at least plausible. I have written more than 200 stories, most of which have been published. I don't plan ahead. I never have been able to. I take a situation and see what happens. Given the magic lamp which Mrs. Whitcomb found in the garden, the rest of the story develops naturally.

And, he might have added, "dramatically," for both stories are cleverly plotted and filled with dramatic incident. Perhaps for that reason both attracted the attention of playwrights. Norman Ashton of Yale University adapted "Genie" as a one-act play that was presented by the Roxbury reading club in 1947 as a benefit for the library.

The plans for "Miss Emmeline" were considerably more ambitious, however. Broadway and later TV and film actress Peggy Wood (*Blithe Spirit, I Remember Mama, The Sound of Music*, etc.) was, as she put it, "enchanted" with the story and wrote to

Walter within months of the story's publication that she had "badgered the moving picture business to read it and do something about it."

When this proved unsuccessful, she then set her sights on Broadway, trying for several years to dramatize and produce the story as a starring vehicle for herself. "I am more excited about this idea for a play than I have been about any other project, and I know that if we do a play, we will prove to the stupid movie people how foolish they were not to have seen the possibilities in your story from the first." Unfortunately, despite considerable work on the part of the actress, nothing ever came of her efforts.

Clifford Goldsmith, the creator of the long-running radio comedy "The Aldrich Family," had somewhat better luck with his efforts to dramatize another of Walter's short stories, "Youth Is Stranger Than Fiction," which appeared in *Liberty* for July 2, 1938. Since Goldsmith's signature creation was the character of the "typical" teenager Henry Aldrich, it's not surprising that this—for Walter—unusual story attracted his attention. "Unusual" since this is one of the precious few stories Walter wrote that features a cast of teenagers. Its protagonist, however, is an adult, Mr. Burnham Wicks, a widower whose teenage daughter Dot "realized that at forty-two her father was practically senile and had to be looked after." Weary of her interference and of her and her friends' habit of unfavorably comparing their parents, Mr. Wicks forms the Parents Protective Association that encourages parents to swap teenage offspring with their friends. Naturally, Mr. Wicks winds up with the surly son of the woman he is dating. Complications ensue.

Goldsmith was no stranger to Broadway; in fact, "The Aldrich Family" was based on his long-running Broadway hit *What a Life*. He hoped to turn Walter's story into a vehicle for the successful film actor Thomas Mitchell (who appeared in such classics as *Stagecoach, Gone with the Wind, It's a Wonderful Life,* and countless others).

Walter and Goldsmith entered into an agreement on August 18, 1947, that granted the latter dramatic rights to the story. Another five years would pass, however, before a production was announced. In a letter dated May 1, 1951, Goldsmith reported that Thomas Mitchell, "who will not only play Wicks but will direct the darned thing if ever it comes to an actual production, has been spending several days with me in Tucson" but acknowledged "there is still a hell of a lot of work ahead."

Apparently he and Walter had been corresponding about weaknesses in the play, since the good-natured Goldsmith went on to write (with a wink), "I'm afraid you are right about the tear gas. Either it will have to be handled more skillfully, or something else better will have to be invented." (Maybe Freddy could make an entrance and save the day.)

Finally, the play—now titled *Your Every Wish*—went into try-outs, running for six weeks in summer stock at Easthampton, New York. Apparently it was not well received, since, in a wry letter to Walter dated February 16, 1953, Goldsmith referred to "the fiasco that developed on Long Island last summer when we tried out your play."

Nevertheless, the dramatist reaffirmed his interest in the project and said he was still working on it. No professional production ever resulted, however, and in 1957 the property was leased to the Dramatists Play Service for subleasing to organizations (principally high school drama clubs) for non-professional presentation. The play was subsequently produced in such communities as Johnstown, PA, Chattanooga, TN, and Sheboygan, WI. The last recorded production took place in Bowdon, GA, in 1973.

One interesting side note to this is an undated radio script Walter wrote for "The Aldrich Family." In it, the hapless Henry "borrows" (i.e., takes without permission) his father's dinner jacket to wear at a dance. Before he even gets to the event, however, he manages to drop most of a cherry pie on his shirt, which in due course will lead a number of people to think he has been shot. Several scenes also take place in the local public library where Henry has been sent to pick up a book for his mother and, in the process (don't ask), becomes interested in pursuing a career in the diplomatic corps.

Though not altogether unamusing, the script creaks with contrivance and never gains any significant comic momentum. In rejecting the effort, Goldsmith diplomatically wrote, "Just to thank you for your efforts and to tell you I still think you're a grand writer. I hope, in case we decide to get in touch with you later on, you will at least be on speaking terms with us."

14

The Forties

D ESPITE THE OCCASIONAL INTEREST OF DRAMATISTS, Walter's short story output shrank significantly in the 1940s, from sixty-six in the previous decade to a relatively modest thirty-nine (though this is still an average of nearly four a year) and, as previously noted, twenty-two of the thirty-nine were Ed stories. Walter never offered any reason for this apparent decline in his productivity, but one might assume that it was because he had less financial incentive to write. For beginning with *Wiggins for President*, which appeared in 1939, he was now publishing a Freddy book every year and the growing popularity of the series meant he was earning significantly more income from it; the advance Walter received for *Freddy and the Ignormous*, for example, was reportedly three times as large as that for *To and Again*. And the book got what, as *Publishers Weekly* reported in its 11/1/41 issue,

> few juveniles get—a national advertising campaign of its own. A series of advertisements with Freddy's picture [by Kurt Wiese] and mentioning all the other Brooks titles has run and is running in newspapers in New York, Los Angeles, and Boston; and "Freddy" will, of course, be featured in the considerable general juvenile advertising which Knopf plans for the rest of the year. The publisher has also prepared and sent out to libraries and schools both a pictorial band for the Brooks titles, and an illustrated circular.

The forties was also the first decade in which Walter began publishing short stories for children; in fact, three of his seventeen non-Ed stories were for children: "The King of Smithia" (1946), "His Birthday" (1948), and "Jenny and the Dragon" (1949) (more about these later).

As for the relatively meager total of fourteen non-Ed adult stories, nine involved magic of one sort or another. In addition to witchcraft and genies, readers could encounter time travel (twice), flying carpets, sea serpents, driads (twice), and a magic powder that—à la Alice in Wonderland's mushroom—could shrink you or grow you to gigantic proportions. Three of the remaining five stories were more examples of Walter's staple— meek husbands (or swains) finding untapped reserves of assertiveness that finally win the hearts of their fair and always hot-tempered ladies.

The final two stories, though, featured a different kind of discovery, one that evidences Walter's lifelong fascination with finding unexpected treasure. In these stories the discovery is of valuable antiques, the sale of which will save their previously unwitting owners from financial ruin. In their own way, these stories are almost as fantastic as those featuring traditional magic. And while they are not as technically successful as "Miss Emmeline" and "Mr. Whitcomb's Genie," both have their intriguing aspects.

The first—published as "The Aristocrats" (*Liberty*, 12/14/46) though Walter's title was "Pride Goes After A Fall"—is yet another reworking of the story of the formerly wealthy but still aristocratic old lady who has fallen on hard times. Like "Plant Early" it is even set on the water in Connecticut and features a nouveau riche neighbor. This time, however, Walter's sympathies seem to lie with the neighbor, Mr. Stigler, who is warm-hearted, friendly, filled with down-to-earth wisdom, and generous to a fault—as is his sweet-natured son, Joey, who even offers to marry Miss Abigail Thaxter's neice, Clelia, to save the Thaxters from impending impoverishment. Clelia declines with good grace. Her heart belongs to Mr. Dillway Preed, the impoverished scion of another old, local family, but she is thrilled when Mr. Stiker pays her $400.00 for half-a-dozen old plates she has bought for a quarter apiece. Of course, it turns out they are "a collector's dream," being thirteen-star plates made in

Philadelphia after the Revolution. And the generous Mr. Stigler then gives Clelia three of the plates as a wedding present when she finally marries her no-longer penniless sweetheart.

There is a good deal more to this complicated and not completely successful story. And so it's a relief that the second story with this theme, "Whistle for My Love," is much more straightforward, considerably more charming, and—for Walter—pleasantly sentimental. When Felicia Stark's father and aunt die within months of each other, she is forced to auction off the contents of the family home and barn, including some apparently worthless books, one of which turns out to be the only known copy of the first book published in the American colonies. An unscrupulous collector (collectors and dealers are always unscrupulous in Walter's stories) attempts to buy it on the cheap and it's left to an elderly gent named Phineas Greet to save the day, with some help from Felicia's boyfriend, Bill Peabody. Like most of Walter's lovers, Felicia and Bill spend most of their time fighting and so, of course, it will also fall to Mr. Greet to trick them into each other's arms and then to the altar.

Phineas is the foxy grandpa type that Walter had been creating since the days of Cicero Betts; the character's interest to Freddy fans soars beyond an appreciation for Walter's skill in creating such types, however, when it is revealed that he has an old farm "up back of Centerboro"! If Walter had only given him whiskers, he might well have been Mr. Bean's long-lost brother.

"Whistle for My Love" turned out to be Walter's last story of the 1940s, since the same year it was published Knopf sent him on his first national tour to promote *Freddy Goes Camping*—another sign of the burgeoning popularity of the series. That same busy year, on October 22, Walter's sister Elsie died suddenly of a heart attack at the age of sixty-eight. Though, as previously noted, Walter had no special fondness for his brother-in-law, he and Elsie seem to have remained close, visiting often and exchanging gifts at Christmas. The stress of her death was exacerbated by the fact that it occurred while Walter and Anne were busy moving to their new home in Roxbury. The two-story wood house they bought on Upper Main Street had been built sometime in the early 1850s and stood in the most historic part of the village. It was apparently the product of two houses having been joined together. The older part at the back consisted of two large rooms on the ground floor—a kitchen and a dining room—that extended the width of the house. Upstairs were three low-ceilinged bedrooms; the largest, which had a view of the back yard, served as Walter's office. The front part of the house, which faced Main Street, consisted of a library and a parlor downstairs and two large bedrooms and a bath upstairs.

Walter now owned three houses—well, two houses and a cabin—and the stresses of managing and maintaining them were, his friend Bellamy thought, the catalyst for Walter's then having a major heart attack in the late summer of 1949. There is no record of the exact date, but it seems to have occurred on an August Sunday following services Walter and Anne had attended at the local Reformed Church. At any rate Walter subsequently received a note from the church's pastor, Glenn W. Young, which reads, in part, "On one other occasion an auditor reacted rather badly to a sermon of mine. He turned on the gas after what I considered a rather hopeful Easter address." In a later letter at Christmas, the Rev. Young expanded on this:

The Roxbury house

Happy to report that you were my last fatality since that "Black
Sunday" in Roxbury in the summer. I know of no way to account
for it unless it is because your conscience was over-sensitive. As
far as I can find out, you, WRB, are the first listener I have had
who applied the sermon directly to yourself. You should be told
quite plainly that in time-tested Christian tradition, members of
the congregation apply the sermon *to one another*—NEVER to
one's self. Now don't let such a thing happen again.

The probable cause of Walter's illness, of course, was not
the sermon but a simple matter of genetics, since his mother
had herself died of a heart attack and heart trouble was common throughout the Stevens family. For Freddy's sake, it was
fortunate that the illness didn't strike until late summer, since
that meant Walter had already finished the next title in the
series, *Freddy Plays Football*, which was published, on schedule,
in October. Providentially, this also gave Walter a number of
months to recover from what had been a truly life-threatening
event before it was time to greet a new decade and to start
work on the next Freddy book.

Walter autographing Freddy Goes Camping *for young fans, 1948*

15

The Final Decade

W ALTER NEVER COMPLETELY RECOVERED FROM THE near-fatal illness of 1949. He spent the next nine years in and out of the hospital, according to his second wife Dorothy, and the precarious, debilitating nature of his health meant that his creative output continued to decline. Though he was still somehow able to produce a Freddy book annually until his death in 1958, he managed to create only seven short stories in the 1950s, four of these being for children. Two of the three adult stories were whimsical entries about animals, while the third adult story—the last one Walter ever published—was titled "The Nicest War in the World" and perfectly epitomized what Walter once wrote about his adult stories being roughly the same as his children's stories. It was a pleasantly nostalgic way to cap his career.

Though Walter's life in the fifties was a quiet one, it was not completely uneventful. Most notably, it was marked by the unexpected death of his first wife Anne, following routine surgery, in October 1952. This was a shock not only to Walter but also to their friends, one of whom, Pauline Hopkins, candidly noted that everyone had expected Walter, because of his fragile health, to be "the first to go."

But life is full of surprises and the community was surprised—and, according to one source, "scandalized"—when, only four months after Anne's death, Walter remarried. His second wife was Dorothy Carman Collins, whom he wed on January 6, 1953, just three days before his sixty-seventh birthday.

Walter and Dorothy Collins in the 1940s

On May 18, 1953, Walter wrote the following letter to Mrs. T. Howard Smith of Eagle Grove, Iowa, to explain the circumstances:

Dear Louisa:

I was really very glad to get your letter. There was, I think, some disapproval of our marriage—natural enough, for it was no doubt too soon. But I couldn't take it alone and I was quite sure Anne would have approved not only of Dottie but of our marrying as soon as possible. The situation was that when I got back here, she seemed to be the only person who could bring me back to reality. I knew very soon that she would be necessary to me if I was to go on living here. I knew that materially I could be useful to her but that, of course, wasn't enough. It was lucky for me that that didn't have much weight in her final decision. The whole thing was incredibly lucky for me and so far—after 5 months—I haven't had a minute of doubt about it. I write at this length because you are a friend of Anne's as well as of mine and some of our friends to whom I didn't talk at all have seemed to disapprove or misunderstand. The local gossips can make what they like of it, but I do want my friends to know that our marriage was, by both of us, a carefully considered step, thought out and talked over with no reservations on either side.

Aside from which everything runs smoothly. I hope it does for you. I hope also that you'll be coming East again for a while at least before long. It's nice and rainy and foggy. The usual spring weather. Also, by some error today is fine.

Dottie sends her best as do I.

Sincerely,
Walter R. B.

Dorothy, who was born September 16, 1907, was twenty-one years younger than Walter. She and her first husband, Norman Collins, had come to Roxbury shortly after World War II to work at the local school, he teaching science and she, the third grade. The couple had two children, Diana and Stephen. When their marriage failed, the husband left Roxbury and lost touch with his former family.

Walter and Dorothy Brooks

It was then, sometime in the late 1940s, that Dorothy and Walter first met. She had by that time become friendly with the Hopkinses, a family of local artists. The wife, Pauline, in fact, taught art at the local school but it was the husband, James, who invited Dorothy—herself an amateur artist—to join him for a day of painting on the hillside adjacent to the Brookses' summer cabin. And it was at some point during that day that he introduced the two. Walter, as he always would, invited them into the cabin and fed them what Dorothy recalled with a shudder as being "truly awful orange caviar on crackers."

Dorothy would occasionally return to that hillside to paint, sometimes taking her young son with her, and each time Walter would invite her in. One is not sure how Anne felt about this, but Dorothy recalled one occasion when, in a temper, she sniffed, "Artists!" and stormed into her bedroom. A volatile personality, red-haired Anne—herself an artist, of course—was apparently in the habit of doing this sort of thing, regardless of how many guests she had.

On the other hand she could be quite vivacious and entertaining, talking ("holding court" as Pauline Hopkins put it) for hours, while a bemused Walter sat silently in a corner, observing. Walter never talked about his own work on such occasions but Anne did, often calling her husband "the American Kenneth Grahame." Recalling this, Pauline Hopkins mischievously allowed it was an apt comparison, since whenever Walter got behind the wheel of a car, he was every bit as bad a driver as Grahame's Mr. Toad! "Jimmy and I feared for our lives," she wrote. "I think the imprint of my fingernails is still in my hands." Anne was also prone to debilitating headaches, during the course of which Walter would sit at her side, patiently stroking her forehead "for hours." ("He babied her terribly," another local woman once tartly observed.)

Despite all of this, Walter was truly devastated by Anne's unexpected death and, concerned now about the state of *his* health, his friends the Hopkinses decided he couldn't live alone and had to remarry. Happily, a candidate was at hand in the person of Dorothy, upon whom Walter already had "quite a case," as Pauline recalled. Whether it was he or Pauline who

Anne Brooks at the cabin in Roxbury

took the initiative is unclear but one thing is certain: Walter owned a doll's tea set that Pauline coveted. Knowing this, he promised her a single dish each time she arranged for him to see Dorothy. Recalling this some years later, Pauline said, with a satisfied smile, "I got the whole set!" And Walter—well, Walter got Dorothy—and her two children.

This might have been problematic, for like many other children's book authors, Walter—though kindly—was not terribly comfortable around children. Indeed, the few newspaper photographs of him on book tours when he was surrounded by them show him displaying emotions that range from uncomfortable to plainly terrified.

Nevertheless, Diana, the older of the two children, has warm memories of Walter. Though her younger sibling Stephen may have been less comfortable with his mother's second marriage (he admits to having run away from home at least once), the union seems to have been a good match. Though there was an element of convenience to the marriage, the couple had genuinely tender feelings for each other. Also, like Walter, Dorothy—a biologist by education—was interested in nature and was known locally as an avid gardener; in fact, the local newspaper printed a feature article about her famously green thumbs. Walter may have had less luck in this department, once reporting ruefully that in Roxbury he "runs a large garden, raising a crop of distorted vegetables, flea beetles, cut worms, etc." There were other crops, as well, however, since he also recalled, "I have been acquainted slightly with a good many cows, and have even had arguments with some of them when they got into my garden and stamped around on the vegetables and tore the corn up by the roots."

Walter was an enthusiastic hobbyist and one of his other nature-related passions was collecting seeds. He kept a handwritten list of them, in fact—chervil, cumin, marjorum, anise, etc.—along with the companies that sold them—Burpee, Schling, Henderson, etc. He also liked to help out on his neighbor's farm (several blurry photos of him seated atop a hay wagon survive) and, in general, enjoyed the sounds and sights of the natural world. As he wrote in the Knopf promotional magazine "Borzoi Battledore" for September 1945:

In the city, when I look up from my typewriter, I see the room and its familiar furniture, the window, beyond which are the brick walls and blank windows of opposite houses, whose dullness drives me back upon my work. But in the country, whenever I look up my eye meets something that poses a question. On that tray is the chervil I cut yesterday; it must be shaken up so it will dry evenly. In the corner is the gun. I haven't cleaned it since I missed that fox the other day. I look up at the roof and there is the spot where it leaked during the storm last night. Have to get the ladder and the roofing cement.

If I look out the window, there is, first, the weather, which I pay no attention to in the city. They're making the hay in the big field; I wonder if they want me to run the tractor for the bailer. The monkshood is blossoming; it ought to be staked up. And was that a fox barking or the crash of a falling tree far up in the woods? Hard to tell with the door shut. I'd better go listen. Take the gun along: he's probably after another chicken. . . .

In various other jottings Walter often noted that he had "a dozen or so" hobbies, although that might have been an exaggeration. Aside from gardening and seed collecting, we know that he also enjoyed learning languages (a new one every other year or so) and claimed a reading knowledge of six—among them, German, French, Swedish, and Italian. As previously noted, he also painted, but was artistic in other ways, too, playing the guitar and banjo, doing woodcarving, chair caning, cooking, bread-baking, and enjoying the process of remodeling. When he and Anne moved to Roxbury, for example, he supervised the installation of a fireplace in the parlor. This project served a dual purpose, since it was necessary to create a hole in one wall to allow moving the furniture from his New York home into the Roxbury house, all the doors and windows of which were too small to accommodate his large Victorian furnishings.

And, of course, he was also a book collector. The eight floor-to-ceiling, built-in bookcases in his library housed a collection of nearly 2,500 volumes at his death. The large number of titles in German, French, and Swedish evidenced his love of language, just as the large number of volumes by Longfellow, Rosetti, Tennyson, Edwin Arlington Robinson, Kenneth Rexroth, Robert Frost, Shelley, Kipling, Masefield, and others confirmed that he, like his late mother, loved poetry. There were numerous works of natural history, as well, including the complete works of John Burroughs. Much in evidence, too, were books about antiques and collectibles. As for fiction, Walter seems to have been a particular fan of Henry James, Thomas Hardy, George Meredith, Joseph Conrad, H. G. Wells, Charles Dickens, G. K. Chesterton, Stephen Crane, and such fantasists as E. R. Eddison, Mervyn Peake, C. S. Lewis, J. R. R. Tolkien, Lord Dunsany, William Morris, Algernon Blackwood, Ambrose Bierce, A. E. Coppard, and Arthur Machen. Himself a humorist, he showed discerning taste in this area of his collections, too, since browsers there would find extensive runs of Robert Benchley, Don Marquis, Ring Lardner, Ludwig Bemelmans, and the somewhat lesser likes of Milt Gross, Gellett Burgess, Hilaire Belloc, and others.

The library in Walter's Roxbury house

When it came to books, though, Walter was not only a collector but also a part-time dealer, operating what he called
"The Brooks Book Service" out of the upstairs office and attic
in his Roxbury home. According to an article in the nearby
Walton, NY, *Reporter*, he had 6,000 books in his house.

"How do you find books for people?" the reporter asked.

"If I don't have the one they want," Walter explained, "I
advertise in magazines for it. Almost everybody has books on
their shelves that someone else is looking for."

Walter also loved going to auctions (which is obvious from
the several short stories mentioned above) even though, he
allowed, "The Catskills are a poor section for books."

Walter had been searching for books for years, of course;
when he was summering in Connecticut in the early thirties, he
wrote that he was also "hunting in any attic I can get into for

rare books. Have done this for years but never found anything very choice."

He also wrote about this predilection in an article called "The Shoestring Book Collector" that appeared in *Bookman* magazine for March 1932. "Not one in ten of my books," he noted there, "have I bought in the usual way through a regular bookstore. I can't afford to. If it is a new book that has just come out, sooner or later I pick it up for a quarter or seventy-five cents in a second-hand store or a lending library discard counter." (In fact he acquired a beautiful set of Jane Austen when it was discarded from the Roxbury Circulating Library.)

He also received books as gifts throughout his life, principally from his family—his mother, his aunts, a family friend named Nannie Dow (to whom *To and Again* is jointly dedicated, along with Anne), his wife, and his sister Elsie. And whenever family members died, Walter seems to have inherited their books, too, since there are volumes in his own collection that had previously belonged to his Grandfather Brooks, his various aunts and uncles, his mother, and his sister.

In the last decade of his life, Walter typically devoted half a day to operating his book service. The other half he spent answering fan letters and working on the latest Freddy title. He jotted down notes for his stories on index cards that he then pinned to a large bulletin board, which hung from the ceiling. His writing was done on a small, portable Corona typewriter of World War I vintage. Walter was a hunt-and-peck typist and when he worked, he sat, sometimes cross-legged, in a deep armchair before his typewriter, which stood on a tripod. Evenings and weekends he devoted to hobbies and to reading—sometimes aloud. He shared his E. Nesbit books in this way with Dorothy and Stephen. Dorothy returned the favor—especially in her husband's last years—by reading aloud to him from his own Freddy books.

Walter was, withal, a very private—and rather formal—person. He always dressed for dinner, for example, though he refused ever to buy new clothing for himself. Many of his jackets looked as if they had been around since the Civil War, Pauline Hopkins observed, and Dorothy said, more than once, that she had to darn the darns on his socks. In the winter, the Roxbury house tended to be cold, partly because it was drafty but also because the thrifty Mr. Brooks kept the thermostat set low. To forestall chilblains, he crafted from an old blanket what his stepson-in-law Peter Halpern describes as "a monk's robe"—complete with cowl—that he wore around the house.

Though Walter couldn't abide waste and resisted spending money on himself, those who knew him said he was always generous with favors, especially if they involved book appraisals, bibliographic assistance, and the like. For his friends he could be even more generous, as we have seen in the case of Bellamy, who continued to visit Walter on holidays when he could afford it, and with whom he continued to correspond faithfully through the fifties. Others also benefited from this aspect of his character. A former Roxbury resident recalls that when her mother, a close friend of Walter's, separated from her husband and didn't have enough money to buy a small house in the village, she went to Walter for assistance and he gladly took the second mortgage. "He was a kind and generous man," she recalls, "and a good friend to our family."

Though not, Dorothy reminisced, a "funny ha-ha" person, Walter had a keen but very dry sense of humor and an endless supply of funny horror stories about former tenants in his Bank Street house. He also enjoyed wryly noting that, as a life-long Democrat, he was doubtless regarded by his conservative, upstate neighbors as being a Communist. When he was amused, Dorothy recalled, "the corners of his mouth turned up slightly and his eyes sparkled."

Both of his step-children, Diana and Stephen, have described that sense of humor as being positively "impish." This sometimes manifested itself in his public life—especially in the 1940s when he was still an active member of the community, belonging to the local Grange and the Reformed Church, while also serving as a trustee of the Roxbury Public Library from 1945 to 1958. This meant taking part in village programs and fund-raisers, where he sometimes appeared as a "musician." With a straight face he would mount the stage carrying a violin case, Pauline Hopkins recalled. Very seriously he would then set it down on a stool, open it and remove—not a violin, but a pencil that he would then use to tap out selections from Beethoven's Fifth Symphony (dah-dah-dah-dum, dah-dah-dah-dum) on his teeth. Or his instrument of choice might be his own head. Sadly these performances took place long before the days of the now ubiquitous camcorder, so they are lost to history.

However, a few of the mock-serious letters he continued to enjoy writing still survive. One of these was sent to his step-daughter Diana, who had married a local man, Peter Halpern, in 1956. Some months later, when Walter came across a news-paper article announcing the marriage of a young woman in Poughkeepsie to another Peter Halpern, he couldn't resist sending Diana the following missive:

Dear Madam:

You are perhaps unaware that your husband, Mr. Peter Halpern, has recently contracted a bigamous marriage with one Loretta E. Buesford. Proof of this revolting fact [a clipping of the article] is enclosed. Incensed by the barefaced effrontery of this crime, committed within a year of your own marriage to Mr. Halpern, we are offering you our legal services at cost. We believe that you will be able to get a very handsome settlement from Mr. Halpern. We are meanwhile searching the local records to make sure that there are no other marriages previously contracted. If such there are, as is more than likely, your own marriage will, of course, be void, but we believe that you can still wring from this wretch a sufficient sum to assure your future and that of your child. We trust that you will contact us immediately.

Sympathetically yours,
Brooks & Collins
Attorney at Law

Once Walter moved to Roxbury, he and Bellamy began a lively correspondence, and newspaper clippings provided the occasion for much of this, too. For example, Walter clipped the

following ad with its irresistible headline, pasted it to the back
of a postcard, and mailed it to his friend:

> **Please forgive me, Frank**
> Forgive me Frank [the accompanying ad read], and I prom-
> ise to take you to see the 1957 DeSoto, the most exciting car in
> the world today! It will be on display at our DeSoto Plymouth
> dealer's October 30th.

To the bottom of this Walter has taped the word "Brooks,"
which he has carefully clipped from another newspaper.
Beneath this earnest entreaty Bellamy wrote, "No, Brooks. It
ain't enough." And mailed it back.

Walter also corresponded with two local professional men,
Dr. Ives and Dr. Sweatman (appropriately the former was a
"people" doctor and the latter, a veterinarian). In one letter
Walter pretended to be a purveyor of post holes. In another he
wrote asking to be made a full partner in his friends' "slightly
soiled second-hand cellars, chimneys, and springs" business.
To this, Ives and Sweatman replied:

> We have decided to permit you to handle our branch office deal-
> ing in unheard echoes. One of the objections to making you a full
> time partner is the fact that you asked for an assignment of 30%
> of the present assets of the firm. This, of course, is not one-third
> of the assets, 33 1/3% being a third. Mr. Sweatman feels that if you
> can make errors of that sort, that you will have to go through the
> second and third grades of mortgages to become more familiar
> with figures and I have suggested that in order to make you more
> conversant with figures, you attend quite a number of the bathing
> show contests this season . . .
>
> Yours until our removable springs run dry,
> IVES & SWEATMAN

Walter clearly kept his sense of humor until the end, but as
the decade wore on and his health continued to decline (he
spent two months in the hospital in 1957), he grew increasingly

concerned about leaving Dorothy well provided for. An opportunity to do this presented itself unexpectedly when Walter received an offer for the television rights to the Ed stories from Hollywood's Arthur Lubin.

The well-known producer-director was no stranger to talking animals, having directed the first six Francis the Talking Mule movies for Universal.[10] Walter accepted the offer and a contract was signed on October 5, 1957. Though a script for a pilot episode was completed by late February of the following year, there is no evidence that Walter saw it. And since the TV show itself didn't debut until 1961, three years after his death, it went unseen and unremarked by Ed's creator—just as well, perhaps, since the campy series bore almost no resemblance to the original Ed stories.

Walter's final published work was a lengthy fantasy titled "The Nicest War in the World," which appeared in *Good Housekeeping* magazine for May 1958. It was the third and final story in an unofficial series about a little girl named Jenny who lived in the Kingdom of Smithia. Jenny had debuted in the story "The King of Smithia," which appeared in the children's magazine *Story Parade* for December 1946. In this first story, Jenny, a clever little girl, outsmarts a very nosey king named Roscoe. Jenny returned three years later in a two-part story titled "Jenny and the Dragon" (*Story Parade* March and April 1945). Filled with charming anachronisms, this gently humorous story of a dragon that likes smiling faces and a knight-errant that doesn't like dragons was surely inspired by Kenneth Grahame's story "The Reluctant Dragon."

Ultimately, as all little girls must, Jenny grows up. She then marries Prince Elmer, who succeeds his father on the throne and Jenny becomes Queen of Smithia. Her final appearance, as noted above, is in "The Nicest War in the World," a charming valedictory effort about a series of wars between Smithia

---

10. It has occasionally been claimed that the Ed stories were inspired by Francis but, if anything, the opposite is the case. The Francis films were based on the novel *Francis* by Peter Stirling, but it was not published until 1946, and by that time all twenty-five Ed stories had already been published.

and the nearby kingdom of Lory, which is located just on the other side of the Debatable Mountains.

Though the story was actually written in 1954, it was not published until just three months before Walter's final heart attack and death on August 17, 1958. It makes a nicely apposite final creative statement, since its tone—both wistful and sweetly whimsical—has an almost elegiac air, as if Walter somehow knew when he wrote it that it would be his final word. Of course it wasn't *quite* his final word. Even more suitably, that would be the last Freddy book, *Freddy and the Dragon*, which appeared posthumously on October 20 of that year.

In a melancholy note in *The Bozoi Quarterly* for the fourth quarter of 1958, publisher Alfred A. Knopf, in listing the four books for young people he would issue that season, wrote:

> Finally [there is] what may, I fear, prove to be Walter R. Brooks's last book—*Freddy and the Dragon*. Mr. Brooks, who has appeared in these pages so often, died August 17 in his home at Roxbury, New York, at the age of seventy-two. Thus ends, to our sorrow, a long and happy association extending over more than thirty years, for we published *To and Again*, the first Freddy book in 1927. And in our current catalogue I find listed twenty-five titles by this charming and popular writer. At my age I suspect I will be recording the death of old friends in every issue of the Quarterly. (p. 4)

Following a funeral service at the Jay Gould Memorial Reformed Church in Roxbury on August 20, Walter's remains were cremated and laid to rest—next to his grandfather, the first Walter Rollin, in the Brooks Family plot in Hamilton, New York.[11]

If the life of his other grandfather, Sam Stevens, had been, as the newspaper obituary noted, "a useful one," Walter's own had been that, too, and more: a delightful celebration of the imagination and the creative spirit. He, after all, had written a

---

11. While a Tiffany window memorialized Dr. Brooks in Hamilton's Baptist Church, Dorothy more practically presented an electric organ in Walter's memory to the Episcopal Church in Margaretville.

total of 205 stories and two adult books, along with countless columns and reviews, which commented with wit and insight on literature and the arts, the culture and the consumables that informed four decades of American life. But most importantly, he left, in the twenty-five Freddy the Pig stories, a series of authentic classics of American children's literature and, in Freddy, one of the greatest characters in the body of that literature. He also captured and preserved, on the Bean Farm and in the nearby village of Centerboro, a uniquely American moment and setting. Though ostensibly located somewhere in upstate New York, the books' true location is now and always will be in the hearts of readers—young and old.

What Happened After

UTHORS' LIVES DON'T END WITH THEIR DEATHS, OF course, because their work lives on. This was certainly the case with Walter. Many of his short works were often anthologized and reprinted, while two of his short stories for children, "Jimmy Takes Vanishing Lessons" and "Henry's Dog Henry," were republished as hardcover monographic works by Knopf in the 1960s, while The Overlook Press reissued its own edition of "Jimmy" in 2008.

Also, as we've previously noted, the "Ed" stories found new life as the inspiration for the now cult classic TV sitcom, also of the sixties, *Mr. Ed*. A selection of nine of the stories, *The Original Mr. Ed*, was published as a paperback original by Bantam in 1963. To his credit, Bellamy orchestrated this for Dorothy's benefit. Walter's lifelong friend outlived him by fourteen years, dying on February 3, 1972, in Castine, Maine.

Sadly, too, the Freddy books began to die, going quietly out of print in the sixties and seventies, and as a result the pig o' our hearts languished, for a while, in limbo. But not for long. In 1984 Toronto playwright Dave Carley founded The Friends of Freddy, a literary fan club determined to lobby Knopf to bring the pig back into print. The members had some success; Random House, Knopf's parent, reissued eight of the books in 1986 (see Part II for particulars). Unfortunately, in an effort to modernize Freddy's appearance, the publisher redesigned the covers with entirely inapposite art by illustrator Leslie Morrill and also failed to market the mini-series release with any notable energy or imagination. As a result, the volumes were quickly remaindered.

The Friends of Freddy remained steadfast, however, and began holding biennial national conferences in 1986. The first two were held at the rustic Kass Inn, located between Roxbury and Margaretville, New York. It was at the second gathering that the Friends established the Walter R. Brooks Memorial Fund, proceeds from which have since been donated to the Roxbury Library, which Walter—and later Dorothy—served as a trustee. The third conference was held in Walter's hometown of Rome, New York, and the conference has moved about the general area of the Catskills in the years since. Until her death in 1994, on the very eve of that year's Friends of Freddy gathering, Dorothy Brooks was the guest of honor at each event.

The Friends remained committed to bringing the series back into print and—thanks to the good offices of long-time members Wray and Loni Romiger, owners of the Purple Mountain Press in Fleischmanns, New York—finally succeeded in 1998. The Romigers were long-time acquaintances of publisher Peter Mayer, who had retired as head of the international publisher Penguin, and was then devoting his attentions to the mid-sized publisher The Overlook Press, which he and his father had started some years before. When the Romigers suggested he consider reissuing the Freddy books, he was intrigued and agreed almost immediately to do so. Thanks to Overlook, all of the Freddy titles are now back in print in gorgeous hardcover facsimile editions. At the same time the children's publisher Puffin (an imprint of Penguin) issued ten of the titles in beautifully designed trade paperback editions. Over the years various production companies have held options on the series for possible motion picture or television development but, to date, nothing has come of this.

Meanwhile thanks to its Internet presence (www.freddythepig.org), the Friends of Freddy are flourishing. They are presently engaged in an ambitious project designed to donate copies of the Freddy books to schools and libraries while happily remaining committed to spreading the name and fame of Freddy the Pig and his creator, Walter R. Brooks, throughout the known universe.

Who knows? Perhaps Freddy will make it to Mars yet!

Part II
THE WORK

Fanfare for Freddy

THOUGH WALTER PRODUCED A PRODIGIOUS AMOUNT OF work for adult readers, it is his twenty-six[12] Freddy the Pig books for children that are his more important—and enduring—accomplishment. Indeed, they are now widely regarded as classics of American children's literature and Walter has been called an American Kenneth Grahame (*The Wind in the Willows*), A. A. Milne (*Winnie the Pooh*), or Hugh Lofting (*Dr. Dolittle*). Still others have suggested he is the natural successor to L. Frank Baum, whose *Wizard of Oz* is regarded as the first truly American fantasy.

I knew none of this, of course, back in 1950 when, at the age of nine, I had my own first encounter with Freddy in the pages of my third grade reader, *On Longer Trails* (Arthur I. Gates, et. al., eds. Macmillan. 1945). There, in the section called "Fun with Farm Animals," I discovered a droll story called "Adventure in a Swamp." It was about a group of such animals that encounter a gang of hungry alligators in a swamp. Though nearly sixty years have passed, I still recall the fun I had reading the story and the pleasant frisson the characters' narrow escape gave me. That might have been the end of my story had I not, several weeks later, been browsing the shelves of the children's room at my hometown public library in Logansport, Indiana. I was an avid reader and already a habitué of the library, and finding a shelf of books there with a

---

12. In addition to the twenty-five Freddy stories, a twenty-sixth title, *The Collected Poems of Freddy the Pig*, was published in 1953.

similar format and design alerted me to the fact that this was a whole series by one author—my favorite kind of reading. I eagerly (and randomly) pulled one of the volumes off the shelf. Providentially it was *To and Again*. I say "providentially," because, flipping through its pages, I quickly realized this was an entire book about those funny farm animals. Indeed, this was the very book from which the story in my reader had been excerpted. I quickly grabbed an armload of other titles from the series to accompany the one already in my hands, ran to the check-out counter and—well, the rest is history.

I immediately fell in love with Freddy and his friends. And when I had read my way through all of the Freddy books the library owned, I nagged my mother until she took me to the local post office, so I could buy a postal money order and send it off to Kroch's Bookstore on Michigan Avenue in Chicago, along with my laboriously printed order for *Freddy the Detective*, the first book I ever bought with my own money. I was still only nine but somehow I discovered within the next year that late each fall the *Chicago Tribune,* the big city newspaper we bought on our way home from church each Sunday, published a special children's section in its book review and somewhere in its pages I would find an ad from Knopf, Walter's publisher, announcing the new Freddy book for that year. Then, off to the post office again; another money order, another letter to Kroch's, and then days of impatient waiting until, running home from my nearby elementary school, I would finally (*finally!*) find a package in the mail box with the latest addition to my own small—but steadily growing—personal library.

Why was I so head over heels in love with the Freddy books? Well, first and foremost there was Freddy himself. For Freddy was the pig o' my heart, a bright, creative, complex, multidimensional character who, though sometimes so frightened that his tail came uncurled, always gritted his teeth and did the right thing. And usually that right thing was helping his friends. How I longed to have a friend like that! And speaking of friends, Freddy's own—both animal and human—were reason number two for my enchantment. I never tired of their company, not even that of the self-important, longwinded rooster, Charles, whose speeches inevitably gave Walter an opportunity to puncture pomposity. Pity the pompous and pretentious in the Freddy chronicles, for they shall come to grief—to the reader's delight. And to Walter's, for we have seen in Part I of this book how he loved to lampoon those who took themselves too seriously. As a child who often felt powerless in the face of adult authority, I delighted in seeing this happen, and I suspect that is the case with many young readers.

Children love animals and stories about them, another reason for the series' popularity. But there's more to it than that: Walter obviously loved animals, too, but he also understood them and, though he often anthropomorphized them, he always managed to capture the essence of their respective animal natures, to which they remained true. Consider Robert and Georgie, the dogs, who are loyal, trustworthy and companionable, while Jinx, the cat, is a firecracker with fur, but when it comes to his friends, he is as loyal as the dogs. Old Whibley the owl is wise, yes, and grouchy in the daytime (and sometimes at night, if it comes to that!) but also a trifle dangerous, a bit—dare I say it—predatory? Then there's gentle, placid Mrs. Wiggins, common sense with a mouthful of cud. And here comes Charles again: strutting around the barnyard, in love with his own voice but horribly, well, *hen*pecked by his wife, Henrietta (could she have had another name?), a termagant with feathers and a beak. But, deep down, we know she loves her husband and is actually rather . . . proud of him. It is departures from essential type like these that lend dimension and interest to the characters.

Sometimes, of course, it is the very departure that defines the character and we have a happy exercise in the humor of incongruity. Think, for example, of Freddy's good friend, Leo, whose predilection for getting his mane permed is most unlionlike (and, hence, quite funny). Indeed, so un-lionlike is Leo that the reader—and even Freddy—tends to forget he *is* a lion. Until, as in *Freddy the Pied Piper*, he reminds us of it.

> He crouched and lashed his tail, and began to creep towards Freddy with a ferocious grin.
> Freddy backed away. "Hey, quit that!" he said. "I—I don't like it."

The lion didn't move a muscle. He stared at Freddy with his ferocious yellow eyes, and then suddenly he twitched his whiskers, and Freddy jumped convulsively backward and fell over a chair. (pp. 103–4)

And, thus, in this delightful scene Walter finds humor not in the incongruous but, for a surprising change, in the congruous!

As a character, Freddy—being both congruous and incongruous—is the most difficult to classify and the one that most often must fight stereotypical thinking about his essence. Pigs are lazy; pigs are greedy, pigs are dirty, etc., etc., ad nauseam. Of course, Freddy is none of these (well, he may be a wee bit lazy); but nevertheless it was inevitable that Walter should have often been asked why he chose a pig as his series hero. In answer he would profess—a bit disingenuously—not to really know himself and then would add something vague about Kurt Wiese drawing such appealing pigs. The fact is, as any Freddy fan knows, the pig wasn't the hero of the first or even the second title in the series. He grew into the part, but what surely appealed to Walter from the start was the fact that pigs are highly intelligent animals. How does he introduce Freddy in *To and Again*? As "the youngest and the *cleverest* of the pigs on the farm."[13]

Walter prized intelligence and intellectual curiosity and in a pig he got both—as well as a character that enjoyed spending hours sitting in an armchair and writing! Walter clearly identified with Freddy, whom he even came to resemble, at least a bit. Henry S. F. Cooper, formerly of *The New Yorker* magazine, once observed that when as a fourteen-year-old boy he met Walter, who had been invited to lunch at the Cooper home, his first thought was that the great man looked like Freddy in one of his disguises.

There are many other parallels between Freddy and Walter, of course. I listed some of them in my introduction to *The Wit and Wisdom of Freddy the Pig* (The Overlook Press, 2000). Here they are again: both were poets, both were news-

---

13. As a boy, Walter, remember, was himself the youngest—and perhaps the cleverest—of his gaggle of Stevens cousins.

paper editors, both played guitar—and football! Both were
artists, both were book lovers, both had banking in their blood,
both disliked winter—and hard work. And both were head
over heels in love with words. This last is yet another reason
why I loved these books: their effervescent use of language, for
they are filled with word play, funny names (could there be a
better name for an ineffectual villain than Herb Garble?), comical expressions ("Well, tear off my collar and necktie"), and
the salubrious, even unrestrained use of polysyllables, which
Walter never edited out of his pages. Why? Because he never
wrote down to his readers. Indeed, as he once wrote of *To and
Again*, "I used the same language in telling the story that I
would have used telling it to grownups. Why not? Children are
people—they're just smaller and less experienced. They are
not taken in by the smug playfulness of those who write or talk
down to them as if they were dull-witted and slightly deaf."
(Knopf promotional brochure, ca. 1945)

Walter was never smug, but he was often playful in the
humorous interaction of characters and in their conversations,
especially those between Leo and the circus owner Mr.
Boomschmidt. His playfulness was almost never jokey, though
he sometimes resorted to slapstick; e.g., Freddy's misadventures on a bicycle (though a pig on a bicycle is also an exercise
in incongruity) or the consequences of the bungling Mr.
Bismuth's household "repairs" in *Freddy and the Space Ship*. This
title also offers a good example of how Walter playfully used
situation for humorous purpose; e.g., the travelers on Uncle
Ben's space ship think they are landing on their target, Mars,
but are in actuality back on Earth, a situation that has all sorts
of comical consequences.

Speaking of situations and consequences, what about
Walter's plots? Well, plots were nearly always secondary and a
good thing, too, since plotting was not Walter's strong suit.
And so the chief criticism of the books that was offered over the
years—that they were too episodic—has some lingering validity.
But that isn't necessarily bad. Walter was, first and foremost, a
short story writer. As a result, his book-length works are collections of moments, yes, but beautifully realized moments that

then conspire with the characters. It is their interactions, their conversations, their failings and foibles that cause these disparate parts of the plot to cohere and become a shining, downright scintillating whole that glitters in the reader's imagination like Mrs. Church's jewelry in the afternoon sunlight.

Ah, Mrs. Church. And Mr. Camphor, too, of course. Isn't it interesting that in the Freddy books two of the most sympathetic characters should be two of the wealthiest? This was almost never the case in the adult stories, where the rich people more often resemble the *un*sympathetic rich folks in Freddy—people like Mrs. Underdunk and Mr. Margerine, who commit the unpardonable sin of being snooty, pretentious, and controlling. As for Church and Camphor, though, they are always down-to-earth, unpretentious, refusing ever to stand on ceremony (Mr. Camphor has a butler, Bannister, for that purpose, after all!) and—at least in the case of Mrs. Church—unfailingly commonsensical, as demonstrated by her refusal to wear real jewelry when the dime store variety glitters just as brightly—at a fraction of the cost!

This does not stop some unscrupulous and unwitting types from coveting the glittering jewelry, though. Indeed, in her very first appearance in the series, Mrs. Church, in *The Clockwork Twin*, gives away her jewelry to the gypsy chief in an effort to ransom the kidnapped Byram. Greed, the desire for material gain, covetousness, and the willingness to step outside the law to satisfy these desires are thus established as the chief motivation—and modus operandi—for villains in the Freddy series. Most notable among them, perhaps, are the evil real estate agent Mr. Anderson and the hapless Herb Garble, who is so often thwarted by Freddy that revenge becomes at least a secondary motive for him, as it does for Simon and his family of rats.

So, how do I love these books? Let me recount the ways: first and foremost there is the individual character of Freddy, that pig of many parts; then there is the larger consideration of characterization and the fact that so many of the most memorable characters are animals, a circumstance so dear to the hearts of young readers. The fact that these characters are so well drawn and developed that readers feel they are their own friends feeds into the strength of the series nature of Walter's enterprise. What reader would not wait breathlessly for the next volume to appear, simply for the sake of finding out what old friends are up to now? Then there is the wonderful use of language—and in this context Walter's respect for his readers and his willingness to challenge them. Then there is his very celebration of intelligence, of books, of writing. And his delightful use of humor in its many forms and types, ranging from satire to wordplay, from slapstick to situation and back again.

To all of these I would add one more: the consideration of setting. Just as Walter loved his characters, so he obviously loved the farm and the nearby village of Centerboro where most of them—animals and humans—lived. And, in a sense, where *he*, too, had lived as a boy, for he acknowledged that Centerboro was really the Rome of his childhood. To write about it was, thus, a kind of exercise in time travel for him. Not to the real past, of course, but to an idealized, reimagined version of it, a place where animals and humans could communicate, where friendship was the gold standard, and helping others was the order of the day. Oh, sure there were villains. Otherwise, things would have gotten dull. But the good guys—er, good animals—always won in the end, which was a happy thing. In a way the Bean Farm was Walter's peaceable kingdom and maybe even his idea of paradise. And for readers like me, who sometimes found the real world a little *too* real, it became a place of sanctuary and refuge, a place where one could escape simply by opening up any of the famous Freddy the Pig books by that American master Walter R. Brooks and, turning to page 1, starting to read.

What perfect bliss.

Pleasures and Particulars: Notes and Commentary on the Freddy Titles

1. *To and Again.* Illustrated by Adolfo Best-Maugard. New York: Alfred A. Knopf, 1927. 196 pages. Later re-titled ***Freddy Goes to Florida*** and reissued with new illustrations by Kurt Wiese. New York: Alfred A. Knopf, 1949.

> *Dedicated to Anne and Nannie (Anne Brooks and family friend Annie Dow)*

Reissued as *Freddy Goes to Florida* in a Dell Yearling (trade paperback) edition with cover art by Bob Jones. New York: Dell, 1980.

Reissued as *Freddy Goes to Florida*—with cover art by Leslie Morrill—in both hardcover and trade paperback editions with an introduction by Michael Cart. New York: Alfred A. Knopf, 1986.

Reissued in a hardcover facsimile edition by The Overlook Press in 1998.

Reissued in a trade paperback edition by Puffin Books (as part of "The Freddy Collection"). New York: Puffin Books, 2001. (Puffin also issued this as a trade paperback in a dual edition with *Freddy the Detective* in 2001).

Reissued in *The Freddy Anniversary Collection*. With an introduction by Michael Cart. Woodstock: The Overlook Press, 2002.

Published in England as *Freddy's First Adventure*. Illustrated by Geoffrey Higham. London: John Lane, The Bodley Head, 1949.

Excerpted in *On Longer Trails*. Edited by Arthur I. Gates, et. al. New York: The Macmillan Company, 1945.

Here is the first book in the series and the one that Walter R. Brooks himself reckoned was the best of the bunch ("the first one usually is," he wrote). Published in 1927, the book is notable not only as the first title in a landmark series, but also as a book that helped usher in modern American children's literature, especially in its wonderful use of realistic language and humor. Though we know when *To and Again* was published, we don't know precisely when it was written. All Walter allowed for the record was, "I wrote it . . . when I was alone in Washington one hot summer doing publicity for the Red Cross."

The only problem with this statement is that Walter worked for the Red Cross for nearly a decade, from roughly 1917 to 1926 and was in Washington periodically throughout that time. Over the years he would tell reporters and interviewers that it took him anywhere from two to five years to find a publisher for the manuscript (his second wife, Dorothy Brooks, asserted it took seven years); nevertheless, 1923 seems to be the most likely date, since he spent an unusually large amount of time in D. C. that year. All that said, precisely how long the quest for a publisher took is of secondary importance. Of primary importance is what Walter acknowledged in a brief autobiography for *The Junior Book of Authors*: "I wrote [*To and Again*] for my own amusement."

In this first Freddy book, the plot is quite amusing: Tired of long, hard winters, the animals of the Bean Farm, somewhere in upstate New York, decide to take a vacation trip to Florida. The book—which begins, appropriately, at daybreak—recounts their travels and the adventures they encounter on their way to and (back) again, including besting a brace of burglars (inspired by the traditional tale of the Bremen Town Musicians), outwitting a group of hungry alligators, and discovering buried treasure, which they take back to the farm and present to their impoverished owner Mr. Bean, who vows, in turn, to make their lives easier. Along the way Walter shares his vision of the good life: "About eleven o'clock they would stop under the shade of a big tree by the road-side, and lie about in the grass and talk until late in the afternoon. And then they would go on for awhile until they found a good camping-place. When they came to a river or a pond, they would all go in swimming. It was the pleasantest life you can imagine."

This book is also distinguished as the only one in the series illustrated by Adolfo Best-Maugard (1891–1964). Every other title is illustrated by the accomplished Kurt Wiese, who would also create illustrations for the 1949 reissue of *this* book, then re-titled *Freddy Goes to Florida*. Best-Maugard was, himself, a distinguished artist, though, one of the first modern Mexican artists to exhibit in New York. An educator and theorist, he also served as Mexico's Director of Arts Education and developed a method of creative design that was widely used in Mexican schools. His three books—*Creative Design*, *Human Figures*, and *Draw Animals*—were all published in the United States by Knopf. The third title may have been the catalyst for Knopf's inviting Best-Maugard to illustrate Walter's book about animals. Though some reviewers praised the artist's efforts, his animals appear in such a highly stylized and self-consciously *designed* way as to clash, unhappily, with Walter's straightforward, conversational style and easy humor. Best-Maugard was a close friend of Frieda Kahlo and Diego Rivera, the latter of whom painted an elegant portrait of his friend in 1913.

Thirteen of the Bean Farm animals make the journey to Florida: Freddy, of course, Jinx, Charles and Henrietta (who have the good sense to leave their ten children and her eight sisters behind), Mrs. Wiggins, Robert, the collie; Alice and Emma, the ducks; Hank, the old white horse; and the four mice: Eek, Quik, Eeny, and Cousin Augustus. Also along for the ride are the spiders, Mr. and Mrs. Webb, who—in later titles—will prove to be inveterate travelers.

Several minor characters are introduced who will appear only sporadically in later volumes (if at all). Among these are Hank's Uncle William (Walter also had an Uncle William, though there is no indication that he was a horse!); Jack, a dog belonging to the villainous man with the black moustache and his son, the dirty-faced boy; and the collie Jock, Robert's older brother. Walter demonstrated his thrift by recycling many of his characters—especially his villains—and though there are altogether 650 named characters in the series, many of them make only cameo appearances or are only mentioned in passing.

Though he already has "a very inquiring mind" and is "a very good parchesi player," Freddy is still a work in progress. Most of the other characters are already fully formed, though Jinx is a bit wilder in his first outing than he will be later. He is, Walter says, "rather careless of appearances and a bit too free in his speech," though the artistic talent that will serve him well in later titles is already established. While Jinx is still a bird-eater, he has made a pact with the mice not to ingest them, though they still seem a bit nervous in his presence. Mr. Bean, too, is gruffer than he will become in later titles and is not above threatening to fricassee Charles for Sunday dinner if the rooster oversleeps again! And, we sense, he means it.

Walter's satirical treatment of politicians, however, is unwavering. On the way to Florida the animals stop in Washington, D.C., long enough to meet the president and their senator who, of course, can't resist making a speech that reads, in part: "To welcome a delegation of the home folks to the Nation's Capital is one of the few pleasures that cheer the burdened brow of those whose stern duty it is to keep their shoulder always to the wheel of the ship of state. And that reminds me of the story of the two Irishmen . . ."

Another sometimes humorous but always genial device that Walter introduces in this first book is what might be called the "grand generalization." This is usually a declaration about an animal trait but sometimes addresses larger issues, as well. We learn, for example, that "Spiders are apt to be very firm in their decisions." "Cats very seldom make promises, but when they do, they always keep them." Also, "All cats are good at tying knots." And "Like most cows [Mrs. Wiggins] had a stout heart."

Freddy's heart was faithful, if not always stout, but his gift with words is evident from this first outing in which he creates a number of poems that the animals sing as they march along. The first of these occurs as early as page 25 and begins, "Oh, the sailor may sing of his tall swift ships / Of sailing the deep blue sea / But the long, white road where adventures wait / Is the better life for me." Like Freddy, Walter enjoyed traveling. Indeed, his friend Bellamy once wrote, "And from time to time Mr. Brooks has packed his knapsack and taken a trip 'round the world."

Not all of Freddy's poems are so elaborate; on page 89 he delivers only a single verse: "'Fraid cat Jinx / His tail's full of kinks! / He doesn't dare slide down the hill! / See how he shrinks." And sometimes his efforts are aborted. On page 94, for example, he starts, "The weather grew torrider and torrider / And the orange blossoms smelt horrider and / horrider / As we marched down into Florida." When Robert protests that the blossoms don't smell horrid, Freddy tries again, to much better effect, with a two-verse song that begins, "Oh, the winding road to Florida / Is a dusty road and long. . . ."

"They all liked this song better," Walter observes, "and as they went along, they sang lustily."

A final poem on page 196 begins, "Oh, a life of adventure is gay and free / And danger has its charm / And no pig of spirit will bound his life / By the fence on his master's farm." And yet home has its attractions, too, as Freddy's final lines—and the final lines of the book—attest: "And however they wander, both pigs and / men / Are always glad to get home again."

Once one has tasted danger, however, home tends to lose its savor and the appetite for adventure demands to be satisfied, as we will see in our discussion of the next story of Freddy and his friends.

2. *More To and Again.* Illustrated by Kurt Wiese. New York: Alfred A. Knopf, 1930. 306 pages. Later re-titled *Freddy Goes to the North Pole*. New York: Knopf, 1951. (An oddity of this later edition is that Wiese re-did the illustration facing page 27; otherwise the pictures are exactly the same. One wonders if the original plates might have been damaged.)

Published in England as *Freddy the Explorer*. Illustrated by Geoffrey Higham. London: John Lane, The Bodley Head, 1949.

Reissued in a hardcover facsimile edition by The Overlook Press in 2001.

Reissued in a trade paperback edition by Puffin (as part of "The Freddy Collection"). New York: Puffin Books, 2002.

Reissued in *The Freddy Anniversary Collection*. With an introduction by Michael Cart. Woodstock: The Overlook Press, 2002.

This title is memorable as the first to be illustrated by Kurt Wiese (1887–1974). The man who gave recognizable faces—and forms—to Freddy and his friends was born in Minden, Germany, and was trained in the export trade, which took him to China from 1909 to 1914. When World War I erupted, he was taken prisoner by the Japanese who turned him over to the British. He spent the next five years as a prisoner of war in Australia and, though he had no formal training, began drawing local animals and scenery and thus found his true vocation, art. He returned to Germany in 1919 and, three years later, set sail for Brazil. He lived there for three years illustrating textbooks and children's books for a Brazilian publisher before wanderlust once again called him away, this time to the United States.

In short order Wiese landed both a job with *Collier's Weekly* and also the commissions for his first two books. By the time Knopf hired him for *More To and Again* he had illustrated those, as well as thirteen others. Unfortunately his debut on the Bean Farm stage was not terribly auspicious. As critic Anne Carroll Moore wrote in *The Horn Book* magazine, "Mr. Wiese's drawings . . . are not his best work and they are given poor reproduction."

Happily, he found firmer artistic footing in his next effort, *Freddy the Detective*, and by the fourth book, *The Story of Freginald*, he was working at the top of his form, which was formidable, indeed. Barbara Bader, in her definitive study, *American Picturebooks from Noah's Ark to The Beast Within*, wrote that Wiese had "an outstanding visual memory; he could work in a variety of mediums and styles, draw animals and people with equal sympathy, convey ideas and information effectively; and he became, almost immediately, the most versatile and productive artist in the field of children's books."

To say he was "productive" is an understatement, however, since over the course of his long career he illustrated not only all of the Freddy books, but more than four hundred other books as well. Whenever Walter finished a manuscript, he sent a copy directly to Wiese, who was always anxious to receive it. And he wasn't the only

Illustrator Kurt Wiese

one, for, as he wrote Walter, "The children around here just wait for the librarian to bring your [new] book down!" "Around here" was rural New Jersey, where Wiese lived on the banks of the Delaware River. "It's a good life," he wrote many years later when he was in semiretirement. "Now when I cannot move around so much, I can sit at my window and the animals come to me. They make me understand how they live so I write stories about them."

The story Walter wrote about his animals in *More To and Again* is not as successful as its predecessor, but at 306 pages it *is* longer—the longest volume in the series. The plot is basically a rehash of the first, except that this time the animals go north instead of south—all the way to the North Pole, in fact, where they meet Santa Claus and, along the way, discover treasure, this time in the form of two children named Ella and Everett, whom they rescue from their abusive aunt and uncle. The animals then take the kids back to the farm, where the childless Beans gladly adopt them.

Freddy is a more prominent character in this book but is still not quite center stage. He does move a good deal of the action, though, it being his idea to start the wildly successful Barnyard Tours, Inc., which he serves as President. Jinx is Secretary and Mrs. Wiggins, Treasurer. Thanks to one of the company's most popular excursions, the one to Scenic Centerboro, we learn (among other things) that its main street is lined on both sides with elm trees and that there is a Centerboro Public Library that is really "very beautiful, built in the gothic style." There is also a Presbyterian Church; the local newspaper is called "The Gazette" (it will later become "The Guardian," of course); and there is "a fine view from the hill behind the Trumbull Place." Alas, familiarity breeds contempt and the animals soon get sick and tired of touring Scenic Centerboro—at which point it is, again, Freddy who hatches the idea of launching a new enterprise, an expedition to the North Pole.

As for other familiar characters, we learn a great deal of miscellaneous information about them. Jinx, for example, reports having a dozen brothers and sisters in this neighborhood. More startlingly, while he is still "inclined to be a little vulgar in his speech," it is he, we discover, who has taught Freddy to read! And in that context we have the first mention of Freddy's prize possession, *The Complete Works of Shakespeare* in one volume, which had formerly been used by the Beans to prop up a legless corner of their bed. He also owns a copy of *Grimm's Fairy Tales* and numerous old newspapers and advertising folders (written by Walter, perhaps?). But how did the cat, himself, learn to read? Why, by sitting on Mrs. Bean's lap while she read the newspaper, of course. And speaking of Mrs. Bean, there is a disquieting scene early in the book in which she urges Jinx to pursue and eat his mouse friend, Eeny: "Look, Jinx. Go chase the mouse. See? Nice fat mouse! M'm! Mice, Jinx, mice!" Happily, Mr. Bean is less bloodthirsty than his wife and has actually mellowed a bit since the first book. We also learn that he has "farmed this place, man and boy, for fifty-two years."

As for Charles, he is pompous as ever and is now reported to have eight daughters and seven sons (the numbers change in virtually every book!). Several new characters are introduced, too. One is Peter the bear, a second is Ferdinand the crow, a third is Cecil the porcupine, and a dozen others comprise the rather tiresome crew of the whaling ship, *The Mary Ann*, and their blowhard captain, Mr. Hooker (this will be their only appearance in the series).

We are treated to more of Walter's grand generalizations; e.g., "No dog in the history of the world has ever been known to tell a lie," and "Like all roosters [Charles] had plenty of courage when he was angry" (this will be memorably demonstrated in *Freddy and the Ignormous*). And Freddy continues to mature as a poet, offering up seven rhyming creations this time (see pp. 179, 186, 209, 215, 249, 259, and 287). One of these is particularly memorable. It begins, "Oh, east is east, and west is west / And never the twain shall meet—"

"Then," Walter tells us, "he stopped and frowned. 'Reminiscent somehow,' he muttered: 'Wonder if it's too metaphysical. It's darned good, though.' He went on: "Until they come to the end of the earth / To Santa Claus' retreat. / Where east is south and west is south / And north is south also. / Where all directions are the same / Whichever way you go."

Ultimately, of course, where the animals will go is home to the farm. "And everybody was thoroughly and completely happy."

3. *Freddy the Detective.* New York: Alfred A. Knopf, 1932. 264 pages. Also published as a Junior Literary Guild selection.

Dedicated to Elsie (Walter's sister Elsie Brooks Perrin)

Published in England as *Freddy the Detective.* Illustrated by Geoffrey Higham. London: John Lane, The Bodley Head, 1950.

Reissued in both hardcover and trade paperback editions with cover art by Leslie Morrill and an introduction by Michael Cart. New York: Knopf, 1986.

Reissued in a trade paperback edition by Scholastic Book Services in 1967.

Reissued in a Dell Yearling (trade paperback) edition with cover art by Bob Jones. New York: Dell, 1979.

Reissued in a hardcover facsimile edition by the Overlook Press in 1998.

Reissued in a trade paperback edition by Puffin Books (as part of "The Freddy Collection"). New York: Puffin Books, 2001.

Reissued in *The Freddy Anniversary Collection*. With an introduction by Michael Cart. Woodstock: The Overlook Press, 2002.

See also "A Literary Pig Turns Detective" in Young Wings, *the magazine of the Junior Literary Guild for July 1932. This also includes a piece by Walter titled "You Can Make Up a Story, Too," which is reprinted in the book* Writing Books for Boys and Girls, *edited by Helen Ferris. New York: Doubleday, 1952.*

At last, Freddy receives star billing, assuming the part that will be—of all the others he later plays—the most prominent. Inspired by a book he has found in the barn, *The Adventures of Sherlock Holmes*, the intrepid pig decides he will become a detective. Fortunately for his nascent career, Mrs. Wiggins the cow agrees to become his partner, for they are a match made in heaven: ingenious Freddy will supply the imagination, while his partner will provide the common sense, the foundation upon which the soon legendary firm of Frederick and Wiggins will be built!

Freddy's first case is already at hand: Everett's toy train has gone missing. After surveying the scene of the crime, which is lousy with clues, Freddy correctly deduces that the train has been stolen by . . . *rats!* Enter Simon and his extended family of thieving rodents, who have returned to the barn, from which they had been expelled by Jinx several years before. They are now using the train cars as protective armor while they steal Mr. Bean's grain. Well, it is one thing for Freddy to uncover the identity of the thieves; it is quite another to foil their nefarious plot, for Simon is a wily—and oily—antagonist, a Professor Moriarty to Freddy's Holmes. Simple force is not enough, as Freddy discovers when he attacks the train and succeeds only in breaking one of his teeth. "Freddy, the sleuth," the delighted rats sing, "He busted a tooth / He's a silly old bonehead, and that is the truth."

This irritates Freddy "frightfully" and goads him to action, but first he must solve several other cases that intrude—the mystery of Egbert and the even more baffling case of Prinny's dinner. Well, neither case is *that* baffling but they keep the pot of the plot simmering while tension builds until, with the help of Mrs. Wiggins's common sense, Freddy hatches a scheme that finally foils the robber rats. But then, wouldn't you know it, *human* thieves enter the already crowded stage and now Freddy must foil them, too. This requires that he don his first disguise; thanks to "quite a large wardrobe" he has assembled for this purpose, he finds an old suit of Mr. Bean's, a false mustache, and a cap like Sherlock Holmes's. Putting them on, he becomes "a very small tramp with a very long nose." For once, a disguise works—well, not quite, but at least well enough to enable the pig to bring the thugs to justice. "Freddy was now a made pig," Walter writes. Alas, Jinx is also made—the chief suspect in the apparent murder of a crow, that is. In due course this will lead to the first in a series of comic trials that will enliven the pages of many subsequent Freddy books.

As the Canadian critic Sheila Egoff has pointed out, the Freddy books are shaped in the classic comedic mode: they begin in order, proceed to disorder, and, at last, return to order. But order is dull, and in the closing pages of this exceptionally fine book, Freddy and Jinx, finding themselves bored when all the mysteries have been solved, decide—not for the last time—to take to the open road in search of adventure. As they leave the farm, they are heard by the stay-at-home Mrs. Wiggins singing one of Freddy's finest songs (and the only one by him in this entire book): "Then it's out of the gate and down the road / Without stopping to say goodbye / For adventure waits over every hill / Where the road runs up to the sky / We're off to play with the wind and the stars / And we sing as we march away / O, it's all very well to love your work / But you've / got to have some play."

A source of the increasing success of the rapidly evolving series is that, for Walter, this kind of writing was not work; it was play; it was diversion. And there is delight in diversion—for both author and reader. It is a never-ending source of delight for the reader to watch Walter, in each succeeding book, discover new things, both about his characters and the nature of the world they inhabit, and then finding just the right way to describe then.

For example, when the pig and his friend Jinx finally manage to wrest the train away from Simon and his family, a sea of angry rats comes boiling out of every corner of the barn loft. How does Freddy react? Here's the way Walter describes it: "Freddy, feeling that his work there was completed, saw no reason for staying longer. In fact he fell down the last eight steps of the stairs, so eager was he to get away." With this dry understatement, Walter cleverly establishes Freddy's—well, call it "prudence." In the next breath he establishes something else: "But outside, by the captured train, he recovered himself and thanked Mrs. Wiggins generously for her part in the victory."

Handsome is as handsome does and Freddy clearly is, in his generous sharing of credit, a very handsome young pig. Of course, Walter has already begun to establish the generosity of spirit and power of empathy that make Freddy so enduringly attractive. In an earlier scene that follows a confrontation with the angry rats, Freddy says to Jinx, as they walk home, "You know, there's really something in what they say. It must be rather hard to be driven out of your home and hunted from pillar to post."

If this statement is true to Freddy's emerging character, Jinx's reply is equally true to his: "You have a sympathetic nature, Freddy," he says. "It does you credit, but your sympathy is wasted on these rats. Nobody'd hunt 'em if they'd behave themselves. And anyway," Jinx shrewdly adds, "if all animals behaved themselves, how could you go on being a detective? There wouldn't be any crimes for you to detect."

Invoking the "b" word—"behavior"—raises an interesting point. As the series continues to evolve and the reader gets to know the characters better, Walter becomes engaged in an increasingly delicate balancing act; i.e., trying to balance his animal characters' innate natures with their acquired, or imposed, human traits. With one glorious exception he almost always succeeds. The exception, of course, is Freddy, who may have a near fatal fondness for food and naps but who, in every other important regard, is clearly not a pig at all, but rather Walter R. Brooks with a snout and trotters!

In terms of the characters' context, though, Walter is still finding his footing and, as a result, there continue to be moments that may bring the reader up short. In *More To and Again*, for example, this occurs when Mrs. Bean urges Jinx to eat Eeny. It also happens with the first appearance of Sheriff Higgins, who will become one of Freddy's most stalwart allies in later books. The point is made that Freddy already knows him "well." How so? Because the sheriff "owned some pigs who were distant relatives of Freddy's." By now the idea of humans "owning" animals is discomfiting, for it transforms the latter from characters into property. Of course, readers are probably still aware—at some level—that the Beans themselves own their animals, but Walter is far enough along in his transformation of the Bean Farm into a peaceable kingdom that the very notion of these animals being owned like, well, *animals* is jarring. For by now the Bean animals have nearly become Mr. Bean's partners, not his property. And as such they work not for him but with him, and not only with him but also with his wife. As Walter writes, "The smaller animals always helped Mrs. Bean with the housework, and were in and out of the house a good deal all day, so when Jinx and Freddy went in the kitchen door and up the back stairs, Mrs. Bean merely glanced up from the peas that two rabbits were helping her shell and said: 'Be careful of those stairs, animals. They're pretty steep. I don't want you should hurt yourselves.'"

There is a subtle transformation at work here, as the animals begin to assume a kind of dual citizenship. In a real world sense, they are still animals, but in another sense—Walter's vividly imagined one—they are also becoming children, members of an extended family. Accordingly, the Beans are becoming their parents—Mr. Bean, the gruff but kindly and always fair father, and Mrs. Bean, the increasingly gentle, concerned, and loving mother. And so the animals' work has now become a labor of love, a kind of free-will offering of their help. Only one thing remains for the transformation to become complete, which will happen in the next title in the series: the animals will finally find the ability to talk not only with each other—an ability they already have—but with human beings, as well.

4. *The Story of Freginald.* Illustrated by Kurt Wiese. New York: Alfred A. Knopf, 1936. Also published as a selection of the Junior Literary Guild.

Dedicated to A.S.B. (Anne Shepard Brooks)

Published in England as *Freddy and Freginald*. Illusrated by Kurt Wiese. London: John Lane, The Bodley Head, 1952.

Reissued in a hardcover facsimile edition by The Overlook Press in 2003.

In *More To and Again* a frustrated Mr. Bean says, "Consarn it, I wish we could talk animal talk; then we'd know" (where the animals are going, that is). Well, there is an old saying that goes something like, "Be careful what you wish for; you may get it." And sure enough Mr. Bean's wish comes true in a book that some readers regard—for several reasons—as being not quite in the canon. One reason is the book's uncharacteristic design with its large format and two-color illustrations. The second and more important reason is that Freddy plays only a cameo role in it— and even that doesn't occur until the story is nearly concluded.

By then, though, the reader has come to know and enjoy the adventures of its new protagonist, an engaging young bear. "Most bears are named Ed or George or Bill," Walter acknowledges, but this one is named "Louise." Because he has a girl's name, the other bears make fun of him and generally shun him. And so, to keep from being lonesome, he starts making up poetry. Here is a sample verse: "Oh, the rabbits play with the rabbits / And the hares like to play with the hares / And I'd like to play with my own people—/ I'd like to play with the bears."

When, one day in the woods, the solitary Louise encounters a lion who, hearing his name, calls it "amazing" and "magnificent," the flattered youngster gladly accepts his invitation to meet Mr. Boomschmidt, the owner of the circus that Leo is with. The ebullient Mr. Boom is equally delighted with the name and invites Louise to join his struggling show.

"I—I'd like to, sir, [says the bear] But do you really think I'd help the show, sir?"

"Help it! [exclaims Mr. Boomschmidt] You'll be the show. A bear named Louise! Not a man, woman or child in the United States has ever seen—yes, or even heard of such a thing."

Walter might also have noted that none of these folks would ever have heard of a man blithely having a conversation with a bear, but, as he did in his adult short stories, Walter simply introduces this bit of useful magic here with no comment whatsoever. Many years later, though, he did comment in a letter to a young fan: "In the first 3 books about Freddy the animals only talked to one another. But in *The Story of Freginald*, they began talking to people. I think the reason I changed was that it was more fun to have them talk to people. But I never explained it in the stories, because what explanation could you give? I just thought nobody would notice it. And of course everybody did!"

Walter's own attraction to talking animal stories is probably rooted in his youth for, as he once wrote, "I had always liked stories about animals talking, and my tales about the animals on the Bean Farm are, I suppose, echoes of the stories of Lily Wesselhoeft, which were my childhood favorites." Elizabeth Foster Wesselhoeft (1840–1919), like Walter, became a children's writer at mid-life. Another area of commonality was homeopathic medicine. Walter's brother-in-law was a homeopathic physician, and so was Lily's husband, Dr. Konrad

Wesselhoeft, who—like Walter's father—attended the University of Leipzig (though fourteen years earlier)! Konrad had the further distinction of being Louisa May Alcott's personal physician. A publisher's note in Lily's first book, *Sparrow the Tramp* (Roberts Brothers, 1888), states, "The lamented author of 'Little Women' in her last days read with great delight the manuscript of this little story; and its publication is owing greatly to the interest which she had in it." As a child, Walter owned a copy of this book, plus two others: *Old Rough the Miser* (Roberts, 1891) and *The Winds, the Woods, and the Wanderer* (Roberts, 1890).

The Story of Freginald may not be a traditional Freddy tale but it is indispensable to the series, for not only does it give voices to the animals but it also introduces the circus, which will become a staple presence, along with Mr. Boomschmidt and Leo, who will become two of Freddy's best friends. These characters are fully formed from the outset—at least they are once Leo has had his mane permed for the first time! As for Freginald, though, he was too much like Freddy as a character to have a lasting place in the series; in fact, this is his only major appearance, though he shows up in passing in *The Clockwork Twin*. A pity because he is an engaging and sensible character, as well as a good poet, perhaps because he understands that "the simpler [his poems] were, the better people liked them. He was rather smart to notice this, for lots of really important people never find it out at all."

5. *The Clockwork Twin.* Illustrated by Kurt Wiese. New York: Alfred A. Knopf, 1937. Also published as a Junior Literary Guild selection.

Dedicated to Bernice Baumgartner (who handled the foreign rights to Walter's work for his agent, Carl Brandt).

Reissued in a Gibraltar Library Binding edition as *Freddy and the Clockwork Twin*. New York: Alfred A. Knopf. (no date)

Reissued in a hardcover facsimile edition by The Overlook Press in 2003.

See also "A Clever Pig and a Clockwork Boy" in Young Wings, *the magazine of the Junior Literary Guild, for January 1938. This also includes a brief profile of Walter, titled "A New Friend and an Old One."*

Well, let's see: First, the animals rescue a boy named Adoniram R. Smith from the ravages of a flood and then, again, from his wicked aunt and uncle (Walter certainly seems to have disliked uncles and, especially, aunts. The latter are antagonists in many of his adult short stories and figure in such later "Freddys" as *Cousin Weedly* and *Camping*).

Following his rescues, Adoniram (pronounced like "Uncle Hiram") comes to live on the farm. The Beans are once again childless, at least temporarily, since Ella and Everett from the North Pole have gone abroad for a year with Mrs. Bean's sister. They must have had a splendid time abroad, since they never returned! (Walter, of course, never acknowledges this; the two simply disappear from the series.) When the animals realize that the boy is lonely by himself, they ask the taciturn Benjamin Bean, Mr. Bean's inventor uncle (whom Brooks clearly does like—as do the animals), to build another boy out of wood. The result—powered by clockwork—is amazingly life-like and a dead ringer for Adoniram, since Jinx, who has painted the face, has only the model of Adoniram to work from. The "twin," whom Uncle Ben names "Bertram," is able to do many of the things a normal boy would do, though he must be operated from within by Ronald, a rooster who becomes Charles and Henrietta's son-in-law.

The plot then turns to the animals' quest to find Adoniram's flesh-and-blood twin, Byram, who has been missing for years. Needless to say, this is a job for Freddy the detective. And, to the reader's delight, the case gives Freddy a chance to try out what will become his most famous disguise—that of little old lady, complete with a gingham dress of Mrs. Bean's, a large sunbonnet with two pinned-in corkscrew curls, and a pair of black lace mitts. Over the years Freddy seems to spend as much time in this dress as out of it, leading the reader to think Walter must have found such sartorial incongruity particularly hilarious. And apparently he did. In his Mohegan Lake Academy diary entry dated December 3, 1902, he notes, "Posed as Ruth and Boaz with Baker in Whiting's room for Mike Kimberly's benefit."

Reading this, one wonders fleetingly whether Walter was

Walter as the Biblical Ruth, 1913

Ruth or Boaz. The answer might be found in this photo-graph—taken in Jerusalem in 1913. One can only guess why Walter wanted to be photographed in this exotic outfit. Was he saluting his schoolboy lark? Was he, like Freddy, in disguise? Who can know? All one can say with certainty is that he makes a much better-looking Ruth than Freddy ever could . . .

Freddy's inevitable discovery of a boy named Byram R. Jones only poses a further problem: how to establish that the two boys are, indeed, brothers? If Freddy had been Shakespeare, he might have asked, "What's in a name?" For the middle initial "R" that the two share is, each admits, the first letter of his real surname (Smith and Jones being adoptive names). Trouble is, both boys think the name is so silly that they refuse to tell anybody—even each other—what it is. It's up to Freddy to devise a way for the boys to reveal the name to each other: they take turns whispering alternate letters into each other's ear. When they've finished, "'They're the same!' shouted Byram. 'We're brothers!' shouted Adoniram. And the two boys solemnly shook hands, while everybody cheered."

At first the boys still refuse to tell anybody else their name, but they finally relent and tell Freddy, who is so overcome with laughter that he finally races out of the barn and disappears into the night, still "yelling and almost sobbing" with laughter. Perhaps he's laughing still. . . .

This, by the way, is the third book in which Walter has included characters who actively dislike their names and either refuse to tell others what they are or change them; i.e., Peter the bear (in *More To and Again*), Louise the bear in *Freginald*, and now the boys, Adoniram and Byram. One wonders if Walter might have had similar feelings about one or both of his given names. One is tempted to think that perhaps that tantalizing "R" stands for Walter's own middle name, Rollin. The only problem with this is that the boys' name has seven letters, while "Rollin" has but six. On the other hand, Walter might have enjoyed the idea of both revealing and at the same time obscuring the truth. It is certainly something to ponder.

While we do that, let's also note that in addition to the inventor Uncle Ben, several other major characters are introduced in this title: among them are Jacob the wasp, Sniffy Wilson the skunk, Georgie the little brown dog, and the wealthy Mrs. Winfield Church. Journalist John Rowen (see his article "Roxbury's Dr. Doolitte" in the fall 2006 issue of *Katskill Life*) has insightfully suggested that the character of Mrs. Church was inspired by Helen Gould, whose family had funded the Reformed Church in Roxbury. It's an intriguing possibility, since Brooks first came to the village in 1937, the year that *Clockwork* was published. And he might well have known about Gould even earlier. At any rate, whoever served as her inspiration served well, since Mrs. Church is a thoroughly delightful character and Freddy becomes so fond of her that he hangs a framed picture of her in his study alongside his pictures of Abraham Lincoln and Sherlock Holmes!

This is the reader's first look inside Freddy's sanctum sanctorum, by the way. Walter describes it thus: "Freddy's study was a comfortable little room that he had fixed up in a corner of the pigpen. Here were all his books and papers, and his typewriter, and an old easy chair that he could sit in when he wanted to think or take a nap or both." A visiting Jinx begins looking—uninvited—through a heap of magazines and clippings that are piled next to him.

> "H'm," he says, "Cross-word puzzles. Old St. Nicholas with half the leaves torn out. Recipe for pumpkin pie—what use is that to you, I'd like to know? . . . 'How to make your own lipstick at home' ha-ha! Freddy you slay me! And an 'Ode to Spring' from the Centerboro Guardian. Listen to this, Freddy this is rich!" And he reads, "O spring, O spring / You wonderful thing / O spring, O spring, O spring! // O spring, O spring / When the birdies sing / I feel like a king. / O spring." "Six verses of it," Jinx crows. "Golly, what stuff! And signed 'Shakespeare, Jr.' Can you beat that? Boy, how he fancies himself!—Why, what's the matter, Freddy?"

The matter is, as the reader has already surmised, that this is the first poem the pig ever wrote. Happily, several of the poet's more mature works are also included in this volume (see pp. 29, 53, and 241). As for that matter, are some more of Walter's glittering generalizations. Among them: "There never yet was a rooster that couldn't be flattered into doing something he didn't want to do." And "There is no animal more curious than a pig." And "Like most doctors he was never very much surprised by anything he found inside his patients." And, finally, "But there's one thing about a pig—he seldom loses his head."

A good thing, too, since Freddy will need all of his wits to rise to the many challenges he encounters in his next adventure.

6. *Wiggins for President*. New York: Alfred A. Knopf, 1939. 253 pages.
Later reissued and re-titled *Freddy the Politician*. New York. Alfred A. Knopf, 1948.

Reissued as *Freddy the Politician*—with cover art by Leslie Morrill—in both hardcover and trade paperback editions with an introduction by Michael Cart. New York: Alfred A. Knopf, 1986.

Reissued in a hardcover facsimile edition by The Overlook Press in 2000.

Rather improbably the Beans plan to go to Europe for six long months on a much-needed vacation but are uncertain about the advisability of leaving the farm in the animals' care. Anxious to demonstrate their responsibility, the animals decide, first, to found a bank and, second, to create a government. Interestingly neither of these bright ideas is Freddy's; instead both come from Georgie, the little brown dog. "Gosh, you're full of ideas tonight," Jinx says admiringly. The dog's subsequent idea, to call the proposed republic "Animalia," is not so well received, however. And the animals opt instead for the simpler "First Animal Republic" or, as it comes to be known, simply the "F.A.R."

The theme of responsibility is established in the opening scene, which takes place in the Bean's kitchen in the middle of the night. Present are Jinx, the two dogs, Robert and Georgie, and the four mice. Outside, a howling windstorm seems intent on tearing the world to tatters, but inside it's warm and cozy. Jinx, who has been wakened by the wind complains about the noise, but Robert says, "I kind of like to lie here all snug and warm and listen to the wind." The literary critic Jerry Griswold, in his marvelous book *Feeling Like a Kid* (Johns Hopkins, 2006), posits the idea that five themes recur in classic and popular works of children's literature. The first of these is snugness, which this scene certainly epitomizes. Snugness also manifests itself, I would argue, in the feeling of security or safety that is fostered by familiarity and predictability. This is surely a reason why series fiction—like the Freddy books—is so popular. This is also why people who have discovered the books as children enjoy coming back to them as adults, when the experience of opening a Freddy book is as sweetly nostalgic as coming home for the holidays. Nothing seems to change there. Hank still has the rheumatism in his off hind leg, Charles is still pompous, Henrietta is still a scold, Jinx is still breezy, and Freddy still falls asleep whenever he has to think about anything for more than two minutes.

But *this* book is all about dramatic and unsettling change, starting when the wind blows the kitchen door open to admit a stranger, a woodpecker who has been flying home to Washington,

D.C., and has obviously been blown badly off course. The next morning he self-importantly explains that he comes from "a rather famous family" that has lived for generations in a sycamore tree on the lawn of the White House. His grandfather was actually born in the executive mansion and since then all first-born sons have borne the names of presidents. His own name is John Quincy (though he's often called, simply, "JQ") and he is amused to find himself in such "a little, unimportant place" as New York State, which is so far "out on the edge of such a big country."

This set-up recalls an adult story, "Discovery of America," that Walter had written for the *Atlantic Monthly* two years earlier about a pair of sparrows, Hubert and Enid, self-styled sophisticates who move from Manhattan to the village of Aeschylus Center, where they receive a well-deserved comeuppance. JQ seems in no danger of that, however, for the animals are so awed by his grandness that they invite him to serve as president of the bank they're starting. "I admit you tempt me," JQ replies. I have often thought I should like to spend a summer among the plain country people, sharing their simple pleasures." And so he accepts and in short order is joined on the farm by his father, Grover, and his son X (the family is so large all the presidents' names have already been used up).

Though Freddy is warned by John the fox not to trust the woodpeckers, he lets himself be quickly—well, *outfoxed* by the devious, power-hungry birds, who wrest control of the bank from him. "Freddy was a good executive," Walter writes, "that is, he never liked to do any work he could get anyone else to do for him." And since banking is hard work, Freddy is not too concerned about the coup until Grover announces his candidacy for president of the newly formed First Animal Republic and Simon and his family show up in support. Meanwhile, at Freddy's urging, Mrs. Wiggins has agreed to run, as well, but things get weird when a dark horse enters the race, too—a scatterbrained rabbit named Marcus. Disorder—and then some—ensues; the nascent republic falls, and Grover becomes a de facto dictator. Is this the end of Bean Farm life as we know it? This is a spoiler-free zone, so it must suffice to say that Freddy is at his best when facing impossible odds—and in disguise!

As usual, there are a number of interesting ancillary attractions along the road to thematic development. We learn that the three wealthiest depositors to the First Animal Bank are all birds: the ducks, Alice and Emma, and the crow, Ferdinand. Another point of interest is a slip-up on Walter's part. On page 25 Jinx tells JQ that Freddy is the only animal on the farm that can read or write—and yet in *More To and Again*, Walter has told us it is Jinx himself who taught the pig to read! We also learn in this book that Freddy is a "wonderful" dancer; that he owns an encyclopedia and has a stamp collection (consisting of seventeen stamps, eight of which are the same—ordinary three-centers!). We also learn another fact about his family (in *Detective* we had learned he has a sister); now we learn his father was not only "fleshy," he was enormous. John the fox—to whom Freddy confides this—replies, "I remember your father. When I was little, he used to come down to the woods for acorns. We liked him so much. Always a laugh and a joke for everybody."

Among the cavalcade of famous firsts in this volume: Freddy rides a bicycle; a field mouse named Winthrop is the first to cast a ballot in the election for president of the F.A.R.; Mr. Weezer the banker is introduced to the series and, for the first time, his glasses fall off at the mention of a sum less than ten dollars; Mrs. Bridget O'Halloran makes her first appearance (Freddy in disguise, of course, and speaking with a bloodcurdlingly bad Irish brogue). Other first-timers are John the fox, the owls, Old Whibley and his niece Vera, and the smarmy detective Jason Binks. And for those who are keeping count, Charles and Henrietta have twenty-seven children in this volume.

There are only two poems in this book and, at that, one of them is by Jinx! Amusingly enough, it's the poem beginning "Hooray for the spring! What a glorious feeling!" that Walter had written some years before for his "Prose and Worse" column. Fortunately Freddy's single contribution is not only new but also significant: it is Mrs. Wiggins's splendid campaign song, which is sung to the tune of "The Battle Hymn of the

Republic" and has, as its refrain, the stirring words, "Hail, all hail to Mrs. Wiggins / Hail, all hail to Mrs. Wiggins / Hip, hurray for Mrs. Wiggins / For our next Pres-i-dent!"

Walter ends the decade of the 1930s on a high note with this title, as *Wiggins for President* is arguably *the* quintessential Freddy book in its rich humor, its serious themes, and its generous characterizations. And with both banking and politics to satirize, Walter must have been in hog heaven, for his readers assuredly are.

7. *Freddy's Cousin Weedly*. New York: Alfred A. Knopf, 1940. 283 pages.

Reissued as a hardcover facsimile edition by The Overlook Press in 2002.

Though always diverting, Walter's first Freddy adventure of the 1940s is, frankly, more lightweight than his previous six efforts. In this one Jinx "adopts" Freddy's timid young cousin William, whom everyone calls "Weedly," and teaches him courage and self-reliance. Though the cat always puts up a bold front, Walter has already told us—in *Wiggins for President*—that Jinx is one of those who are brave because they are afraid to act scared. He has his reputation to think of, after all. This consideration of reputation is a theme that, once introduced, will recur in a number of subsequent adventures, though it is usually Freddy's good name that is at stake, not the cat's.

But back to the story: Not knowing the Beans are still on vacation in Europe, Mr. Bean's aunt and uncle, Effie and Lucius Snedeker, show up at the farm for a visit and, not understanding that the animals are capable of running the place in the Bean's absence, decide to stay a spell. Unfortunately Aunt Effie also decides that this is the perfect opportunity to claim as her own the silver teapot that her mother had left to Mr. Bean instead of her—an act that has always rankled. The animals, led by Freddy, must find a way to foil this nefarious attempt. In the meantime Jinx's efforts to stiffen Weedly's spine have been all too successful, and the young pig has become bold to the point of obnoxiousness. A humbling encounter with Old Whibley cures him of this and his further effort to stymie the Snedekers completes his redemption.

In the meantime Walter has amused himself—and his readers—by using the Snedeker's relationship to poke fun at marriage. Aunt Effie is a dominant type, tall, stiff, and prim. Uncle Snedeker is, well, the opposite. Though a bit of a milquetoast, he is second only to Leo ("Well, dye my hair") the lion as a source of funny expressions and sayings. Among them: "Why, shine my Sunday shoes." "Well, curl my eyewinkers." And "Well, tear off my collar and necktie." To which Aunt Effie tartly replies, "Snedeker, I will *not* have this awful swearing. Remember there are ladies present."

Not that he is ever allowed to forget that. His partnership with his wife can be summed up in Walter's tongue-in-cheek observation, "Uncle Snedeker was usually considered to be a pretty good husband. That is, he almost always did what Aunt Effie told him to."

When Walter isn't busy with the Snedekers, he is having fun with the poetic side of Freddy's nature. The pig muffs his chance to spirit the teapot away from Aunt Effie when he is distracted by the quiet and coziness of the Bean's parlor. For "he was a poet, as well as a pig of action," Walter notes. Accordingly, he cannot resist sinking into a red plush chair and—pretending he is a guest at a tea party of the sort Aunt Effie is planning for the animals—begin making up a poem: "When day is done and shadows creep / Across the lawn, then set to steep / The teapot on the table-top. . . ."

Alas, he dawdles too long and, leaving the room, is surprised by Aunt Effie who commands him to relinquish the teapot and sit down. Unfortunately the nearest seat is a little ottoman with a pattern of red roses on a pink background. Freddy does as she-who-must-be-obeyed commands but he is hideously uncomfortable, "partly," Walter tells us, "because he had been caught but partly, too, because he knew that pink wasn't his color. It made him look very fat."

Ah, poets! They're so darned sensitive! But creative, too, for Freddy proceeds to write an entire play in verse, which the animals perform for the Snedekers and other friends of the farm. Freddy's motivation for doing this is to keep the visitors on the premises until the Beans return from Europe, but

Walter's inclusion of the entire drama slows the action and seems self-indulgent in the extreme. Perhaps *his* motivation was simple nostalgia for his own childhood efforts at writing and producing plays for the delectation of *his* aunts. In any event, all's well that ends well, as another dramatist once observed, and the teapot will find a home that satisfies every member of the Bean family.

Though episodic and discursive, *Weedly* is a very funny book, filled with examples of Walter's signature humor, including a sample of the sheriff's use of the ornate and polysyllabic language of the law to terrify and intimidate (though, since the person he's trying to terrify and intimidate is the formidable Aunt Effie, he obviously fails). In her review of this title, the noted critic May Lamberton Becker went so far as to write, "Comparisons are never fair but, all things considered, I think I can safely call Mr. Brooks the Wodehouse of American juvenile fiction. Nobody else has just this ability to put over the incredible and make it seem the most natural thing in the world . . . and, what's more, the knack of keeping this up for book after book, practically all alike but preserving the illusion of difference. . . ."

Walter's stock company of players is now so sizable that only a few new characters—other than the Snedekers—appear in this title, but one worth mentioning is Mr. Muszkiski, who runs the Grand Palace Motion Picture Theater in Centerboro and will figure in later episodes. Meanwhile, though Walter has developed a number of running jokes, too, a new and delightful one appears in this volume: Mrs. Wiggins chides Freddy on how terribly dirty his pigpen window is. "Why, you can't even recognize your friends three feet away through that glass." Freddy explains why he likes it that way: "It gives me ideas when I'm sitting here working on my poetry. Everything outside looks a little different than what it is. When you go by, for instance, if the window was clean, why I'd just think 'There goes Mrs. Wiggins. But if the window's dirty, I'd think: 'My goodness, what can that be? Is it an elephant?' And then I'd have something to write about." Needless to say, Mrs. Wiggins is not flattered by this explanation.

This window had a real-world counterpart. In the *Borzoi Battledore* for September 1945, Walter writes about the distractions of creating in the country. Describing his summer cabin in Roxbury, he says, "The small-paned windows of wavy glass make everything appear twice as interesting. Thanks to the distortion the flora and fauna take on a dreamlike character. That mixed herd of camels and giraffes pursued by a two-headed giant is only the cows being driven down to the barn." Alas he doesn't mention if Mrs. Wiggins is among them, only that "This phenomenon scared the wits out of me the first time I noticed it. But it is always interesting." (p. 7)

Always interesting, too, are Walter's glittering generalizations and there are several new ones to report: "As you probably know, when a cat makes up his mind you might as well let him do what he wants to, for he'll do it anyway." And, "Like all scary people, he began trying to scare himself worse, by thinking of all the terrible things that could have happened until he was in a regular panic." And, lastly, "Mr. Webb, who like most spiders was rather short-tempered. . . ."

Though never preachy, the Freddy books do contain some, well, call them lessons in ethics and practical morality. Walter disarms the critics' potential charge of didacticism, however, by always following such points with a leaven of humor. One example will suffice: Weedly has gotten himself into a pickle, thanks to some outrageous misbehavior and has received a dose of his own medicine administered by Dr.—er, Whibley. When, in the aftermath, Jinx begins lecturing the little pig, Whibley interrupts:

"Don't be too hard on him, cat. It's easy enough—telling somebody else to be a good sport. Remember the time that rat down in Macy's barn—"

"All right, all right," Jinx interrupted hastily. "We haven't time for all this talk. It's Weedly's bedtime."

"Put him to bed, then, and don't lecture," said the owl. "He hasn't done so badly, and if he's still mad at me, I guess I can bear it."

"I'm not mad at you, Mr.—Mr. Whibley," said Weedly.

"Good," said the owl. "Just remember there's two ends to a joke. Depends on which end you get hold of whether it's fun or not. Now get along . . ."

Point taken. We, too, must get along now—to our assessment of the next title.

8. *Freddy and the Ignormus.* New York: Alfred A. Knopf, 1941, 286 pages.

Reissued in a hardcover facsimile edition by The Overlook Press in 1998.

Reissued in a trade paperback edition by Puffin Books (as part of "The Freddy Collection"). New York: Puffin Books, 2001.

Calling itself "The Ignormus," something—nobody is quite sure what—is terrorizing the farm and extorting food from the animals by threatening to eat them. Because the creature lives north of the farm in the eerie Big Woods, which the animals shun, thinking it haunted, The Ignormus (if there is an Ignormus) quickly takes on larger-than-life proportions.

Meanwhile Freddy is challenged by Theodore the frog to prove his bravery by going with him into the Big Woods. Our hero is terrified, but what can he do? His reputation is at stake. And so, off the two animals go, briskly enough at first but the closer they come to the woods, the slower their pace until finally, when they reach the road that defines the southern boundary of the woods, they come to a dead stop. However, Theodore is heartened to discover that the famous Freddy isn't any braver than he is and, thus emboldened, he gathers his legs under him and makes a single, long leap into the woods. "I'm *that* much braver than you, Freddy," he says. Well, Freddy can't be outdone and so he dashes after the frog, who then takes another leap, and Freddy another dash, and soon the two are rushing headlong into the dreaded forest until they're stopped short by an impenetrable thicket of bri-ars. Only then do they realize what they've done. And how very quiet it suddenly is. As Freddy will later write, "It was dark in the woods / It was very, very scary. . . . Dim and dark and very solitary."

Well, you know what happens: "If the race into the woods," Walter writes, "had been to decide which of them was the braver, the race out was to decide which was the scareder. And it, too, was a tie."

Tearing out of the trees, Freddy almost trips over Simon the rat, who has come back to the Bean Farm following a lengthy stay in Iowa, "where," he tells Freddy (rather nastily), "the pigs make pork, not poetry!"

The reader may wonder why Freddy doesn't "smell a rat" when Simon then goes on to reveal a surprising amount of knowledge about the Big Woods and the creature that lives there. Indeed, it is he who reveals its name as "The Ignormus." But Freddy, anxious to get back to the farm to alert the other animals to the rat's return, simply tells Theodore, "Simon is the worst liar in three counties. If he tells you anything, you can be sure that the truth is something different."

Ah, but what is truth? For it turns out that this is but the beginning of a very tangled tale, indeed, one that will threaten the future of the Bean Farm and force the animals into launching an all-out war against their enemy. Meanwhile, an undeclared war is being waged on Freddy's reputation. It starts when he makes the near fatal mistake of "borrowing" Mr. Bean's gun without permission for an investigative foray into the Big Woods and, alas, loses it. Then *someone* robs the First Animal Bank of many of its depositors' winter supplies of food and Freddy, as president, is responsible for making reparations. Then, to make matters worse, *someone* plants a bag of stolen oats in the pigpen, and not only the animals but even Mr. Bean think Freddy is the thief. Only Jinx remains faithful. "I'm with you to the last claw," he tells Freddy. "I'm not much at detecting but when it comes to a scrap—boy, Jinx is there!" Well, Jinx will have his scrap and much, much else will happen before order returns to the farm (I told you it was a tangled tale).

This title is one of the most enduringly popular in the series, perhaps because of the suggestion of the supernatural that overlays the book. Also, the tale is simply great fun to read, since Walter does an exceptionally fine job of managing suspense by mixing it with some very funny scenes—Mrs. Wiggins in a swing, Charles attacking the strange creature who is the Ignormus's bagman and then nearly fainting with fright when he discovers it is a rat in disguise. Then there's Freddy's habit, whenever he mentions the Ignormus, of adding parenthetically "if there is an Ignormus" and, well, a good deal more. New York's radio station WMCA recognized the widespread appeal of this title by featuring it on its popular children's program "Let's Listen to a Story" on October 2, 1954.

For the record *Ignormus* marks the first appearance not only of Theodore but also of Randolph the beetle, Jeffrey the thousand-legger, and Jinx's maddeningly gabby and overbearing sister, Minx. It also provides our first glimpse of the old Grimby House in the Big Woods. *And* it serves as the inspiration for a later adult story Walter wrote about those sparrows Hubert and Enid, titled "The Dread Ignormus," which appeared in the March 1953 *Esquire*.

As for the chicken children count, there are twenty-six offspring to report in this one! And in the poetry watch department, we learn that there are two things that one needs to write poetry: quiet and coolness. Freddy is so busy in this adventure that he has very little quiet yet manages to create two poems—the one already quoted about the Big Woods (p.185) and the second a poem for an alphabet book in verse that he is writing—"probably the first book for animals ever written." The verse he completes is the celebrated one titled "Ants, Although Admirable, Are Awfully Aggravating" (p. 68) that ends with the memorable couplet: "Yet though I praise his boundless vim / I am not really fond of him."

But readers *were* really fond of Freddy, and not only readers but also reviewers. May Lamberton Becker—who had previously called Walter the American Wodehouse—had this to say of his chief creation in her review of *Ignormus*: "I don't know that anyone has called attention to a basic likeness in character between Freddy and [Winnie the] Pooh; Freddy is not a pet, he is less wistful, but he has the same innocent vanity and boundless good will." *Unlike* Pooh, who was, of course, a bear of little brain, Freddy is distinguished by his intelligence. And so is Jinx, as he demonstrates by making the sage observation that ends this book: "There'll always be Ignormuses." "And personally," Walter adds, "I think it was the wisest thing he, or any other cat, is ever likely to say."

9. *Freddy and the Perilous Adventure.* New York: Alfred A. Knopf, 1942. 245 pages.

Sold to Editorial Juventad in June 1947 for publication in Spain.

Reissued in hardcover and trade paperback editions with cover art by Leslie Morrill and an introduction by Michael Cart. New York: Alfred A. Knopf, 1986.

Reissued in a hardcover facsimile edition by The Overlook Press in 2001.

Freddy gets himself into a fix! Thinking he has volunteered only to give a speech at a hot-air balloon ascension, he discovers—to his horror—that he has unwittingly volunteered to go aloft, too—along with the ducks, Alice and Emma. Afraid to appear afraid, he has no choice but to follow through, all the while thinking, "That's the trouble with a reputation for bravery: you have to live up to it. Oh, dear, I wish I wasn't such a fearless character!"

Not only fearless but soon speechless, too, when—rising to the occasion—he unthinkingly bites down on some taffy the sheriff has brought him and discovers his teeth are stuck together. Mistakenly thinking Freddy's so scared he can't talk, some of the rougher elements in the crowd begin to boo as the balloon is released from its mooring and soars aloft . . . into more trouble. For now the valve cord is tangled in some ropes and Freddy can't release any gas to return to earth. With that the wind picks up and Freddy and his passengers (the Webbs, too, have come along for the ride) sail off into the lofty Empyrian, leaving the impression among the earthbound that the intrepid pig has stolen the balloon.

After a number of narrow escapes (one of the more hilarious involving the man with the black mustache and the dirty-faced boy), plus several encounters with the bald eagle Breckenridge that give Walter a chance to satirize the lofty language affected by America's national bird ("Welcome, oh, pig, to the starry upper spaces of the blue empyrean"), the balloon finally returns to earth. The pig, knowing he is wanted by the police, borrows some clothing from a scarecrow and, disguised as Jonas P. Whortleberry of Orinoco Flats, hightails it to the farm—just in time to see Mr. Bean pay the balloon's unscrupulous owner, Henry P. Golcher ("The Bounding Balloonist"), $200.00 to make up for his loss of business. What to do, what to do? There's no way for Freddy to prove he didn't take the balloon on purpose—or is there? Delightful complications ensue as the pig goes into hiding with the circus, where his friends help him try to recover the balloon *and* his good name. Leo is especially forthcoming: "Whatever I have is yours, Freddy; you know that. Teeth, claws and a good loud roar. That's all there is. But if you can use 'em. . . ."

A subplot involves the return to the farm of the ducks' pompous and self-important Uncle Wesley, who was probably Brooks's rather acid portrayal of his domineering Grandfather Stevens. In a scene that brings the book's thematic concern—dramatizing the difference between bravado and real bravery—full circle, the elderly duck must finally admit to himself that he isn't brave at all and, showing more wisdom than the reader would have thought he could muster, realizes he doesn't care. "Why, it relieves me of a tremendous strain, the strain of always having to act up to something I wasn't."

With that, the other animals crowd up and shake hands[14] with him and pat him on the back. Wesley's reaction is worthy of actress Sally Field: "'Why, you like me!' he exclaimed, and began to cry."

For the reader, the real emotional payoff is the final scene when a triumphant Freddy is able to return Mr. Bean's $200.00. Freddy finds the farmer sitting on the front porch and lays the packet of bills on the man's knee:

> "Eh?" said Mr. Bean looking at him sharply, and then he took up the bills and counted them.
> "By cracky!" he said. "By cracky!"

---

14. Walter describes animals who don't have hands as shaking hands with each other so often that, after a while, the reader no longer even notices the anomaly.

Mr. Bean never said "By cracky!" unless he was pretty deeply moved, and now he had said it twice. Freddy felt very happy and he went up and rested his chin on Mr. Bean's knee.

A bit later Mrs. Bean comes to call her husband to dinner and this is what she sees: "Mr. Bean, with his unlit pipe in his mouth, was rocking peacefully to and fro in the old willow rocker, and Freddy was sitting in his lap!" Truly a moment to savor, and Kurt Wiese's illustration of this scene (p. 237) is priceless.

Though this book opens with Freddy in a poetic mood—the ducks find him delicately sniffing a buttercup, which has no smell!—there's precious little poetry in this volume. Only three efforts are featured: one of these is incomplete and a second is mangled by the eagle; only the third is offered in full (see pp. 4, 54, and 64). There are even fewer (only two) of Walter's glittering generalizations: "Like all birds, the eagle was curious. . . ." And, "That's a cat all over. Let him think you don't want him to do something, and he's crazy to do it."

10. *Freddy and the Bean Home News.* New York: Alfred A. Knopf, 1943. 230 pages.

Sold to Editorial Juventad in June 1947 for publication in Spain.

Reissued as a hardcover facsimile edition by The Overlook Press in 2000.

Reissued as a trade paperback edition by Puffin Books (as part of "The Freddy Collection"). New York: Puffin Books, 2002.

Up to this point the Freddy books have existed in some pleasant "somewhen" outside of time. Yes, their settings are vaguely contemporary but they are also filled with old-fashioned elements. Some people in these books drive cars, but others—like the Beans—are equally likely to travel in horse-drawn buggies. And on farms horsepower is still supplied literally by horses, not by gasoline-powered engines. New-fangled devices such as radios—which Walter detested—are seldom, if ever, in evidence. All in all, it often seems that the unspecified year of the setting might be any that fell within Walter's memory and could fluctuate considerably within the progress of any given story. This is about to change, however.

In the real world that Walter inhabited a great war was now being waged. Too old to fight, the author busied himself with civil defense work and raised a victory garden. It is, perhaps, inevitable that his characters should begin doing the same. In this instance it is a scrap drive that fuels the engine (if we may put it that way) of the plot. With Freddy in the lead, the animals are determined to bring home the prize being offered to he who brings in the most scrap. The trouble is that scrap is in short supply, since a similar drive had been held the year before when Mr. Bean collected, on his farm alone, three tons of old iron. The patriotic animals vow to do their best, however, though as the pickings become slimmer and slimmer, their efforts must become more creative. Jinx, for example, pulled into town in the phaeton by Hank, begins giving late-night concerts on back alley fences. His "audience," wakened from their peaceful slumbers, "applaud" by throwing at him whatever household good comes to hand. The animals load the haul into the buggy and head back to their scrap heap. This inspires Freddy to create one of his most celebrated poems. Surely you remember it? It begins, "Listen, my children, while I discourse / Of the midnight ride of Hank, the horse / 'Twas in April, nineteen forty and three / Robert and Sniffy and Georgie and me / With Jinx, our leader, to set the course. . . ." We can presume that Longfellow would have been honored!

When even such lively stratagems begin returning almost nothing on their investment of creativity, the animals begin to look longingly (all right, *covetously!*) at the cast iron deer that adorns the lawn of the wealthy Mrs. Humphrey Underdunk. Alas, she is—to put it mildly—no friend of Freddy, for he has had the bad luck of (literally) running into her on the sidewalk in Centerboro. But there's more to it than that. A year earlier Freddy's picture had run on the front page of the local newspaper, the Centerboro *Guardian*, immediately adjacent to a picture of, you guessed it, Mrs. Underdunk. This might have come to nothing if the woman hadn't shown the paper to old Mr. Lawrence, who didn't see very well and mistook Freddy's picture for her. "Fine likeness," he wheezed. "For the first time

I see a look of your father in your face." Of course, the story spread like wildfire and the humiliated Mrs. U. took her revenge by wresting control of the paper from its editor/publisher, Mr. Dimsey, who unfortunately owed her money. When the dynamic Freddy discovers this, he retaliates by starting his own newspaper, the *Bean Home News*, which quickly threatens to run the *Guardian*—now edited by Mrs. Underdunk's truculent brother, Herb Garble—out of business. Is it any wonder that the sister and brother, who will appear regularly in later Freddy titles, make it their life's work to capture Freddy, pack him in a crate, and ship him off to Montana?

Things get really complicated when Charles then decides to take on Mr. Garble himself. Ever since he bested a rat in a fair fight (see *Ignormus*), Freddy observes, "he's had these spells of thinking he can lick the whole world." Charles is still Charles, however, and though he gets as far as the newspaper's office, he has nearly run out of steam until Mr. Garble makes his fatal mistake: he refers to Charles as a "chicken," fighting words to any rooster. Enraged, Charles flies at the hapless man and—becoming a veritable hurricane of claws and wings and beak—actually drives him from his office.

The malefactors of great wealth seize on this as an excuse to have a warrant issued for Freddy's arrest (surely you're not surprised?) and the pig, disguised in an old sailor suit that belonged to Mr. Bean as a boy, assumes the identity of the sheriff's nephew, Longfellow Higgins, and takes shelter where no one will think to look for him: in the Centerboro jail. Alas, Mrs. U. hires a detective—the smarmy Jason Binks—who, in a dazzling display of deviousness for which he will pay dearly, actually manages to discover Freddy's whereabouts.

And so Freddy is brought to trial (not for the last time, either!) and Walter has a wonderful time in the courtroom, creating a memorably satirical set piece starring Old Whibley as Freddy's defense attorney (again, not for the last time).

Well, could there possibly be any more to report? Why, yes—remember that iron deer? And how about—well, suffice it to say that setting his story in the real world of 1943 seems to have caused Walter's pot of creativity to boil over.

But if some things have changed, as a consequence, others have remained gloriously the same. Once again, Walter has fun satirizing a politician, this time in the person of the pompous and long-winded Senator Blunder, a shirttail relative of Mrs. Underdunk. Mr. Bean continues to eat those enormous breakfasts, Freddy's windows go unwashed, generalizations get made (e.g., "Like most cows, Mrs. Wiggins always said what she meant." And "Like most hens, [Henrietta] thought she could crow as well as a rooster can"—though she really can't!). And, somehow, Freddy finds time for poetry, taking on not only Longfellow but also Sir Walter Scott: "Breathes there a pig with soul so dead / Who never to himself hath said / 'This is my own, my native pen?'" Other poems can be found on pages 219, 220, and 222.

In addition to the two new villains, Walter also introduces another engaging new character: the ant, Jerry Peters (and, of course, his pet beetle, Fido). Jerry is clearly a character after Walter's own heart—he is an ant who dislikes work! What he really likes are things that are of no use to him, "such as watching the clouds on a summer day, or taking walks to nowhere in particular, or listening to the wind in the grass." You can almost hear Walter's sighs of pleasure at these sentiments. Sadly, Jerry appears in only one other title—*Flying Saucer Plans*.

Freddy's creation of a newspaper gave Knopf a bright idea for promoting this and other Freddy titles. The editors wrote and printed two mock copies of the *Bean Home News*. The first is a four-page edition that includes ads for Frederick & Wiggins and for The First Animal Bank. The second, less ambitious offering is a special edition in the form of a broadside. Both of these have become collectors' items.

11. *Freddy and Mr. Camphor.* New York: Alfred A. Knopf, 1944. 244 pages.

Reissued in a hardcover facsimile edition by The Overlook Press in 2000.

Reissued in a trade paperback edition by Puffin Books (as part of "The Freddy Collection"). New York: Puffin Books, 2003.

Freddy is bored. In fact, he'd probably be bored stiff if he weren't so limp from the heat. It's not just the heat, though.

Freddy is exhausted, and he wonders if he has, perhaps, taken on too much extra work. Yes, that must be it! "Oh, what a terrible thing is ambition!" he exclaims. "Why could I not have been content to remain in obscurity, happy in the simple quiet round of daily tasks, busy with my books and my poetry? I might in time have made quite a name for myself as a poet."

"And then," Jinx observes dryly, "you'd have to address even more societies and women's clubs." It's Weedly who suggests a remedy: "I think what you need, Cousin Frederick, is change."

And so it is that Freddy applies for a summer job as caretaker of a nearby estate. His vision of the job is positively palmy. As Walter observes, his summer "was evidently to be the most comfortable and luxurious summer spent by any pig that ever lived. 'And you'll come to visit me,' he said [to Jinx and Weedly], 'and we'll lie out in hammocks under the trees on the lawn and have ice cream and cakes and ginger ale brought to us on little trays, and . . .' 'Yeah?' sensible Jinx interjects at this point, 'Who's going to carry the little trays?'"

Even that isn't enough to dampen Freddy's enthusiasm, but of course reality never meets expectations and the reality is that his summer will be spent as a virtual prisoner of the man with the black mustache and his son, the dirty-faced boy, as he also tries to fight an invasion of the property by Simon and his gang. Some summer!

But first things first: it turns out the estate is owned by an eccentric rich man with the wonderful name of C. Jimson Camphor. His estate is on the shore of Otesaraga Lake, only three miles north of the farm if you go cross-country or eight miles by road. Odd that Walter can be so precise in measuring the distance, since he doesn't seem to be quite sure where the farm itself is—in various titles it is said to be anywhere from four to seven miles either north or northwest of Centerboro. Walter doesn't seem to be any better at geography than he is at math! However, he did once go on record in a 1948 letter to a fan as saying:

I guess Centerboro in my stories is probably Rome many years ago, or Hamilton, where my grandfather lived. The lake is sort of a composite—partly Adirondack, partly Cazenovia Lake. And the farm, which started out near Phelps, in the western part of the state [actually, it's in the Finger Lakes region and, today, serves as a bedroom community for both Rochester and Syracuse], is now apparently outside of Roxbury, in Delaware County, where we live in the summer. This is all frequently rather confusing to me, and as I didn't have the sense to have a map of the farm and its surroundings in the beginning, I have to do a good deal of research in my own works to find out just where the roads go and who lives in which house.

Regardless of precisely where Mr. Camphor lives, he remains among Walter's most delightful creations. A "short, red-faced man," he is one of Walter's few rich characters who is also agreeable and sensible. One of the most attractive things about him is his refusal to stand on ceremony. "Never had much dignity," he tells Freddy. "That's why I keep Bannister here. He has to be dignified for the two of us." Bannister, "a very tall, dignified man in a black coat with tails," is, of course, Mr. Camphor's butler. How dignified is he? "He was so dignified that he didn't even lower his eyes to see who had rung the bell."

Though starchy, Bannister seems to be a nice man. When Jinx apologizes for having clawed him (when the man accidentally stepped on the cat's tail), Bannister's response is, "Pray don't mention it, sir. I should no doubt have clawed you if you'd done the same thing to me." And he and his employer seem to have what is, at heart, an easy and bantering relationship, which is rooted in their mutual love of proverbs and their even greater love of arguing with each other about them. When Mr. Camphor sagely observes, "Money is the root of all evil," Bannister replies, "I don't agree with you, sir," adding, "I don't think you believe it either, sir. If you did, you'd give all your money away, wouldn't you, sir?" Mr. Camphor cannot argue with that but he is so intrigued by the thought of having a banker as his caretaker that he hires Freddy on the spot.

Freddy settles into his quarters, a delightful houseboat on the lake, and Mr. Camphor and Bannister head off to Washington, D.C., where Jimson will be working for the government all summer (it's still wartime, remember), and the disorder begins. First, Freddy discovers that Simon and his family are living in the attic, and then who should drive up to the front door but the man with the black mustache and the dirty-faced boy! It turns out that Mr. Camphor's cook, Mrs. Winch, is the man's estranged wife. Now, in his third appearance in a Freddy book, the villain's name is at last revealed to be Zebedee Winch and the boy's name is Horace. They move in, make Freddy a virtual prisoner in his houseboat, and proceed to trash the property. When Mr. Camphor returns for a visit, he blames Freddy and gives the pig the sack. Well, now it's personal, for Freddy's reputation is at stake (again)! How Freddy goes about restoring his reputation—and getting rid of the rats—makes for diverting reading, involving a secret passage in the house, a dark, stormy night, and another of Freddy's disguises.

The action is interrupted, however, by another of Walter's set pieces. Further evidence that it is wartime is the presence of Mr. Bean's victory garden, which is being threatened by an invasion of insects. Mr. and Mrs. Webb hold a patriotic mass meeting, hoping to persuade the neighborhood creepie-crawlies to spare the patch. The sign they have woven nearby reads: "Patriotic Mass Meeting. Tonight at 8:30. All Bugs, Beetles, and Caterpillars Invited. Fireworks, Music, Dancing. Mr. Webb will speak." Some sign! One wonders if it might have been the inspiration for E. B. White's *Charlotte's Web* and *her* woven signs—among them "Some Pig!"[15]

Well, Freddy—himself some pig—carries the day with a little help from his farm friends and such others as the eagle, Breckenridge, and Sheriff Higgins. Walter's inclusion of the latter gives him another opportunity to have fun with the complicated and taxing language of the law. Meanwhile Freddy has added a new talent to his portfolio: he becomes a painter as well as a detective, poet, banker, and newspaper editor. (But where on earth, the reader wonders, did he come up with that beret and smock he sports in the frontispiece?) He also writes

---

15. The critic Robert Sale offers a lengthy—and lucid—analysis of this scene in his book *Fairy Tales and After.*

his first book in the immediate aftermath of this adventure. It is to be titled *The Care and Management of Friends* but, not surprisingly, it winds up being called *The Life and Times of Freddy by Himself.* Walter notes, perhaps revealingly, that "although he started with that idea" (managing friends) "pretty soon he did what a good many authors do—he began putting in more and more about himself, until when he had finished it was really not a guide to making friends at all, but a complete autobiography." This is a nice justification for my own undertaking of *this* biography without access to many primary sources—except for Walter's own voluminous, self-revealing work!

Speaking of voluminous work, a homesick Freddy adds one new poem to his oeuvre, the one beginning, "The wheels are where the cart is / The jam is where the tart is / And home is where the heart is / But mine is far away." Walter also adds one glowing generalization to his growing body of those: "If more poets would seek the advice of cows, they would be less criticized for impractical behavior."

And speaking of behavior, Freddy demonstrates his mastery of behavior modification when he manages to make the boy, Horace, stop throwing rocks. No sooner has he done that, however, than another boy shows up manifesting the same bad behavior. But that takes us to the pig's *next* adventure. . . .

12. *Freddy and the Popinjay.* New York: Alfred a. Knopf, 1945. 244 pages.

Dedicated to Anne (Anne Shepard Brooks)

Reissued in a hardcover facsimile edition by The Overlook Press in 2001.

The most message-driven title in the series, this is a book about transformation—how Freddy transforms an ordinary robin named J.J. Pomeroy into a popinjay (bad mistake, Freddy!) and a boy named Jimmy Witherspoon from a rock-throwing pest into an ally and friend.

Of course, all this is easier said (by me) than done (by Freddy)! The robin's transformation starts out as an innocent exercise in self-defense; the near-sighted bird has mistaken Freddy's tail for a worm. Freddy's first reaction is an intemperate "Eeeeee*yow!* My tail! Oh, my tail!" But then, being Freddy, he offers to help by getting the bird some glasses. But how will J.J. raise the eight dollars to pay for them? Enter Mrs. Church stage right on a bicycle built for two (it's still wartime and Freddy's patriotic friend has given up her car to save gasoline). The pedal power is being supplied by her chauffeur, Riley. Mrs. Church has come to town to have invitations to her niece's wedding engraved with the Church coat of arms (three white churches on a green field, of course); the insignia has a helmet, at the top of which is some kind of bird. Does Freddy recognize it? No, he doesn't, but it gives him an idea: "Why don't you make up a name for him? Why don't you call him—a popin-jay?" Well, one thing leads to another and before you can say "plot point," Freddy—with the help of the local milliner Miss Peebles—transforms J.J. into a popinjay. Mrs. Church hires him to sing at the wedding and to double as her hat for the fes-tive occasion. All of this goes to his head, as well as hers, and he becomes a bit of an egomaniac. Apparently fine feathers don't make fine birds.

Meanwhile Freddy has another problem: young Jimmy Witherspoon, the son of the nearby farmer Zenas Wither-spoon, has taken to throwing rocks at him and the other ani-mals. Mrs. Wiggins, who is still president of the First Animal Republic, appoints a committee of three—Freddy, Jinx, and Henrietta—to address this problem. Their first solution doesn't work too well. They have a pit dug and lay small branches over it and cover them with leaves and grass. The idea, of course, is to trick Jimmy into chasing a small animal across the trap; he'll fall in and the animals will have him where they want him. Henrietta explains this is how elephants are caught in India. (How she knows this is a mystery. "I doubt very much," Walter observes dryly, "if she or any other hen had ever gone in much for elephant hunting.")

Of course, it's not Jimmy but Mr. Bean who falls into the trap and the animals figure it's curtains for them. But, no, Mr. B. likes being in the pit! "This is first time since I started farm-ing, fifty years ago, that I've been in a place where I can look around me and not see a lot of work that has to be done. . . . If

I had a mug of cider, I'd be as happy as a moth in a blanket." Calling the pit his "thinking place," Mr. Bean becomes a regular visitor and, presumably, a "deep thinker" (forgive the pun!). In the meantime a wildcat named Mac has moved into the neighborhood and the animals, fearing for their lives, enlist the wasps' aid in chasing him away. They chase him, all right—right into the elephant pit on top of Mr. Bean! Fortunately, Mr. Bean can take care of himself and, before you know it, the wildcat—and also his wife and three children—have been transformed into model citizens.

As for Jimmy Witherspoon, it turns out his misbehavior is a product of his being ashamed of looking like a scarecrow. His father is a miser who refuses to buy the boy any new clothes or to pay for a decent haircut. "Zenas is always suspicious," Mrs. Bean tells Mr. Bean, "when any of his folks look happy: he thinks maybe it's costing him money." "He's ashamed," Freddy later explains, "not to have what other boys have. If people try to be nice to him, he thinks it's because he's poor, and he snubs them." To change Jimmy properly will mean changing his father, too, and that takes nearly an entire village—but, finally, it gets done. (The four-page lecture Mrs. Bean gives him doesn't hurt, either. . . .) And somewhere along the line, the puffed-up Mr. Popinjay, who started all this, gets his comeuppance and is transformed back into plain Mr. Pomeroy.

So many transformations! So many lessons! Among other things we learn, "The more honest you are in an argument, the better chance you have of winning." "If you like people a lot, it doesn't matter what they look like." "There's always two sides to every question. And the funny part of it is, both sides are usually right. There wouldn't ever be any arguments if one side was always right and the other, always wrong." Well, maybe. . . .

Chicken children count: the number has now risen to thirty! And speaking of children, this title marks the fourth and final appearance of Adoniram and Byram (see also *Clockwork Twin*, *Politician*, and *Weedly*). After this, they—like the earlier Ella and Everett, indeed like all children—will simply vanish from the series without comment. Also, it's no surprise that in such a philosophical work, there are a goodly number of glittering generalizations, including the following: "Being a banker's wife, she was hard to please." "I guess it's just advertising. If it sounds nice, nobody expects it to mean anything." "Like most cats, Jinx never worried much about hard looks as long as they weren't accompanied with broomsticks." "Like all owls, he was a terrible arguer." (This last refers to the screech owl Uncle Solomon who makes his debut in this book.)

Despite all the philosophizing, Freddy finds time to write four new poems in this book, including the memorable "Oh, for a Waggable Tail" (see pp. 2, 12, 116, and 200). We also learn something about poetry: "Now one of the great difficulties of writing a poem—and I have mentioned several, but this is perhaps the greatest," Walter lectures, "is that poets feel like writing poems much oftener than they have anything to write about." By this stage Freddy, of course, has had a great deal, indeed, to write about. So much that he thinks, "Perhaps I owe it to the American people to see that it has the opportunity to read my poems." And so he decides to publish a collection of them. His fans will know that it takes him another eight years to get *The Collected Poems of Freddy the Pig* published (see below), but surely they will agree the effort is worth the wait. In the meantime, another adventure looms.

13. *Freddy the Pied Piper*. New York. Alfred A. Knopf, 1946. 253 pages.

Reissued in a hardcover facsimile edition by The Overlook Press in 2002.

"It had been a hard winter," Walter writes. So hard that Freddy is all but snowbound in the pig pen. When Charles braves the elements to tell him that Jerry, the rhinoceros from Mr. Boomschmidt's circus, is in the cow barn, having walked all the way from Virginia to see him, Freddy knows he has to get down to the barn. But how? The snow is over his head. Well, where there's a Freddy, there's a way. Not always a good way but a way, and the pig, after many hilarious false starts, finally manages to reach Jerry and learns that it's been a hard winter for the circus, too.

Indeed, the last four years have been an ordeal. Because of the war, the circus has been unable to tour. No tour means no income and, though Mr. Boomschmidt had put some money aside to tide them over, he forgot one little thing: to budget money for food for his animals! The larger ones must go to zoos; as for the rest, they must live off the lean of the land. Jerry and Leo, the lion, decide to head for the Bean Farm to solicit Freddy's help. Thinking they will be less conspicuous traveling alone, they split up. And now Jerry has arrived safely, but where is Leo? They don't call him Freddy the Detective for nothing and, soon enough, the pig learns that Leo is being held prisoner in a pet shop in Tallmanville, some two hundred miles to the south. No matter, Leo is their friend, so Freddy and Jinx unquestioningly head to the rescue—on foot. Fortunately they are overtaken by Mrs. Church who is on her way to a wedding and gives them a lift. Disguised as the wealthy Mrs. J. Perkins Vandertwiggen, Freddy checks into the Tallman House Hotel and begins plotting how to rescue his friend, Leo. This brings him up against one of Walter's funniest villains, the pet shop owner Gwetholinda Guffin, who may be a force of nature but who, in a hilarious sequence of scenes—some of the funniest in the entire series—will prove no match for our hero.

Returning to Centerboro with Leo in tow, Freddy must now figure out how to save the circus. It will take at least a thousand dollars, according to Mr. Weezer, to get it back on the road. Freddy is a well-to-do pig but he doesn't have nearly that much money and so he hatches yet another scheme: he will become a demouser! All of the houses in Centerboro—and even the bank—are overrun with mice that have come indoors to escape the wretched winter weather. If he charges $5.00 per house, Freddy figures he should make enough to help Mr. Boom. At this point the law of unintended consequences kicks in and Freddy discovers the four mice, furious about his plan, have stopped speaking to him. Old Whibley grumpily agrees to adjudicate the dispute and works out a plan: Freddy will use part of his proceeds to rent a good tight barn where he will house and feed the city mice until spring. Everybody is satisfied.

Now, "Freddy could have moved the mice over into the barn quietly without any fuss, but that was not his way of doing things." Instead, he takes out a big ad in the newspaper with the headline "THE PIED PIPER OF CENTERBORO will free your town of mice Monday, at 2 p.m." At the appointed hour Freddy, resplendent in a pied piper costume that Miss Peebles has helped him fabricate, appears at the corner of Main and Elm, pulls a tin fife out of his pocket and, tootling the first seven notes of "Yankee Doodle Dandy," starts up Main Street. The mice have their instructions and come tumbling out of the houses as Freddy passes, falling in line behind him, "dancing and squeaking." This is a bit overwhelming for some of the more timid citizens and Old Mrs. Peppercorn is so scared she swarms up the trellis on Judge Willey's porch and the fire department has to come to get her down.

With the mice safely taken care of and $1,726 dollars in his pocket, Freddy sets off for Virginia, accompanied by Jinx, Leo, and Jerry. Their trip south passes with surprisingly little incident—but don't worry, Walter has more conflict up his sleeve. Arriving in Virginia the animals find themselves at a racetrack where a most unusual race is about to begin. A free-for-all, it is open to any animal *except* horses and the purse is $200.00. The animals decide to enter Leo and Jerry (who will be ridden by Jinx), pay the entry fee, and they're off! Unfortunately, Jerry's weak eyesight fails him and he veers off the track, charges through the judges' stand, and vanishes into the nearby woods.

Alas, one of the judges, Mr. Bleech, has observed Freddy taking money from the saddlebags attached to Jerry's saddle. He follows the rhino and, taking advantage of the fact that Jerry isn't exactly the sharpest knife in the drawer, steals the dough and hurries home. The outraged animals follow and try a frontal assault on the house—well, actually, Jerry does, literally using his head this time, as he charges the house and scores a direct hit between the two front windows. This causes some dandy damage, though Mr. Bleech's main response is to drawl, "Just for your information, this house ain't mine. I rent it." Unfortunately he *does* own the gun he produces, and the animals must retreat.

Freddy is devastated. "I'd rather leave the farm for ten years," he says bitterly, "than to disappoint Mr. Boomschmidt like this." This is an especially bitter moment for the pig, since he had earlier rejected Jinx's warning that he has tackled a job that's too big "even for you," saying, "Maybe so. But I've got to try. Mr. Boomschmidt is my friend and so are Leo and the others."

Freddy needn't worry. Walter guarantees that nobody will be leaving the farm nor will Mr. Boomschmidt be disappointed. To make that happen, he produces a series of cleverly conceived and exceptionally funny scenes. Indeed, page for page this book may have more genuinely, joyfully funny scenes and lovely, hilarious complications than any other title in the series (with the possible exception of *Space Ship*, as we will see). It is also, in Freddy's selfless determination to help Mr. Boomschmidt and his animals, Walter's most heartfelt exposition of the enduring importance of friendship. It is this writer's personal favorite of all the Freddy books.

As for poems, there are an unusually large number: six in all (see pp. 23, 24, 26, 109, 124, and 243), although not all are by Freddy. One is by—of all people—Mr. Bean. It is the verse he has crafted for a homemade valentine to Mrs. Bean, and it's worth quoting in full: "I love my pipe / and my tobaccy / I love you / I do by cracky! // I can't write pretty / For I ain't a poet / But I love you / And don't I know it. // If you ditched me / I sure would pine / So I hope you'll be / My valentine."

We meet at least two new animal characters in this title. One is the omnivorous Phil the Buzzard, whom Walter named for a Roxbury boy, Phil Caswell, whose mother often typed Walter's manuscripts. "I was known as Phil the Buzzard for decades," he wrote to Kevin W. Parker, then president of the Friends of Freddy. The other character is Willy the boa constrictor, who will play a major part in the foiling of Mr. Bleech. When greeting friends, Willy enjoys giving them a "little hug," often squeezing until their eyes bug out. This is presumably a sample of snake humor. Willie is also the occasion for another of Walter's generalities. "Like all snakes," he tells us, "Willy had a tendency to lisp when excited." As if this weren't memorable enough, the book concludes with what Walter judges "was really one of the smartest things Freddy ever said." To find out what it was, turn to page 253 in *Freddy and the Pied Piper*.

14. *Freddy the Magician.* New York: Alfred A. Knopf. 1947. 258 pages.
Reissued in a hardcover facsimile edition by The Overlook Press in 2002.

Freddy becomes an amateur magician—performing as "Professor Frederico"—and arouses the ire of Signor Zingo (great name!), the Boomschmidt Circus's professional prestidigitator. This leads to a hilarious grudge match of magic and mummery between the two (guess who wins?). There is no firm evidence that Walter himself ever undertook the practice of magic, but he did write one adult short story, "The Hand Is Quicker than the Eye," about a man who was an amateur magician. Published in 1945, it may well have been the inspiration for this novel, published a scant two years later.

Jinx's sister, the tiresome Minx, makes an encore appearance in this one and is every bit as annoying as before. In an effort to reform the chatty cat, Freddy and Jinx play a trick that backfires, leading to Zingo's attempt to rob the First Animal Bank. A further sub-plot involves the magician's similar attempts to defraud the Centerboro Hotel and offers a delightful first appearance by its polysyllabic proprietor, Ollie ("I've always had a predilection for this here sesquipedalianism") Groper. Disguised as Mr. Groper's nephew, Marshall (there *is* a family resemblance between the pig and the portly hotelier!), Freddy takes up temporary residence in the caravansary, while also preparing for his epic showdown with Zingo.

He is not, however, too busy to write three exceptionally fine poems (see pp. 67, 145, and 177), including his epic about worrying. Surely you remember it, the one that begins, "When life's at its darkest and everything's black / I don't want my friends to come patting my back / I scorn consolation, can't they let me alone? / I just want to snivel, sob, bellow, and groan."

Freddy has a great deal to worry about in this adventure and so, perhaps, do his fans, who may find a number of vaguely disquieting elements in this uneven volume. Zingo and his assistant, the white rabbit Presto, are hands-down the nastiest villains to date. Presto, for example, is a liar who ingratiates himself with Mrs. Wogus and Mrs. Wurzburger and then cruelly insults them behind their backs. As for Zingo—he's a thief, for starters. Not only does he try to defraud the hotel and steal money from Freddy, he also gets caught stealing a thousand dollars from the Circus and, as a result, is fired. He has a terrible temper and—taking advantage of circumstances that prevent Freddy's retaliating—twice slaps the pig and twice pinches him, viciously. He also carries a handgun and shoots at Freddy with clear intent to kill.

In a twist, Old Whibley winds up in possession of the pistol and uses it, unsuccessfully, to hunt prey—an amusing idea, but somewhat less amusing is an earlier scene in which the owl is shown trying to catch a field mouse for dinner. We are reminded that he is a predator but the point seems to be that this is all right so long as he doesn't hunt the four farm mice. When the Beans are shown sitting down to a chicken dinner, the reader wants to rush out to the hen house to make sure that Charles and Henrietta haven't gone missing! As for Zingo, he purposely orders an extra helping of ham in Freddy's presence.

As a result of these and other episodes, *Freddy the Magician* is the most violent title to date. On the other hand Walter uses the incidents with Zingo to show Freddy's innate goodness and talent for sympathy and empathy. For example, as Freddy watches a performance by the thoroughly unpleasant Zingo fall to pieces, he at first has "an awfully good time," but then "he couldn't help feeling a little sorry for the magician. Zingo was a crook; he had stolen from Freddy and cheated him and abused him; and yet Freddy had begun to feel that he wanted to help him. Some people would think this was pretty weak of Freddy and others would say that it was simply good sportsmanship not to jump on an enemy when he was down. You'll have to decide that for yourself."

Still later, when justice is being administered to Zingo in an unusual way, it is Freddy who first says, "I think we ought to let him go. He's had enough." It's clear that Freddy's motivation is not revenge; if anything, it is (once again) to redeem his own sullied reputation and, in the case of Mr. Groper, to help a friend. Walter also makes the point that Freddy has one advantage over Zingo: he knows how to hold his temper. And so he does. For though Freddy is occasionally miffed and even a bit outraged, he is almost never shown to be angry during one of his adventures—a reason, perhaps, that he is always such an appealing character.

Another appealing character, Sheriff Higgins, is featured prominently in this book and, like Mr. Bean, assumes a father-like role to those in his charge, i.e., the prisoners. He worries about them and is concerned about their comfort and well being—to the extent that he turns the jail into a "home from home" for them. For this reason, when a prisoner has served his time, he often commits some minor infraction on release so that he can be returned to the jail, as Red Mike does in this volume. Indeed, the sheriff is devastated when an occupant of the jail actually steals a pie. "Can't understand it," he tells Freddy, "such a thing has never happened before in all my years as sheriff. My boys here are better behaved and honester than most of the folks outside, and I know that for a fact." When Freddy discovers the identity of the thief, the sheriff's punishment is to send the offender to his room!

Readers also meet a less appealing character in this title, Mr. Metacarpus, the manager of the Busy Bee Department Store on Main Street, whose chief characteristic in this and later titles seems to be his officiousness. At least readers get their first real look inside the store, the motto of which is "The customer is always right, but never admit it."

It is Mr. Groper, though, of whom Walter seems to be fondest, perhaps because—like the hotelier—he, too, has always had "a predilection for this here sesquipedalianism" and Mr. Groper's dialogue gives Walter a chance to indulge it. It's a measure of his respect for his readers that Walter never defines these lavish words, even when a familiarity with them may be necessary to understand a plot point, as when Freddy checks into the hotel and Mr. Groper puts him into a room which he says is "contiguous to that currently occupied by Signor Zingo." One can imagine a young reader asking Walter, "What does 'contiguous' mean?" and Walter blandly replying, "There's the dictionary. Look it up."

So much does Walter like Ollie that he gives him the last word(s) in the book—well, almost. Delighted with Freddy's resolution of his problems, he promises the pig, "'The comestibles prepared in the culinary precincts of my caravansary are your permanent perquisites and upon demand will be served gratis in unlimited quantity to yourself and companions whether extempore or at a predetermined time. This ain't your pecuniary emolument, for which I anticipate you will render a statement, but it is in the nature of an augmentation, subsidy or bonus in recognition of exceptionally sedulous and perspicacious opportunism. I trust you find it adequate.' And he patted Freddy on the shoulder."

Freddy's reaction? "Why—why, sure."

"He wasn't certain it was the right answer," Walter sagely concludes, "But what would you have said?"

What, indeed?

15. *Freddy Goes Camping.* New York: Alfred A. Knopf, 1948. 258 pages.

Reissued in hardcover and trade paperback editions with cover art by Leslie Morrill and an Introduction by Michael Cart. New York: Alfred A. Knopf, 1986.

Reissued in a hardcover facsimile edition by The Overlook Press in 2001.

Reissued in a trade paperback edition by Puffin Books (as part of "The Freddy Collection"). New York: Puffin Books, 2003.

To the reader's delight Mr. Camphor makes an encore appearance in this next title, which is among Walter's finest efforts. The book begins when the short, red-faced magnate cleverly enlists Freddy's help: first, in dealing with his two difficult aunts, who are spending the summer with him and, then, in saving the old resort hotel across the lake, where the ladies would normally stay but cannot this year because the caravansary (look it up!) has closed due to an infestation of ghosts.

We learn the startling fact that, as a boy, Mr. Camphor was orphaned and raised by these visiting aunts, Elmira and Minerva.

Perhaps, as a result, he—like Walter who was also orphaned and (at least in part) raised by aunts—has made "quite a study of aunts. There's two kinds," he tells Freddy, "there's the regular kind and then there's the other kind. Mine are the other kind." What he means by this is that the one, Elmira, is a preternaturally gloomy semi-invalid (or so she claims), while the other, Minerva, is livelier but as cantankerous as a bear with a sore paw—no, make that *two* sore paws. At that, they prove easier to deal with than the ghosts, but Freddy's skills as a detective are once again sufficient to carry the day—helped along, no doubt, by his "Great Detective Expression," which "consisted of pressing his mouth very tightly together and squinting up his eyes so that he looked suspicious and determined at the same time. He had practiced this expression before the looking glass until it was now almost perfect, and strangers were quite often terrified by it." Not so his friends, alas: "But Jinx just laughed. 'You kill me, pig,' he said. 'Look, smooth out that face before it sets that way . . .'"

Once again, the reliably recidivist rats provide much of the villainy, but this time in collaboration with the evil and mysterious Mr. EHA, who has designs on both the hotel *and* the farm. Brooks even manages to invest old Simon with a touch of nobility when the Bean homestead comes under attack and the rat is grievously wounded.

Meanwhile Walter demonstrates his thorough knowledge of camping and the outdoors when Mr. Camphor and Freddy (wearing a coonskin cap) take to the woods near the hotel for some plain and fancy ghost-busting. This occasions a number of hilarious scenes—including Freddy flipping flapjacks over an open fire, a visit to the haunted hotel and a reciprocal visit to the camp by the (shudder) undead, and Freddy paddling a canoe. Further investigation will then take Freddy into Centerboro, accompanied by Georgie the little brown dog, one of Walter's more appealing characters who finally, in this adventure, gets more than a walk-on part. The teasing banter between him and Freddy contributes to the hilarity of the Centerboro scenes when, disguised as Dr. Henry Hopper, Freddy first "examines" a suspect, must then run for his life, and finally—to Georgie's delight—winds up at a wedding in a dress.

The stratagem Freddy contrives to finally foil the villain is satisfyingly complex and calls on the talents not only of animals but also a number of insects and—at the other end of the food chain—Mr. Bean himself. Unlike humans, Freddy doesn't resort to firearms or mayhem, though his display of fiendish imagination this time reveals Georgie's sympathetic nature, while Jinx— well, "My nature's not sympathetic," the cat says, "and I wouldn't miss this for eight pounds of prime catnip. If the guy goes crazy I want to be here to see." Later, when Freddy's plot turns even more diabolical, Jinx ups the ante: "I wouldn't miss it for eight pounds of prime catnip *and* two quarts of cream. I haven't had so much fun since Mrs. Wiggins fell out of the swing."

Freddy himself has quite a lot of fun writing poetry (see pp. 10, 22, 112, 162, and 258), and his biographer, Walter, generously includes poems by Mr. Pomeroy and the rats! Walter also makes room for two more generalizations: "Like all chipmunks, he spoke jerkily, stamping his feet, flicking his tail, and giving continual little jumps as if he felt pins being stuck in him." And, "like a good many snakes, he thought that a good joke never wore out."

The combination of humor and an unusually involving plot promised Walter's readers such fun that Knopf decided to send him on his first national book tour to promote this title. No itinerary survives but newspaper articles suggest that most of the author's appearances were in the East and Midwest. While in Chicago he appeared on the popular NBC radio program for kids, "The Hobby Horse," hosted by Ruth Harshaw, a hearty lady in a hat. The event on November 6, 1948, featured a dramatization of a scene from the book followed by a discussion among Walter, Ms. Harshaw, and a panel of (horrors) children. On a surviving recording, Walter sounds much as one would expect—dry, a bit diffident, and as reluctant to talk as Mr. Bean might have been!

Camping was also featured twice on "Let's Listen to a Story" on WMCA in New York, first on December 3, 1953, and again two years later, on July 23, 1955.

The reviews of this title were gratifyingly enthusiastic. The *New York Times* called the Freddy books "funny and wise" and

*"The Hobby Horse" host Ruth Harshaw, Walter and fans
before the broadcast*

hailed *Camping* as "this wonderfully involved chronicle." The distinguished critic Louise Seaman Bechtel wrote, "What joy to greet again this famous pig who is editor, poet, banker, and detective, all in one solidly enduring character. . . . The new story is good: it has ghosts and surprising details of all the animals out camping. But what one enjoys most is the lively style, the rare conversations, and the inimitable character of Freddy." Hear, hear!

16. *Freddy Plays Football.* New York. Alfred A. Knopf, 1949. 265 pages.

> Reissued as a hardcover facsimile edition by The Overlook Press in 2001.
> Reissued as a trade paperback edition by Puffin Books (as part of "The Freddy Collection"). New York: Puffin Books, 2002.

Walter keeps the inimitable one exceptionally busy in this double-barreled novel, which is both mystery and sports story. The mystery involves the appearance on the Bean Farm of a man claiming to be Mrs. Bean's long-lost brother, Aaron Doty, come—after a thirty-year absence—to collect his share of the family inheritance. You-know-who has his doubts about the honesty of the Doty claimant and, frankly, so do the Beans, but they're so honest that, as long as there's the slightest chance that Doty is who he says he is, they will fork over the $5,000 that is his share. Mr. Weezer agrees to loan them the money, though there's little chance they'll be able to pay it back, and they might lose the farm as a result. To prevent the Beans' coming such a cropper, Freddy collects the loan himself and, with it in hand, goes on the lam. The lam doesn't last, however, and Freddy winds up in a jam, instead—well, in jail, anyway. And there goes his reputation again!

Most painful, for Freddy, is Mr. Bean's failure to trust him and his intentions; even Mrs. Bean is dubious. Ouch. The inescapable fact is that Freddy has—at least technically—stolen the money, even though he never, in his wildest dreams, contemplated keeping it once he had managed to discredit Doty. Nevertheless, he must stand trial. Once again, Old Whibley agrees to serve as his defense, "But this is the last time," he warns Freddy. "I can't spend my life getting you out of trouble. If a person is a born fool, it is a waste of time helping him."

Meanwhile the sports story involves you-know-who becoming a member of the Centerboro High School football team, tossing around the ol' pigskin (!) and once again surviving Herbie Garble's attempts to pack him in a crate and ship him off to Montana. Walter clearly draws on his own days as a football player in private school for gridiron verisimilitude, though one wonders if the Mohegan Lake team ever encountered any like Centerboro's archrival Tushville, whose team contains players with full beards and children at home.

As if he weren't busy enough, to join the football team, Freddy must become a full-time student at the high school. But who has the time? Freddy is so busy in this one, Walter tells us, that "he didn't have much time to be lazy," let alone go to school five days a week. Fortunately Freddy has, in Weedly, a cousin who looks very much like him and is willing to practice a little duplicity of the bait-and-switch kind. This gets them into trouble only once.

As he did in *Bean Home News*, Freddy spends a lot of time in Centerboro in this story and perhaps a few observations are in order about the town. We've already established that Walter himself regarded the Rome of his boyhood (and perhaps also Hamilton where his grandfather lived) as the model(s) for Centerboro. Was one more central than the other? Well, the population of Rome in 1900, when Walter was fourteen, was 15,653. However, in *Football* Walter tells us that the combined population of Centerboro *and* Tushville was "probably not more than 4,000," which would have been approximately the population of Hamilton in 1900. So does this mean the latter is the true inspiration for Centerboro? Not necessarily. The Centerboro shops, businesses, and services that Walter has mentioned thus far in the series suggest a community of a size closer to Rome than Hamilton. Consider that Centerboro—which is governed by a town board—boasts a bank, a daily newspaper (maybe more than one, since, over the years, Walter refers to the local sheet variously as "The Gazette," "The Guardian," and "The Sentinel"), a fire department, a high school (administered by a school board), a thriving department store, a hotel, a hardware store, a music store, a movie palace, a public library, a Presbyterian church, a Methodist church, a courthouse, a county jail, a diner, a tea shoppe, a milliner's (whose sign reads "Harriet—Hats"), an optician, a bus station, a drug store, a grocery store, a butcher, a lumber yard, and a realtor. In later titles Walter adds a bookstore, a country club, a Rotary Club, and a chamber of commerce. The main street, lined by elms, is called, well, Main Street, while other named streets include Elm, Orchid, and Clinton.

Just as Walter never tells us precisely the population of Centerboro, so he never tells us the precise age of the Beans or of few other important characters for that matter (though he does mention that Mr. Camphor is forty). In this book, however, there is evidence that Mrs. Bean is no more than forty-one! Her older brother Aaron has been missing for thirty years, after all, and she was just eleven when he left home. On the other hand, when he mentions having served in the Spanish-American War, which took place in 1898, she snaps,

"You were only two when that war started!" This would mean he was born in 1896 and, at the time of this story, would be fifty-three. It's also stated that he is five years older than Mrs. Bean, so that would make her forty-eight. Either way, her husband, Mr. Bean, is clearly older than she. After all, he has mentioned having farmed his spread, "man and boy" for fifty-two years. If he were ten when he started farming, he would now be sixty-two; maddeningly nonspecific evidence in other books confirms that he is, indeed, probably sixtyish but that is as close as Walter permits the reader to come. Such arcana is of interest only to true Freddy enthusiasts, but if you're reading this, you, no doubt, are among that number and will forgive this digression. . . .

Chicken children count: only seventeen children—all daughters—in this one. Perhaps the Beans have been having chicken dinners *every* Sunday?

Generalizations: Only one but an important one: "Like most lazy persons, pigs work harder, when they do work, than more energetic people. They do this because they are anxious to get through the work as quickly as possible, so they can lie down and go to sleep again. At least that was the way Freddy figured it out. And for that reason, he said, they do just as much work in a week as energetic people and should not be criticized."

The putative Mr. Doty, on the other hand, is genuinely lazy, sleeping each morning until ten or eleven o'clock. This annoys Charles who feels that everyone—human and animal alike—should leap out of bed at the first sound of his beautiful voice. Accordingly, he flutters up to the windowsill of the man's bedroom and crows as loud as he can. Mr. Doty gets up, all right—and throws a shoe at Charles.

Doty is one of Walter's more interesting villains. Though he clearly has a mean streak, he is also fun to be around and, at least once, comes to Freddy's defense. This causes Freddy to think, "Oh, dear, I wish people were all one thing or all the other." But, to Walter's credit, most of his characters are more satisfyingly complex than that. Even Freddy's best friend, Jinx, is flawed. Though faithful and stalwart, he is also vain and, to put it mildly, insensitive. "Boy, is Mr. Bean sore," he tells

Freddy, who is in hiding. "It's the sausage factory for you, kid, if they catch you."

Jinx has brought Freddy one of the wanted posters Mr. Bean has had printed. This leads to a slightly metafictional moment when Freddy says—of the picture of himself that has been used—"Tisn't very flattering. . . . Why couldn't they have used the one that Mr. Wiese drew for Mr. Bean that time he came out?"

As for poetry, the pig is never too busy—or lazy—to versify and there are six poems in this volume (see pp. 56, 77, 90, 159, 182, and 264), though one (p. 182) is not by Freddy but rather by Uncle Solomon, the screech owl, who plays a significant role in this adventure.

17. *Freddy the Cowboy.* New York: Alfred A. Knopf, 1950. 233 pages.

Reissued in hardcover and trade paperback editions with cover art by Leslie Morrill and an introduction by Michael Cart. New York: Alfred A. Knopf, 1986.

Reissued in a hardcover facsimile edition by The Overlook Press in 2002.

This is the first book Walter wrote following his 1949 heart attack and, perhaps in the interest of taking it easy, he borrowed the plot—well, parts of it, anyway—from an unpublished short story he had written a year or so earlier. Titled "Mr. Sparrow-Flint's Double Life," it is about a young man named James Melton Sparrow, who lives in Ulster County, New York, and is the author of a series of successful Western novels. Since he has never been west of Niagara Falls, he writes under the pseudonym of "Cal Flint," for whom he has created quite a colorful persona—an ex-cowhand "with a past full of corrals and lariats and rodeos and other standard West equipment." Mr. Sparrow is careful to keep his true identity a secret for fear of disappointing his readers (and spoiling his sales). But then a dude ranch opens on the adjacent farm and all bets are off, as Mr. Sparrow inevitably runs afoul of the thoroughly unpleasant ranch owner, Sid Prosser.

Cowboy similarly involves the opening of a dude ranch near the Bean Farm and it, too, is owned and operated by a thoroughly unpleasant man named . . . Cal Flint! And, of course, Freddy will run afoul of him. This starts when Freddy, returning from an adventure, comes across a man, dressed like a cowboy, who is beating his horse. Kind-hearted Freddy intervenes and, to save the horse, offers to buy him. The sour and near-sighted owner, Cal Flint, thinking Freddy is a man (the pig is wearing a suit), agrees and Freddy takes him to the First Animal Bank, where he withdraws the money he needs for the purchase. Letting Flint observe this is a mistake that Freddy will later regret. Until then, however, he enjoys developing his new persona as a cowboy, affecting a cowboy hat and thunder-and-lightning shirts (Mr. Sparrow wears those, too). Freddy isn't satisfied with just looking like a cowboy, however; he wants to learn how to ride and shoot and handle a rope, for, as Walter reminds us, "When Freddy set out to do something he was never satisfied with just halfway doing it." Fortunately, the horse—named Cyclone, or Cy for short—is enormously helpful, being savvy about all this stuff and even managing to teach the pig how to ride. After this the two new friends enjoy leisurely canters around the countryside. If this last sounds familiar, it is, for Walter pretty clearly also borrowed the character of Cy not from Mr. Sparrow but from Mr. Ed—*sans* the alcohol.

In yet another disguise—as Snake Peters from Buzzard's Gulch, Wyoming (this character also appears in the short story) —Freddy bests Flint in a rodeo competition. Unfortunately, Freddy's disguise fails him and he must then find ways to save his, as it were, bacon, for the thoroughly unpleasant—and now humiliated—cowpoke vows revenge. Flint also sets out to rob the First Animal Bank. The animals, who mistakenly think the cowboy has shot Freddy, are waiting and, while they don't quite tear him to pieces, they do make his life thoroughly unpleasant for a while (a similar thing has happened to Mr. Garble in *Football*, by the way, when the animals think *he* has shot Freddy). Seeing Mrs. Wogus bounce up and down on the hapless cowpoke is satisfying to the reader but, unfortunately, it leaves the man more determined than ever to track Freddy down and fill him full of bullet-sized holes. Ultimately this will lead to an exciting cross-country chase on horseback that takes the two antagonists into downtown Centerboro and, indeed, right into the Busy Bee, where a hilarious confrontation takes place that leaves Flint humbled, defeated, and smelling much, well, sweeter than he had before.

This title is notable not only for its blood-and-thunder action but also for its introduction of the Horrible Ten, a band of rabbits who—with their ears tied down, brandishing little tin knives, and chanting bloodthirsty chants (which Freddy has written)—become terrifying enough, at least in appearance, to thoroughly intimidate bad guys in this and future books. In fact, the rabbits have so much fun doing this that their number soon swells and they become the Horrible Twenty. ("We are the Horrible Twenty/ Of ferocity, boy! we've got plenty!") and then the Horrible Thirty ("We may be bloodthirsty and dirty . . .").

Though there is only one generalization to report in this book ("Like most fat people [Freddy] had a good sense of balance"), there are an unusually large number of spirited poems (see pp. 86, 87, 89, 113, 122, 141, 166, and 181), though they are all either Horrible chants or songs that Freddy sings while accompanying himself on the guitar, which he has learned to play. (If we accept that Freddy can type, I suppose we must accept that he can also play a guitar!)

Knopf had hired a new children's book editor in 1947, William Hall, who was responsible for Walter's 1948 tour. Apparently, he also encouraged Walter to try to modernize the Freddy saga a bit. If making his hero a cowboy was Walter's initial effort at that, it was a successful one, for the story is exciting and funny and proved very popular with young readers. Indeed, WMCA featured it twice on "Let's Tell a Story," first on December 2, 1950, and again on June 2, 1951. At the same time Jean Poindexter Colby, a former editor at Houghton Mifflin, was operating a review service called "Junior Reviewers," for which children aged eleven to fourteen submitted their impressions of new books. The anonymous reviewer of *Cowboy* gave it an enthusiastic thumbs-up, reporting, "It gets you into hysterics in the end. You laugh out loud and have to be sent out of the living room."

Walter and a young fan in the early 1950s

True, true. Even Walter had such a good time making Freddy a cowboy that he couldn't resist starring this persona in an encore performance in the very next adventure.

18. *Freddy Rides Again.* New York: Alfred A. Knopf, 1951. 240 pages.

Reissued as a hardcover facsimile edition by The Overlook Press in 2002.

Two-gun Freddy is back, and a cowboy craze has swept the Bean Farm. Even Jinx gets the fever and, persuading Bill the Goat to serve as his trusty steed, rides out with Freddy. The villains this time are not surly cowpokes but, instead, fox-hunting city folks—the wealthy and thoroughly obnoxious Margerine family, which has bought an estate near the Bean Farm.

When Mr. Margerine threatens Mr. Bean, an uncharacteristically brave Charles pecks the man on the nose twice and Freddy, to hasten him on his way, fires two blanks into the air. As a result, these two desperadoes are charged with assault and must hide out in the Old Grimby House. Freddy, now disguised as the Comanche Kid from Spavin Creek, Texas, is bemused to then find himself being hired by Mr. Margerine to detect himself. As if that weren't complicated enough, things get really tangled when the rich folks kidnap Mrs. Wiggins and Freddy retaliates by kidnapping the Margerine's son, Billy. And I haven't even mentioned the rattlesnake yet or the sanctimonious Arthur, the Margerine's calico cat, or the Horrible Thirty, or about half a dozen other strands of this tangled—yet not very dynamic—plot. Anyway, things work out and Freddy even manages to teach Billy a lesson or three in humility, while also putting him to sleep with his poetry. There are several other lessons conveyed (too many probably) in Walter's most didactic effort since *Popinjay*.

Chicken children count: back up to twenty-seven.

With the Horribles at their full complement of thirty, it's worth mentioning that there are even more rabbits on the farm than there are chickens—so many, in fact, that few of them have names but are referred to, instead, by number. The most prominent of these is Number 23, who is often described as Freddy's "chief operative." Other named rabbits in the series include numbers 4, 6, 6 Jr., Mrs. 6, 7, 8, 11, 12, 13, 14, 16, 17, 18, 21, 24, 27, 32, 34, 35, 37, 38, 41, 62, 74, and 84 ½.

The poems (see pp. 93, 100, 127, 130, 214, and 235) are, as in *Cowboy*, mostly Horribles chants and cowboy songs, though Freddy gets around to writing another in his splendid series "The Features." This one is about the eyes. Alas, the pig still hasn't managed to publish his collected poems, but in this volume it's mentioned that when he does, he plans to use the title *The Poetical Works of Frederick Bean, Esq.* Thank goodness, he will change his mind.

19. *Freddy the Pilot*. New York: Alfred A. Knopf, 1952. 247 pages.

Reissued in hardcover and trade paperback editions with cover art by Leslie Morrill and an introduction by Michael Cart. New York: Alfred A. Knopf, 1986.

Reissued in a hardcover facsimile edition by The Overlook Press in 1999.

Reissued as a trade paperback edition by Puffin Books (as part of "The Freddy Collection"). New York: Puffin Books, 2001.

After the rather weak tea of *Rides Again*, Walter rebounds nicely with the hearty brew that is this robust adventure. It begins

with the reader's discovery that Mr. Boomschmidt is in a dilemma, though he's not quite sure what that word means. "Same
as quandary," Mr. Bean offers. Well, that helps a lot, doesn't it?
"Ah, yes, quite right—a quandary," the baffled circus owner
says. Leo pipes up: "It's a bird, I think, chief. Kind of a cross
between a swan and a cassowary." This is the kind of patented
patter for which Walter created these two characters and he
has great fun in this outing giving them ample opportunity to
engage in it. Fortunately for the reader—and the advancement
of the plot—Mr. Bean is still there to define the term: "When
there's several things you can do, but they're all likely to turn
out badly . . . you're in a dilemma. You're also in a quandary."

Well, with *that* out of the way, Mr. Boom announces he needs
not only a good detective but "the best detective talent in the
country." Fortunately, the old reliable firm of Frederick &
Wiggins is available, for it is, indeed, a complicated problem. At
its root is a man named Watson P. Condiment, who is determined to marry the circus equestrienne, Mlle. Rose. When she
politely refuses his repeated offers, the unscrupulous Condiment decides to force her to accept by destroying Mr. Boomschmidt's circus. His method is a clever one: he hires a pilot to
dive bomb the big top during each performance. The panicked
audience flees and Mr. Boomschmidt must then return their
money. Alas, no one can prove that Condiment is behind the
plot, nor can anyone figure out exactly where the plane is coming from. To find out, Freddy begins taking flying lessons; Mr.
Bean then buys him his own plane and the pig becomes, ta-dah,
Freddy the pilot! In the meantime the polymath porker has met
Mr. Condiment and discovered he is a comic book publisher.
Freddy has already expressed his (and Walter's) distaste for this
form of expression: "Comics!" he exclaims, "No self-respecting
animal over two years old looks at that trash."

Further learning that Condiment specializes in horror
comics gives[16] Freddy a bright idea, though. Why not turn the

---

16. An already controversial topic, two years after this book was published,
another Freddy—Dr. Frederick Wertham—published *his* book, *The Seduction of
the Innocent*, a scathing attack on comics that almost destroyed the comic book
industry.

tables on the man? He's trying to scare the circus business away. Why not scare him away by appearing to bring his comic characters to life? This leads to some extremely funny scenes featuring Willy, the boa constrictor, as The Great Serpent and Freddy as Lorna the Leopard Woman. For this role Freddy essays a Spanish accent, which reminds us that dialect humor was once a staple form of the comic, but, in our multicultural age, now probably elicits more frowns than smiles. Nevertheless, the farcical nature of the scenes in which Freddy employs it—and scares the wits out of Condiment—remain very funny, indeed. The piece de resistance, however, is Mrs. Wiggins's performance as the Countess Chinitzky, aka The Demon Woman of Grisly Gulch, Wyoming.

Along the way, Freddy is also helped by a coalition of the Horribles and Sniffy Wilson's family—who, inspired by Freddy's copy of *The Adventures of Robin Hood*, have transformed themselves into Merry Men—er, skunks.

Mr. Condiment never has a chance but, nevertheless, the bilious publisher does make a splendid villain. If Ollie Groper is a walking dictionary, Condiment is an ambulatory thesaurus. Consider this sample of his conversation: "Madame, this is not a matter for jests, jokes, witticisms—that is, funny business. Ponder my words, consider them, contemplate them—I mean, think them over." Um, okay. . . .

While we're thinking them over, Uncle Ben, hearing of Freddy's new role as pilot, returns to the farm to try out his latest invention, a bombsight. Since Walter has already established that many of Uncle Ben's repairs tend to turn the broken article into something else entirely, it comes as no surprise that the bombsight will make a dandy self-filling piggy bank. It takes a misadventure involving the U.S. Army to reveal this, however. But that's no problem for the reader, since it gives Walter even more opportunity for his patented form of satire, i.e., poking fun at authority.

The book ends happily when Mr. Boomschmidt learns the real reason Rose has turned down Condiment's proposals. It turns out love, as well as Freddy's plane, is in the air. The element of romance makes this the only love story in the Freddy series. Walter's Roxbury neighbor, Irma Mae Griffin, the local historian who also occasionally typed his manuscripts, always claimed to have given Walter the idea for this plot point, asserting he was too unromantic ever to have thought of it on his own.

Walter's spirited defense of traditional books over comics gives him a chance to add a bookstore to the inventory of Centerboro businesses. It is operated by a Mr. Tweedle, "rather a peculiar person. He never even looked up when a customer came into the store, and anybody that wanted to could stay there all day taking down books from the shelves and reading them." This was Walter's idea of the perfect bookstore, as we already knew, thanks to his 1932 *Bookman* article, "The Shoestring Book Collector." In it he wrote of a certain bookstore he knew: "I went into it one day a year or two ago and was practically thrown out because I said there was nothing I specially wanted, but thought I'd like to look around. 'Just want to look around, do you!' exclaimed the owner. 'What do you think this is, a free library?' Fortunately this sort of boorishness you will very rarely meet."

And certainly, the reader concludes, not in Mr. Tweedle's shop! We don't know if Walter envisioned himself as Mr. Tweedle, but it's clear that Wiese did, for his picture of the bespectacled bookman (see p. 85) is a dead ringer for the now sixty-six-year-old author.

Soaring into the wild blue yonder inspires Freddy to versify. He not only creates a poem about flying ("Oh, the young pigs fly / About the sky // And they zoom and dive and roll . . .") (p. 106) but also manages to create another in his earthbound series on the features—the hair this time (p. 95)—and a new Horribles chant, too (p. 138). His experiences aloft also inspire him to write another book, this one titled *The Sky Is the Limit: A Book on Flying for Animals* (copies are probably available in your local public library).

There are three generalizations worth noting: "Like most detectives, he trusted more to luck than planning." "The sparrow . . . like most sparrows was always trying to be tough without much to do it with." And "Alligators are seldom very experienced in affairs of the heart." Also, Freddy posits a new theory of laziness, to wit: "When a lazy person once really gets started doing things, it's easier to keep on than it is to stop."

Finally, it should be mentioned, at least in passing, that in this book the name of the circus is changed (without explanation) from Boomschmidt's Colossal and Unparalleled Circus to Boomschmidt's Stupendous and Unexcelled Circus. Make a note.

20. *Freddy and the Space Ship.* New York: Alfred A. Knopf, 1953. 262 pages.

Reissued in a hardcover facsimile edition by The Overlook Press in 2001.

Reissued in a trade paperback edition by Puffin Books (as part of "The Freddy Collection"). New York: Puffin Books, 2002.

Walter seems to have had at least the basic idea for this book in mind as he was finishing *Pilot*, for when we last see Uncle Ben in its pages, he is busily drawing plans for a jet plane, preparatory to designing a space ship. Aside from that, though, one wonders if Walter approached the actual writing of his books in the same manner that Freddy approached his detecting, trusting more to luck than planning. The following note to a friend about this title invites such speculation:

> Currently I labor at a new Freddy in which my hero tries to reach Mars. Through miscalculation he gets turned around somewhere in the solar system and lands again on earth thinking it Mars. Complications are setting in and I am now on chapter 13 with 7 more to go. Whether I can get everything straightened out in that space remains to be seen.

Well, seeing is believing and readers have here the evidence of the finished book—with everything neatly straightened out. Uncle Ben has, indeed, built his space ship and is in the final stages of planning his journey to Mars. To accompany him he chooses four of the animals: Freddy and Jinx, of course, along with Charles and Georgie.

Meanwhile, a family named Bismuth moves into the Grimby house in the nearby Big Woods. Mrs. Bismuth is Mrs. Bean's cousin and when the Bismuths fall on hard times, soft-hearted Mrs. Bean invites them to come to the farm and Mr. Bean helps them fix up the old house. Ed Bismuth, the family's fatuous and eternally optimistic paterfamilias (aka "noble Pa") is an almost Dickensian character. When he accidentally burns down the house—and most of the nearby woods with it—he moves his family in with the Beans. "Nothing to worry about," he says, eating Mrs. Bean's cookies faster than Freddy has ever seen anyone eat them before. "Nothing at all! Ha, ha; I should say not! Oh sure, burned up the house, burned up the furniture—but it didn't burn up the Bismuths. Buy another house, buy more furniture—ha ha!—Bismuth is in business again."

When Mr. Bean—annoyed by that little "ha ha!"—asks what the man intends to use for money, the breezy reply is, "A Bismuth never worries about money. Ha, ha. I guess not! You can't keep a Bismuth down." Bluntly put, Mr. Bismuth is a bit of a con artist, as Freddy discovers when the man sells tickets for the Mars trip to a number of Centerboro's leading citizens. Mr. Bean has to bail him out and all but one of the citizens are mollified. The exception is elderly Mrs. Peppercorn who has paid her five dollars and is determined to go to Mars. So determined is she that Uncle Ben decides it's easier to let her come along than to dissuade her. (And besides, she threatens him with her umbrella!)

With the crew complete, the rocket ship blasts off. Next stop Mars. Or not, as the case may be. As Walter has already indicated, a "miscalculation" turns the ship around in mid-flight and it returns to Earth, landing in the burned out Big Woods. The only problem is that the space travelers think they're on Mars. This leads to all sorts of hilarious complications and some nicely mysterious touches—what, for example, is that enormous flying creature that, under cover of darkness, carries off Charles? Could it be a dragon? And what about that mysterious little creature with the big yellow shoes? (Yes, I know: it sounds like Mickey Mouse, but, trust me on this, it's not!)

The truth will finally out but in the meantime Mrs. Wiggins gets arrested for allegedly stealing Miss McMinnickle's pocketbook; the Bismuths are eating the Beans out of house and home; Mr. Bean's garden is flooded; Alice and Emma's fabulous jewelry collection is stolen and their pompous Uncle Wesley disappears. Time for Freddy to don one of his best disguises—painting his face blue and adding various odd bits of facial hair, he becomes Captain Neptune from outer space. He fools everyone but Mrs. Bean, though she doesn't let on. Instead, Walter has her behave most uncharacteristically, saying all manner of cruel things about Freddy that hurt his feelings and leave readers scratching their heads. She even quotes, to "Captain Neptune," poems she alleges are by the pig; e.g., "I am smart and I am bright / When I do things, I do 'em right. / There isn't anything I won't try / Oh, golly, I'm a brilliant guy!" Yes, of course, the point is made that she knew it was Freddy all along but, nevertheless, the experience leaves many readers with a bad taste in their mouth.

The book concludes with not one but two trials and—what's this?—Freddy is the defendant in neither! Walter manages to invest the subsequent ending with a nice touch of the Twilight Zone that leaves readers anxious for more about Mars. They will not be disappointed as Walter soon demonstrates in *Freddy and the Men from Mars*.

But first, a few thoughts on characters: Mr. Bismuth is one of Walter's most inspired creations. He is a thoroughgoing scoundrel, yes, but is also the source of most of the hilarity in this very funny book. Even when he's offstage, he's the source of humor, as when Freddy—in the wake of Bismuth's inept efforts as a handyman—visits Dr. Wintersip and, surveying the consequences, takes a header into a rain barrel. Mr. Bismuth's awful family—wife Ambrosia and children Carl and Bella—add to the dark fun. One's feelings are a bit more mixed about the elderly Mrs. Peppercorn, who has been little more than a face in the crowd in earlier volumes. Some may wish Walter had left her there, for she proves to be more than a bit of a termagant, which is bad enough. But then, inspired by Freddy, she begins writing poetry, some of the most excruciatingly, run-screaming-for-the-exits awful stuff ever written. Who can forget such couplets as "Some stars are large and some are small / and some are quite invisiball" and "The light from some far distant stars / Does not reach earth for yars and yars." Not me, no matter how hard I try!

Speaking of poetry, Mrs. Wiggins also catches the bug—to, believe it or not, worse effect than Mrs. P! ("Although in jail in Centerboro / I do not fret or stew or worro.") Even Freddy's work, represented here in only three poems (see pp. 19, 73, and 260), is far from his best; e.g., "Farewell my friends, farewell my foes / To distant planets Freddy goes." Happily, his better work is proudly on display in the volume that follows.

21. *The Collected Poems of Freddy the Pig.* New York: Alfred A. Knopf, 1953. 81 pages.

Reissued in a hardcover facsimile edition by The Overlook Press in 2001.

"Freddy's complete poems are also to be brought out this fall, separately, with a scholarly introduction and explanatory notes by my friend Bill Hall, who is the children's editor at Knopf's," Walter wrote to a friend. Alas, neither the introduction nor the notes came to be. There is, however, a nicely witty foreword by "The Editors" and a generous—though not definitive—collection of poetry by Freddy and assorted others. The poems are divided by subject: The Features, Marching Songs, Self-Praise, Laments, and more. Wiese has provided witty new drawings for virtually every page of what has become an extremely rare book!

22. *Freddy and the Men from Mars.* New York: Alfred A. Knopf, 1954. 246 pages.

Dedicated to Dottie (Dorothy Brooks).

Reissued in hardcover and trade paperback editions with cover art by Leslie Morrill and an introduction by Michael Cart. New York: Alfred A. Knopf, 1986.

Reissued in a hardcover facsimile edition by The Overlook Press in 2002.

Hard on the heels of Freddy's misadventures in space comes the news that Martians have landed in Lanksburg, Virginia, and have joined Mr. Boomschmidt's circus. Freddy's suspicions are quickly aroused when he learns that the Martians' "manager" is none other than Herb Garble. Mrs. Peppercorn, too, has her suspicions, though hers derive from a certainty that the red-clad Martians, who hail from the Red Planet, are Communists.

"They ought to be sent right back to Rooshia, where they come from," she grouchily opines. Freddy pooh-poohs this notion: "My goodness, Santa Claus wears a red suit—you don't call him a Communist, do you?"

"I wouldn't put it past him," the peppery old lady answers, "Seems like you can't trust anybody these days."

This satirical exchange is rather brave of Walter. To be sure, McCarthyism wasn't quite the menace it had been even a year earlier, since the Wisconsin senator's star was in the eclipse by the middle of 1954 when this was written and by the end of that year McCarthy would be censured by his colleagues in the U. S. Senate. Nevertheless, the Cold War—and the attendant fear of Russia—would linger for years to come. Walter had already demonstrated even greater bravery, however, in his adult short story, "The Dread Ignormus," which *Esquire* had published in March 1953 and which contained even sharper criticism of McCarthyism—though somewhat veiled in the form of another of his stories about the sparrows Hubert and Enid.

At any rate both characters' suspicions are justified when Freddy discovers the Martians are not Russians but rats! This poses a really interesting problem. Freddy would have no qualms about discrediting his old enemy Mr. Garble, but revealing the Martians' true identity would also discredit Mr. Boomschmidt, who innocently believes the creatures on display are the real thing. Worse, two of Charles and Henrietta's children are then kidnapped and Freddy receives the following semi-literate note: "Freddy. As long as Marshans are Marshans chickins will be chickins, when Marshans are not Marshans chickens will be et, so kepe your big mouth shut brother."

Dear me, as Freddy would say. Yes, the pig has now refined his Great Detective expression to the point where he manages to look like "a sort of George Washington and Winston Churchill"—but even those two worthies might have been stymied by this latest challenge.

Fortunately, at this point a flying saucer containing *real*

Martians lands in a vacant lot near the circus. Uncle Ben and Mrs. Peppercorn are the only ones to observe this, since the inventor is open to such anomalies and Mrs. Peppercorn— well, as Walter says, "A little thing like a group of visitors from outer space never bothered her." And a good thing, too, since the visitors' appearance is a bit alarming, to say the least: they have three eyes, pear-shaped heads (with feelers), four arms, and no necks. They walk upright but are, well, "not exactly spidery, and yet they reminded you more of spiders than of anything else." Spiders that are two feet tall, that is. Happily there is an ancient genetic link between the Martians and Earth spiders, since this means that Mr. and Mrs. Webb are able to communicate with them, using a common—but ancient—language. On the other hand, the preternaturally taciturn Uncle Ben seems to be doing pretty well on his own, using a combination of grunts, sign language, and drawings.

Well, solutions to many of Freddy's problems are now at hand, though first he will manage to get himself captured by Mr. Garble and nailed into that omnipresent crate, always waiting to be shipped to Twin Buttes, Montana. In a nice twist, however, it is Mr. Garble himself who will get to see the Big Sky country.

If Walter weren't altogether comfortable writing about the space age, he certainly makes the best of it by crafting some very funny scenes that keep readers laughing from beginning to end of this volume. Freddy's scenes with Charles's children, Chiquita and Little Broiler—who are also locked in Mrs. Underdunk's basement along with the pig and his "helper," Red Mike—are particularly delicious. To put the icing on the comic cake, they are joined by a chicken that can whistle "Dixie." A very grand "woman," her name is Mrs. C. Ogden Hapgood. Or "Madame Glorianna Hapgood, on the stage," she frostily and pompously reminds the sheriff. Similarly, Mrs. Underdunk's encounter with the Martians is certainly something to write home about, as is the strategy Walter comes up with to rid the farm of the rats—perhaps forever?

It's interesting that even at this late stage in the life of the series, Walter is still introducing new characters who will reappear in later titles. Chief among them in this title is Mr. Boomschmidt's brother, Mr. Hercules, who looks just like his brother Orestes except for being twice as wide and twice as tall. Alas, he has none of his smaller brother's quick wit, but his mental slowness will be partially responsible for Mr. Garble's downfall.

Just as Walter introduces new characters, he continues to offer new revelations about established ones, too. For example, we learn that Mrs. Peppercorn was once a fifth grade teacher and that Mr. Garble was one of her students, and not a very good one, at that. "I don't seem to remember that you ever knew the answers to anything," she says to him. Mrs. Peppercorn, on the other hand, remembers any number of embarrassing anecdotes involving her former student and is quick to share them with anyone in earshot. One of these, involving an unfortunate encounter with mucilage, inspires Mr. Herc to begin calling the unfortunate Garble "Ol Moosiludge." This is always followed by a heave of heavy laughter, "Uh, uh, uh." Mr. G. gets pretty sick of it. We also learn that Mrs. Underdunk supports her ne'er-do-well brother with a monthly stipend.

For those who love the established order, however, Walter demonstrates that the more things change in Freddy's world, the more they stay the same. The Beans, for example, turn down Uncle Ben's invitation to chauffeur them about in his now atomic-powered station wagon, preferring, instead, to travel by horse and buggy. Mr. Bean remains nervous at hearing his animals talk. And those animals continue to entertain themselves by telling stories, singing, and playing games—sometimes until nearly midnight.

Also blessedly predictable is Freddy's continued plying of his poetic craft—six times in this volume (see pp. 61, 97, 118, 172, 234, and 244). Unfortunately, the malign presence of Mrs. Peppercorn seems to be infecting the pig's work, which is becoming a bit sloppy; e.g., "Way down upon the old home planet / Million miles away / I'm so homesick I can hardly stan' it / There's where the old pigs stay." This, of course, is a take-off on Stephen Foster's "Old Folks at Home" and evidences Walter's continuing fondness for pastiche, as does another not very good poem that is a take-off on Joyce Kilmer, which begins, "I think that I shall never see / Another pig as smart as me. . . ."

At least Freddy has the good grace not to publish this one, being rightly "afraid that it might sound a little conceited."

Alas, not only is Freddy's work beginning to show signs of deterioration, so is Walter's. This typically manifests itself as sloppy or inapposite diction. For example, Leo refers to money as "dough" and Willy the boa constrictor tells an importunate Henrietta to "lay off, sister." Syntax is becoming oddly tortured, rustic to the point of sounding ignorant. It's hard to isolate specific examples but one is when Mr. Garble says, "I want you to take five instead of ten, which it's only fair you should do so." Mrs. Peppercorn is also guilty of such locutions, while the word "ain't" is increasingly evident, though it's always been present, and appropriately so to define character and atmosphere. Now, however, its use seems sometimes careless and indiscriminate. Worst of all, though, is Walter's increasing tendency to include violence (which began as early as *Magician*). Guns are increasingly present and always loaded. Mrs. Underdunk orders her brother, "Shoot, Herb! Shoot that pig!" and, later, she herself takes a potshot at the porker. The rats are becoming more physically violent, too. When they discover one of the Horribles, No. 23, has infiltrated their gang, Zeke—Simon's eldest son—snaps, "Hold him down, boys. Banjo, where are those pliers?" "No. 23 didn't like the sound of that at all," Walter writes. Neither does the reader.

Wiese's pictures, too, are starting to show signs of decay. His once fine and fluid line is becoming sometimes sketchier so that pictures appear rushed and unfinished or heavier to the point of sometimes seeming almost murky (see pp. 34, 44, 96, and 105 for examples of both).

These criticisms aside, all of the succeeding volumes continue to show flashes of both Walter's and Wiese's accustomed brilliance and there is much to savor and enjoy in even the relatively less successful entries.

Chicken children count: thirty-five.

Glittering generalization: "Simon, like most rats, was ticklish."

This one, by the way, is dedicated to Dorothy. She and Walter had been married the year before.

23. *Freddy and the Baseball Team from Mars.* New York: Alfred A. Knopf, 1955. 241 pages.

Reissued in a Dell Yearling trade paperback edition with cover art by Bob Jones. New York: Dell, 1984.

Reissued as a hardcover facsimile edition by The Overlook Press in 1999.

The six real Martians like Earth so much that they decide to stay, becoming a star attraction with the circus. In short order, Freddy is summoned by Mr. Boomschmidt when one of the six, Squeak-Squeak, disappears (this also invites the first-ever mention of a Centerboro police force and even a police chief). Arriving at the circus, Freddy notices the Martians playing a game of catch and has a brainstorm: why not build a baseball team around them? Mr. Boomschmidt is a bit dubious at first but Freddy has good reason to think the aliens would be well-nigh unbeatable. As for Walter, his good reason for introducing baseball into this story was probably that his new editor was passionately interested in America's pastime (and we've already established that Walter's own father had been quite good at this sport, too!).

Of course, there are only five Martians now and clearly more players are needed, so Mr. Boomschmidt, Leo, Oscar the ostrich, Mr. Hercules, and Hannibal the elephant are added to the roster. Freddy, disguised as a cantankerous old geezer named Mr. Arquebus, serves as coach. Why the disguise? Freddy has donned it to shadow the villainous real estate agent Mr. Anderson, whom he's observed also watching the Martians. Coincidence? I think not. Nor is it a coincidence that Mrs. Church soon phones to tell Freddy her house has become haunted and, oh, yes, the ghost has stolen her diamond necklace. Soon thereafter similar burglaries take place, as a crime wave sweeps the area from Buffalo to Albany, from Watertown to New York. Meanwhile, other old friends—er, enemies— show up, too, when the circus team finds itself pitted against the Tushville town team, which is managed once again by the odious Mr. Kurtz and sports the usual full roster of ringers, including Black Beard, whom Freddy had bested in *Football*, and a professional pitcher named Zingwall. You'll have to read the book, though, to find out how Freddy then winds up—in his favorite disguise as Mrs. O'Halloran—in the role of house-keeper to the Kurtzes, and even then you may not be able to figure out what on Earth possesses the pig to fry a skillet full of bacon! Has he lost his mind? Perhaps, for in another departure from character, he has earlier actually struck Oscar the ostrich when he can't retaliate, not once but twice!

Other characters do surprising things, too: Mr. Boom-schmidt decides his circus will winter in Centerboro for the first time; Mr. Bean takes to the ice and proves himself to be an excellent ice skater (who knew?); Henrietta becomes a cheer-leader; Mrs. Peppercorn, not content to visit only her own awful verse on the world decides to rewrite Longfellow ("Under the spreading maple tree / The blacksmith shoppe stands / The Smith, a mighty man is he / With hands like iron hams" and so on and on . . .); Mr. Webb, too, takes up the pen to write a book titled *How to Make Friends and Influence Spiders*; and Leo, Jinx, and even Freddy himself reveal a visceral dislike of children! This last comes in the context of Freddy's declara-tion that he's had too much to do with people of late—"humans, I mean." As a result, he tells his friends, he's started a long poem about "how funny people look compared to ani-mals." One of the verses he quotes is: "The aardvark makes your senses whirl / But he's no curiouser than a girl / To me, quite frankly, it's bewilderin' / How folks can get so fond of children." Which inspires Jinx to add, "Had I my way, I'd put the skids / Under the whole darned race of kids."

Such splenetic musings lead the three to collaborate on a book-length work, in verse, about good manners. "Why shouldn't we point out the things that are bad manners," Leo offers, "and at the same time show that animals don't do them?"

Freddy agrees that such a book would have a big sale among animals and maybe even among humans who wanted to improve themselves. "Yeah?" Jinx acidly asks, "What humans do?"

Well, dearie me, as Jason Binks was wont to say, some ani-mals don't seem too set on self-improvement, either, as they handily demonstrate in the very next adventure.

24. *Freddy and Simon the Dictator.* New York. Alfred A. Knopf, 1956. 244 pages.

Reissued as a hardcover facsimile edition by The Overlook Press in 2003.

The animals are revolting! Simon the rat returns from his exile in Montana determined to turn the farm into a dictatorship. Employing what Walter is now calling "the Communist way," Simon begins spreading the Big Lie about Mr. Bean—that he is a cruel, exploitive master—and keeps repeating it until he has won enough animals to his side to make it possible to take over the farm.

But Simon's ambitions don't stop there: today, the Bean Farm; tomorrow, the entire state. And speaking of New York State, Freddy learns that Mr. Camphor has been persuaded (much against his better judgment) to run for governor. Now recanting his decision, he enlists Freddy's aid in encouraging the nominating committee to withdraw its endorsement. Alas, Freddy's first ploy—to paint Mr. Camphor as a helpless giggler—backfires. "The first new idea in politics in a hundred years," one of the politicos crows. "There's our slogan," he continues, "Laugh and the world laughs with you. Camphor the giggling governor. It's a natural, gentlemen. It will be a landslide."

Needless to say, Freddy—now disguised as Dr. Henry Hopper—must go back to the drawing board. But before he can contrive an alternative strategy, Mr. Camphor vanishes. Good heavens, what next? Well, nature abhors a vacuum, so no sooner has Mr. Camphor disappeared than Herb Garble shows up and we learn that it was he who brought the rats back from Montana and is supporting their revolution. Then Jinx appears to defect and Simon rewards his new ally by appointing him head of the farm. Mr. Bean does not take kindly to this idea, and fortunately he's not alone. Anyone who has read Walter's 1939 story "Till the Cows Come Home" (an inspiration for this book) will know that it is the dogs' continued loyalty that will ultimately tip the balance and cause Simon's glorious revolution to fizzle (and will inspire the single poem in this volume, "The Charge of the Dog Brigade"—pace Alfred Lord Tennyson!).

Walter has his usual (by now somewhat self-indulgent) fun satirizing politics and especially politicians, whose number here include the likes of Judge Anguish, Senator Blunder, Mr. Slurp, Colonel Buglett, and Mr. Glockenspiel. When Freddy finally tries another ploy—suggesting Mr. Camphor will abolish all taxes if elected—Mr. Glockenspiel protests, "But if we do away with taxes, who's going to pay the governor's salary?" "And our salaries?" the self-interested Col. Buglett chimes in. "We all expect to be appointed to political jobs if Camphor is elected." But even this idea backfires and a frustrated Freddy complains, "Golly, Mr. Cam—I mean, Jimson. I think up the craziest things for you to do, and the crazier they are, the more they like them." And, indeed, his craziest idea of all—animal suffrage— is the suggestion that finally convinces the committee that Camphor is absolutely their man. At this point, Mr. Camphor just gives up and in due course is elected governor. His staunch supporter Freddy becomes the political boss of Otesaraga County (who else can deliver the all-important animal vote?) and, later, the pig will even be elected Mayor of Centerboro.

Hmmmm . . . the problem here, I think, is that Walter has two stories going simultaneously and they never quite gel. If he had simply stuck to the animal revolution, he would have had a tighter and better book. By introducing all of the human pol- itics, however, he diffuses the action and introduces, in his satire, a good deal of material that most young readers will simply find dull. It seems a mistake, as well, to actually identify the political party that has nominated Mr. Camphor. It's the Republican Party, of course; this *is* upstate New York, after all, and it is also logical that Freddy—and the farmer Mr. Bean— should be Republicans and that the animal vote should also swing that way. But by introducing this degree of realism, Walter seems to be violating the spirit of genial fantasy that has previously prevailed. Another violation is his new habit of inserting his own name into the text (once here, twice in *Baseball Team*, and again in *Flying Saucer Plans* and *Dragon*). All of these practices are gradually turning Freddy's genially sep- arate world into just another part of the all too dreary real world, a pattern that, sadly, recurs in the next title.

25. *Freddy and the Flying Saucer Plans.* New York: Alfred A. Knopf. 1957. 243 pages.

> Reissued in a hardcover facsimile edition by The Overlook Press in 1998.

More politics, but this time gangs of international spies are trying to steal the plans for Uncle Ben's flying saucer. Freddy gets involved, of course, and through a comedy of errors is branded a thief and a traitor. He goes into hiding, disguised as a gypsy fortuneteller, outsmarts the spies, and clears his good name. He hardly has to break a sweat doing so, since this is the most feebly plotted of all the Freddy books, filled with holes large enough for Hank to pull the phaeton through while flanked by the three cows *and* Uncle Ben's atomic-powered station wagon. And one of the scenes—a lengthy one involving Freddy, Cy, and a state trooper—is lifted, largely intact, from the Ed story "Medium Rare."

The politics involved also get extremely murky, and most readers are put off by the numerous, rather jingoistic references to "good Americans" and Communists. One can only be grateful that Walter didn't require Freddy and the others to take loyalty oaths. In the author's defense, though, loyalty has always been important to Freddy in the context of friendship, so it's only logical that loyalty to his country would be similarly important. One only wishes it were not so clumsily handled. But, again, Walter's health was in steep decline by this time and it is, perhaps, remarkable that he was able to write this book at all.

Like all of the Freddy titles, it does have its agreeable moments. The county jail prisoners' expression of support for Freddy is heartwarming and Walter demonstrates that his talent for creating funny names hasn't failed him: for example, Uncle Ben hopes to sell his plans to an automobile company called "Interminable Motors" and the leader of a band of cannibal ants is named "Grisli." Too, Walter's treatment of the principal spies Penobsky and Smirnoff, though uneven, has flashes of his signature whimsy, as do the several generalizations, from which we learn that "most insects are pretty vain," that "moles in general have a name for being reliable and straightforward in their dealings, though often cranky and irritable," and that "the only thing an ant has to fear in a house is a broom." There are four poems (see pp. 4, 222, 226, and 238), though the last is a re-working of the famous animal song of the open road.

One new major character is introduced: Samuel Jackson, the mole. Far from being Walter's most inspired creation, Samuel is more often annoying than amusing. However, his delight, at the book's end, in finding himself "one of the gang" will resonate with all readers who have ever regarded themselves as outsiders and have found, in the Freddy books, a place where they, too, belong.

The reviews of this book were surprisingly favorable. The *New York Times* noted, "Walter Brooks' lightly satiric touches make this story as funny to grown-ups as to Freddy's legions of devoted young fans," while the reviewer for the *Toronto Globe and Mail* judged, "Walter R. Brooks has combined science fiction, an animal, and a spy story as well plotted as the cleverest detective writer." Only one reviewer—for *Junior Libraries*—offered a dissenting opinion, tartly opining, "Freddy deserves a long vacation. This one lacks the charm and originality of the earlier books."

26. *Freddy and the Dragon.* New York. Alfred A. Knopf, 1958. 239 pages. *Published posthumously with "A Note on the Author" following the text.*

Reissued in a hardcover facsimile edition by the Overlook Press in 2000.

A crime wave swamps Centerboro in this final Freddy adventure, and the Bean Farm animals are the prime suspects. To save his reputation one last time Freddy sets out to solve the case and runs headlong into a headless horseman. Shades of Washington Irving!

In the meantime, young Jimmy Wiggs, from *Perilous Adventure*, makes an encore appearance, asking for Freddy's help with the backyard circus he's planning as a fund-raiser to pay for his baseball team's uniforms. Freddy wisely turns to Uncle Ben, who conjures up a fire-breathing dragon that will not only be the star of the circus but will also be instrumental in Freddy's resolution of the mystery.

As for that mystery . . . its viability depends on the reader accepting the notion that two-thirds of the Centerboro residents would turn against Freddy. Few readers will be willing to make that leap, especially when Walter unwisely portrays the locals as planning to lynch Freddy (and includes Jinx's feeble attempt at a joke about this that is in shockingly bad taste). The plot suffers, too, from the lack of an interesting villain. The perpetrator turns out to be an outsider, a retired big-city crook whom readers never really get to know. Perhaps sensing this weakness, Walter introduces the bad guy realtor Mr. Anderson at the end, but it's a case of too little, too late. Unfortunately, the chapter devoted to Jimmy's circus seems as much a tacked-on afterthought as a similar chapter did in *Perilous Adventure*, though it does offer a satisfying opportunity for the awful Mrs. Underdunk to receive a bit of a comeuppance. It's also a pleasure to learn that Mr. Anderson has finally been sent to the penitentiary for a crime. Perhaps he will be reunited there with Mr. Garble, who was similarly sent to the big house at the end of *Dictator*.

This novel introduces two new characters, Mrs. Peppercorn's elderly aunt, Mrs. Talcum, who is rather engaging, and Percy the bull, who is not—well, at least at first. Initially a member of the gangster gang, Percy is taken to the farm when it is discovered that he is the long-lost father of the three cows! A diamond in the rough type (perhaps a bit like Walter's Uncle Jim Stevens?), he needs a lot of reforming and who better to do that than Samuel Jackson, the mole, who masquerades as the voice of the bull's conscience. For some readers' taste, the mole may sound a little too much like Warner Brothers' animated character Foghorn Leghorn, who, in turn, sounded a little too much like the character Senator Claghorn from the Fred Allen radio shows. At least, however, Walter manages to flesh out his character—as he does Percy's—making both appealing members of his large cast.

There is only one poem from Freddy in this title but fortunately it is an ambitious one. About the eyebrows, it will be the last in his series about the features (p. 138). There is also an amusing poetic exchange among Freddy, Mrs. Peppercorn, and Mrs. Talcum (pp. 140–142). And finally, there are also two of those comfortingly familiar generalizations: "Like most cows, she was inclined to be rather outspoken" and "Like all cats, he was curious." It's nice, isn't it, that these should refer to the great perennnial characters, Mrs. Wiggins and Jinx, respectively.

Knowing this is Freddy's final appearance makes the reading of this novel a melancholy exercise. And yet, to coin a generalization of our own, we might say, "Like all Freddy books this, too, has its delights," chief among them being another opportunity to spend time in the company of one of literature's great characters, our friend Freddy, whom the *New York Times*, in its generous review of this book, called "that charming, ingenious pig." Truer words were never written.

POSTHUMSOULY PUBLISHED

The Wit & Wisdom of Freddy and His Friends. Walter R. Brooks. Illustrated by Kurt Wiese. Introduction by Michael Cart. Contributing Editor Sarah Koslosky. Woodstock: The Overlook Press, 2000. 253 pages.

This is a generous collection of brief excerpts from the Freddy books arranged by topic; e.g. Friendship, Bravery, Imagination, Honesty, etc. The publication of this volume helped launch Overlook's ambitious republication of the entire series in facsimile.

The Freddy Anniversary Collection. Walter R. Brooks. Illustrations by Kurt Wiese. Introduction by Michael Cart. Woodstock: The Overlook Press, 2002. 432 pages.

The collection contains *Freddy Goes to Florida*, *Freddy Goes to the North Pole*, and *Freddy the Detective*.

The Art of Freddy. Edited and with an introduction by Michael Cart. Woodstock: The Overlook Press, 2002. 192 pages.

This lavishly produced, oversized volume contains a generous selection of the best Wiese illustrations from the series, arranged by topic; e.g., The Many Roles of Freddy the Pig, The Many Disguises of Freddy the Detective, Let's Eat! Freddy and Food, Villains Galore! The Many Foes of Freddy and His Friends, and many more. A separate portfolio reproduces—"in glorious, living color!"—the dust jackets of the twenty-six Freddy books.

NOTES ON POPULARITY

So, what's your favorite Freddy book? That was the question posed by Freddy fan Cameron Wybrow in conducting a 2007 online survey of other devotees of the series. The returns were modest in number, but nevertheless instructive, since there is a strong equation expressed in them between popularity among readers and popularity among critics. Thus, the most popular titles with readers—*Freddy the Detective* and *Freddy the Politician* tied for first place—are generally regarded by critics as among the most successful, although *Florida*—sometimes regarded by critics as the best—ranked only sixth in popularity. Contrariwise, the eighth most popular among readers, *Baseball Team from Mars*, would surely rank significantly lower in reviewers' assessments.

As for myself, I admit that my top ten personal favorites would differ somewhat from my top ten critical choices. Here are my two lists:

My Critical Favorites	My Personal Favorites
1. *Detective*	1. *Pied Piper*
2. *Politician*	2. *Politician*
3. *Florida*	3. *Football*
4. *Camping*	4. *Camping*
5. *Clockwork Twin*	5. *Camphor*
6. *Camphor*	6. *Clockwork Twin*
7. *Bean Home News*	7. *Detective*
8. *Ignormus*	8. *Ignormus*
9. *Pied Piper*	9. *Bean Home News*
10. *Space Ship*	10. *Florida*

Selected Books and Articles About Freddy— and His Boswell, Brooks

Cart, Michael. "Freddy, St. Peter and Me." *Children's Literature in Education.* Autumn 1983.

Cart, Michael. "Fanfare for Freddy." *School Library Journal.* February 1986.

Cart, Michael. "What's So Funny? Humor in the Writing of Walter R. Brooks." *The Lion and the Unicorn.* 13 (1990) 131–140.

Cart, Michael. *What's So Funny? Wit and Humor in American Children's Literature.* New York: HarperCollins, 1994. 223 pages.

Cart, Michael. "Freddy the Detective." *Booklist.* May 1, 2002.

Cart, Michael. "The Freddy the Pig Series: A Teacher's Guide" (pamphlet). New York: Puffin Books, 2002. 12 pages.

(*I have also frequently devoted my monthly "Carte Blanche" column in* Booklist *magazine to various and sundry aspects of Walter and Freddy. For examples see my columns of 11/15/94, 3/15/98, 11/15/04, 10/15/06, and 6/1/07.*)

Egoff, Sheila. *Worlds Within: Children's Fantasy from the Middle Ages to Today.* Chicago: ALA, 1988. 339 pages.

Galewitz, Herb. "The Many Disguises of Freddy the Pig" in *The Mystery Reader's Companion,* edited by Dilys Winn. New York: Workman, 1977.

Hochschild, Adam. "Pig Tales." *The New York Times Book Review.* May 22, 1994.

Sale, Roger. *Fairy Tales and After.* From *Snow White* to E. B. White. Cambridge: Harvard University Press, 1978. 280 pages.

Entries about Walter are contained in most of the standard reference works, including *The Junior Book of Authors* (Wilson), *Something About the Author* (Gale Research), *St. James Guide to Children's Writers* (St. James Press), *The Continuum Encyclopedia of Children's Literature* (Continuum), and *The Oxford Encyclopedia of Children's Literature* (Oxford University Press). Walter is also included in *The National Cyclopedia of American Biography* (White).

Non-Freddy Publications by Walter R. Brooks

THE TEENS:

"Haunted" (sonnet). *The Century*. April 1915.

"Harden's Chance." *Forum*. December 1915.

"The Elopement" by "Aeneas B. Hooker." *Breezy Stories*. January 1916.

"Beyond the Border." *The People's Home Journal*. May 1916.

"The Green Jade Earring." *The People's Home Journal*. August 1918.

"Trouble? Red Cross." *Red Cross Magazine*. November 1918.

"Trayner's Wife." *Breezy Stories*. March 1919.

THE 1920s:

"Octopus Pets" (article). *Guide to Nature*. January 1920.

World Traveler (series of nine travel articles). May 1920–December 1921.

"Always a Silver Lining." *Successful Farming*. July 1920.

"Cicero Betts' Best Bet" by "Aeneas B. Hooker" (co-authored with Frances Rufus Bellamy). *World Traveler*. August 1921.

"Lesson from Nature" (poem). *New York Sun*. 4/14/22.

"When City Shadows Jig in the Gloom" (newspaper story). Publisher unknown. March 1922.

"The Piper in the Park." *The New York World Magazine*. 4/16/22.

"Spanish Doubloons." *The People's Home Journal*. May 1922.

"Mr. Cabbit's Marvelous Adventure." *The World Magazine*. 12/24/22.

"You Can't Climb Beanstalks." *The Boston Transcript*. 5/9/23.

The Romantic Liars (six-part serialized novel). *Country Gentleman*. 7/25–9/25.

"How Are Your White Elephants?" and "Yourself and Your Customers" (articles). *The Gift and Art Shop*. Undated.

THE 1930S:

New York: An Intimate Guide. New York: Alfred A. Knopf, 1931. 212 pages.

"The Shoestring Book Collector" (article). *The Bookman*. March 1932. Reprinted in *Reader's Digest*. June 1932.

"Reviewing Made Easy" (article). *The Bookman*. June 1932.

"Imagine That." *Vanity Fair*. April 1934. Also published in New Zealand. (The inspiration for Walter's adult novel *Ernestine Takes Over*.)

"Little Red Hat." *Esquire*. September 1934. Also published in Sweden and in England in *Leisure*.

"Mr. Weller." *Waldorf-Astoria*. 9/15/34. Also published in *World's News* (Australia).

"The Executive Approach." *Waldorf-Astoria*. 9/22/34.

"Mileage or College" (humorous essay). *Waldorf-Astoria*. 9/22/34.

"Major." *Waldorf-Astoria*. 9/29/34. Also published in *Sunday Sun* (Australia) and *The Evening Standard* (England). (Walter's first short story to feature a talking animal.)

Ernestine Takes Over. Illustrated by Herbert Roese. New York: Morrow, 1935. 265 pages. Reprinted in a cheap edition by Triangle Books in 1938.

"The Hermit." *Waldorf-Astoria*. 1/?/35. Also published in *The Evening Standard* (England).

"Fragile." *Waldorf-Astoria*. March 1935.

"Seated One Night at the Organ." *Esquire*. March 1935. Also published in *The Evening Standard* (England).

"I Think It Was Schenectedy." *Esquire*. June 1935. Also published in *The Evening Standard* (England).

"Home Is Where the Heart Is." *Esquire*. July 1935. Also published in *Leisure* and *Argosy* (both in England).

"Nude Interlude." *Esquire*. August 1935. Also published in *The Bystander* (England) and in New Zealand.

"A Wink to Fortune." *Esquire*. November 1935. Also published in *The Evening Standard* (England).

"No Sale." *The Evening Standard* (England). 12/20/35. Reprinted in *Argosy* (also England).

"The Hand Is Quicker Than the Eye." *Evening Standard*. 12/31/35. Reprinted in *Fiction Parade* in 1936, in *The Evening Standard* (England), and in Sweden and Australia.

"Unmanageable Animals." *Evening Standard*. ?/?/36 (England). Reprinted in *Fiction Parade*.

"The Conservative." *Esquire*. January 1936. Reprinted in *Fiction Parade* in February 1936 and in *The Evening Standard* (England).

"A Bare Possibility." *Esquire*. May 1936. Also published in Sweden and New Zealand.

"The Private Life of George and Ermyntrude." *Leisure* (British). 6/16/36. Also published in Australia.

"In the Garden." *The Bystander* (British). 6/17/36. Reprinted in *Town Topics* (date unknown).

"The Jessingham Ghost." *Esquire*. July 1936. Also published in *The Bystander* (England).

"Don't Give It a Thought." *College Humor*. October 1936. Also published in *Leisure* (England) and in Australia and Denmark.

"The House of the Dog." *Home Journal* (British). ca. October 1936.

"I Stood on the Bridge at Midnight." *Esquire*. October 1936. Also published in *Woman's Journal* (England).

"Mr. Cabbitt Walks Home." *Evening Standard* (British). 10/3/36. Also published in New Zealand.

"Ayawahoo." *Woman's Mirror* (Australia). December 1936.

"One Does What One Can." *Liberty*. December 1936 (date sold).

"Like a Diamond in the Sky." *The Evening Standard* (England). ?/?/35. Reprinted in *The Evening Standard Second Book of Strange Stories*. London: Hutchinson, 1937.

"The Worm Returns." *Woman's Journal* (British). ?/?/37.

"A Princess Steps Out." *Esquire*. June 1937. Also published in *Pearson's* (Canada) and in Sweden and Holland. Reprinted in *Help Yourself Annual*, Garamond Press, 1939.

"Blood Is Thicker Than Water." *Evening Standard* (British). 6/9/37.

"Jane Makes Up Her Mind." *Liberty*. 6/19/37. Also published in Holland and Sweden.

"Shake Well Before Using." *Liberty*. 7/10/37. Also published in Denmark.

"Love Is Enough." *Esquire*. August 1937. Also published in *The Bystander* (England) and in Australia.

"Discovery of America." *Atlantic Monthly*. August 1937. Also published in *Woman's Journal* (England) and in South Africa. (The first Hubert and Enid story. This was a favorite story of the artist Grant Wood ["American Gothic"], who once insisted on reading it aloud to the other guests at a dinner party.)

"King's Testimonial." *Esquire*. August 1937. Also published in *Evening Journal* (England).

"Ghost My Eye." *Scribner's Magazine*. August 1937. Also published in *Everywoman's* (England).

"Why I Hate Everybody" (humorous essay). *Esquire*. September 1937. Also published in *The Bystander* (England).

"The Talking Horse." *Liberty*. 9/18/37. (The first "Ed" story.)

"Father's No Fool." *Liberty*. 10/9/37. Also published in *Woman's Journal* (England) and in Australia.

"Organgrinder's Swing." *College Humor*. October 1937. Also published in *MacLean's* (Canada) and in Australia.

"Irish Nightingale." *Evening Standard* (British). 11/13/37. Reprinted in *The Manchester Chronicle* (England).

"Fortune Beckons Mr. Beed." *Liberty*. 11/6/37. Reprinted in *Fiction Parade*. Also published in *Everywoman's* (England) and in Australia and Sweden.

"She Asked for It." *MacLeans* (Canada). 1/1/38. Also published in *The Bystander* (England) and in Sweden.

"They Say It's Catching." *Liberty*. ca. January 1938. Also published in Sweden.

"Plant Early, Two Feet Apart." *Atlantic Monthly*. January 1938. Also published in *Harper's Bazaar* and *Argosy* (both England).

"Requesting No Miracles." *The Passing Show* (British). 1/22/38.

"Live Alone and Look It" (essay book review) *Fiction Parade*. January 1938.

"Everything Is Nothing." *Scribner's*. March 1938. Also published in *Digest and Review* (England).

"He Whose Laugh Lasts." *Atlantic Monthly*. March 1938. Also published in *Plus Living* (England).

"Believing's Seeing." *Esquire*. June 1938.

"Neck's Appeal." *College Humor*. July 1938. Also published in *The Bystander* (England) and in Australia.

"Seen By Appointment Only." *Atlantic Monthly*. July 1938. Also published in Australia.

"Youth Is Stranger Than Fiction." *Liberty*. 7/2/38. Also published in *Everywoman's* (England). Adapted by Clifford Goldsmith as a three-act play.

"The Perfect Scream." *College Humor*. September 1938. Also published in *The Bystander* (England).

"From Worse to Better." *Liberty*. 9/24/38. Also published in *Woman's Journal* (England).

"Horse Sense." *Esquire*. October 1938.

"Love Sends a Little Gift of Polyhedrons." *Liberty*. 10/15/38. Also published in Sweden and Australia.

"Fools Rush In." *College Humor*. March 1939. First published in

Liberty in January 1938 as "They Say It's Catching."

"What the Doctor Ordered." *Atlantic Monthly*. May 1939. Also published in *The Bystander* (England).

"To Break the Monogamy." *Liberty*. 4/22/39. Also published in *The Grand* (England).

"Till the Cows Come Home." *Atlantic Monthly*. July 1939. Also published in *Illustrated* (England). (Inspiration for *Freddy and Simon the Dictator*.)

"Another Little Drink." *Colliers*. 8/12/39.

"Life Is Too Short for Unicorns." *Commentator*. October 1939. Also published in *The Bystander* (England).

"Ed Has His Mind Improved." *Liberty*. 10/14/39. Also published in *Illustrated* (England). Reprinted in *In the Stacks: Stories about Libraries and Librarians* edited by Michael Cart, New York: The Overlook Press, 2002.

"Really You Americans." *Atlantic Monthly*." December 1939.

THE 1940S:

"Remember Tomorrow." *Commentator*. January 1940. Also published in *Everywoman* (England) and in Sweden.

"Ed Shoots It Out." *Liberty*. 6/1/40.

"The Midnight Ride of Mr. Pope." *Liberty*. 8/3/40.

"Just a Song at Twilight." *Liberty*. 9/21/40.

"Mr. Ames and the Dark Enchantress." *Liberty*. 11/2/40.

"Ed Gets a Mother Complex." *Liberty*. 1/8/41.

"Ed Holds a Séance." *Liberty*. 3/1/41.

"Ed Likes to Be Beside the Seaside." *Liberty*. 9/5/41. (Inspiration for "The Wooing of Hester Warren.")

"Ed Takes the Cockeyed Initiative." *Liberty*. 9/27/41.

"Dragon's Teeth." *Argosy* (England). September 1941. (Reprint of "Plant Early, Two Feet Apart.")

"The Rival." *Liberty*. 2/22/41.

"Mr. Beasley's Caller." *Esquire*. June 1942. Also published in *The Strand* (England).

"Mr. Pope Rides Again." *Saturday Evening Post*. 7/4/42. Also published in Australia. Reprinted in *Saturday Evening Post Carnival of Humor* edited by Robert M. Yoder, New York: Prentice-Hall, 1958.

"Bird in the Bush." *Saturday Evening Post*. 9/5/42.

"At the Bottom of the Garden" (another Mr. Beasley story) *Esquire*. November 1942. Also published in *Modern Woman* (England) and in Australia.

"Dr. Atwood and Mr. Ed." *Saturday Evening Post*. 1/16/43. Reprinted in *The Bedside Book of Humor* compiled by Mathilda Schirmer, Chicago: Consolidated Book Publishers, 1948.

"Do Ye Ken Wilbur Pope?" *Saturday Evening Post*. 6/5/43.

"Should Auld Acquaintance Be Forgot." *Liberty*. 10/23/43. Also published in *Argosy* and in *Evening Standard* (both England) under the title "Forget It, Mr. Finch."

"Ed Quenches an Old Flame." *Argosy*. May 1944.

"Ed Signs the Pledge." *Argosy*. June 1944.

"Ed Makes Like a Horse." *Argosy*. August 1944.

"Well, Really, Mr. Pope." *Argosy*. October 1944.

"Ed, the Were Horse." *Argosy*. February 1945.

"Ed Goes Psychic." *Argosy*. April 1945.

"Ed Divides and Conquers." *Argosy*. July 1945. Reprinted in *Story Digest*. December 1945.

"With Teeth and Tail." *Argosy*. September 1945. Also published in Sweden. Reprinted in *Story Digest*. January 1947.

"Miss Emmeline Takes Off." *Saturday Evening Post*. 9/8/45. Also published in *Argosy* (England) and reprinted in *Alfred Hitchcock's Ghostly Gallery*, New York: Random House, 1962.

"Man from Mars." *Liberty*. 11/3/45. Also published in Australia.

"Mr. Whitcomb's Genie." *Saturday Evening Post*. 12/15/45. Also published in *Argosy* (England) and in Sweden, Denmark, Australia, and New Zealand. Reprinted in *Story Digest* (date unknown) and *Country Gentleman* (spring 1982). (This is Walter's most anthologized adult story. It was reprinted in at least seven collections. Radio and television rights were also sold.)

"The King of Smithia." *Story Parade*. December 1946. Also published in book form: *A Story Parade Picture Book*, New York: Grosset & Dunlap, 1947. (First story about Queen Ennyjay.)

"Miss Billings Makes a Sale." *Liberty*. 9/14/46.

"The Aristocrats." *Liberty*. 12/14/46.

"Henry's Magic Powder." *Argosy*. April 1947. Also published in *Modern Woman* (England) and in Sweden and Australia.

"His Birthday" in *Santa's Footprints and Other Christmas Stories*. New York: Aladdin Books, 1948. (Walter's only Christmas story.)

"George's Flying Carpet." *Argosy*. January 1948.

"The Wooing of Hester Warren." *Cosmopolitan*. February 1948.

"Second Chance." *Saturday Evening Post*. 2/14/48. (A motion picture option was taken on this title but never produced.)

"Jenny and the Dragon." *Story Parade*. March and April 1949. (The second Queen Ennyjay story.)

"Whistle for My Love." *American Magazine*. December 1949. Also published in *Modern Woman* (England).

THE 1950S:

"Jimmy Takes Vanishing Lessons." *Story Parade*. 1950 (date unknown). Subsequently published in book form: New York: Knopf, 1965. Also reprinted in *Children's Digest*. (This is Walter's most often reprinted story. It has been anthologized at least thirty-one times and was recently reprinted in hardcover by The Overlook Press in 2007.)

"The Goblins of Dormerville." *Story Parade*. June 1952. Reprinted in *Children's Digest* May 1966.

"Ambrose." *Story Parade*. January 1953.

"The Dread Ignormus." *Esquire*. March 1953. (Another Hubert and Enid story. Though obviously inspired by *Freddy and the Ignormus*, it can also be read as a sly criticism of McCarthyism and its use of what came to be called "the big lie.")

"Henry's Dog Henry." *Story Parade*. 1954 (date unknown). Subsequently published in book form: New York: Knopf, 1965. Also reprinted in *Children's Digest* in January 1959 and in *Favorite Stories Old and New* edited by Sidonie M. Greenberg (New York: Doubleday, 1955) and *Stories for Fun and Adventure* selected by Phyllis Fenner and Mary M. McCrae (New York: John Day, 1961).

"Harold the Honorary Mouse." *Esquire*. January 1955.

"Nicest War in the World." *Good Housekeeping*. May 1958. (The final Queen Ennyjay story.)

In 1945, Walter's agent, Carl Brandt, shopped around a collection of ten of Walter's stories hoping (without luck, alas) to sell them as a hardcover collection. The stories were "Discovery of America," "The Haunted Houseparty," "He Whose Laugh Lasts," "The Jessingham Ghost," "Life Is Too Short for Unicorns," "Plant Early, Two Feet Apart," "Really You Americans," "Remember Tomorrow," "Seen By Appointment Only," and "What the Doctor Ordered."

In 1959 the agent tried a similar strategy (though again unsuccessfully) with the following twelve stories: "The Conservative," "Early American," "Father's No Fool," "The Hermit," "I Stood on the Bridge at Midnight," "The King's Testimonial," "Major," "No Sale," "One

Does What One Can," "That Man's Here Again," "A Wink to Fortune," and "The Worm Returns."

If *I* were to select the best of Walter's stories for an anthology, they would be (in alphabetical order): "I Think It Was Schnectedy," "Jenny and the Dragon," "Life Is Too Short for Unicorns," "Miss Emmeline Takes Off," "Mr. Whitcomb's Genie," "Nicest War in the World," "Organgrinder's Swing," "Second Chance," "Seen By Appointment Only," "The Talking Horse," "Till the Cows Come Home," and "Why I Hate Everybody."

The "Ed" Stories

"The Talking Horse." *Liberty*. 9/18/37.
"Horse Sense." *Esquire*. 10/?/38.
"Mr. Pope's Thoroughbred." *Liberty*. 6/10/39.
"Ed Has His Mind Improved." *Liberty*. 10/14/39.
"Ed Shoots It Out." *Liberty*. 6/1/40.
"Midnight Ride of Mr. Pope." *Liberty*. 8/3/40.
"Just a Song at Twilight." *Liberty*. 9/21/40.
"Ed Gets a Mother Complex." *Liberty*. 1/8/41.
"Ed Holds a Séance." *Liberty*. 3/1/41.
"Ed Likes to Be Beside the Seaside." *Liberty*. 7/5/41.
"Ed Takes the Cockeyed Initiative." *Liberty*. 9/27/41.
"Mr. Pope Rides Again." *Saturday Evening Post*. 7/4/42.
"Bird in the Bush." *Saturday Evening Post*. 9/5/42.
"Dr. Atwood and Mr. Ed." *Saturday Evening Post*. 1/16/43.
"Do Ye Ken Wilbur Pope?" *Saturday Evening Post*. 6/5/43.
"Ed Quenches an Old Flame." *Argosy*. May 1944.
"Ed Signs the Pledge." *Argosy*. June 1944.
"Ed Makes Like a Horse." *Argosy*. August 1944.
"Well, Really, Mr. Pope." *Argosy*. October 1944
"Ed the Were Horse." *Argosy*. February 1945
"Ed Goes Psychic." *Argosy*. April 1945.
"Ed Divides and Conquers." *Argosy*. July 1945.
"With Teeth and Tail." *Argosy*. September 1945.
"Medium Rare." Only in *The Original Mr. Ed*.
"His Royal Harness." Only in *The Original Mr. Ed*. (Inspired by the earlier story "Believing's Seeing.")
"O Sing No More." Unpublished.
"Operation Gratitude." Unpublished.

A collection of nine of the Ed stories were collected in an original paperback titled The Original Mr. Ed. *The book was published by Bantam in January 1963.*

The definitive book about Mr. Ed, *the television series, is* The Famous Mr. Ed *by Nancy Nalven. A 30th Anniversary Collector's Edition was published by Warner Books in September 1991.*

UNPUBLISHED STORIES AND NOVELS

These are presented alphabetically, since virtually all of the manuscripts are undated.

"Any Friend of George's"

"The Beaten Path" (aka "The Barlows")

 "The Burgomaster of Coucelles"

"Death of a Goldfish" (sold to *Esquire* 11/6/52 for $350 but never published)

"Disengaging Marjorie"

"Does She Remind You of Anybody?"

"Don't Be Silly" (aka "Fall and Rise of Benvenuto Smith")

"Double or Nothing"

"Edgar Limpus"

"Epinandus Rides Again"

"Figures Don't Lie"

"F. O. B. Alexandria"

"Footprints"

"Gesture"

"Hanson's Potion"

"The Helping Hand" (aka "Better Angel")

"Henry Sees America"

"Himself" (aka "The Last Conservative")

"The Honest Man"

"I Hate Lawyers" (essay). (There are two versions: one is by Bellamy, and the second, finished one—which incorporates sections of Bellamy's—is by Walter.)

"If You Don't Bother Them, They Won't Bother You"

"The Importance of Being Silly"

"Independence Day Anyhow"

Lie Still and Slumber (completed 3/6/47)

"The Low Pressure Salesman" (aka "Wrong Side Up Is Right Side Down") (sold to *Esquire* 9/27/51 for $300 but never published)

Marionettes

Masquerade

"The Miraculous Lampshade" (aka "Mr. Bedford's Miracle")

"Miss Billings Admires the View"

"Miss Mary" (clearly inspired by Aunts Lucy and Rhoda)

"Mr. Bull Wakes Up"

"Mr. Nelson's New Party Line"

"Mr. Sparrow-Flint's Double Life" (partial inspiration for *Freddy the Cowboy*)

"The Naked Truth"

"On the Threshold"

"Or a Studebaker"

"The Piper in the Woods"

"Farmer Holliday and His Animals" (radio script; *A Bread-time Story*)

"The Red Cross" (poem)

"The Revenge of the Adjective"

"Reverse English"

"Rickert Street"

"The Screaming Began at Ten"

"Seever's Folly"

"Sit Down Beside Me"

"A Hubert and Enid story"

Snake Mountain

"Some of My Best Friends Are Mice"

"Something about the Germans" (five chapters of a proposed book)

"Speak, Monkey, Speak"

"The Stray Lamb"

"Strive and Succeed; or Horatio Alger's Legacy" (literary essay)

"There's Where the Old Folks Stay"

"They Never Learn"

"Thinking of Thee, Love"

"Time Out for Dinner"

"To Those Whom It May Concern"

"The Toll of the Island"

"Truth Powder"

Untitled book on money (outline and sample chapter)

Untitled essay on book clubs (two versions)

Untitled essay on book reviewers

"The Well"

"What Will Lady Selina Say?"

"Why Men Hate Women" (essay)

Sources

A GENERAL NOTE ON SOURCES

In writing this biography I have consulted a variety of primary and secondary sources. For the latter, see the bibliography that follows. As for the former, my principal sources include my interviews with Dorothy Brooks, Pauline Hopkins, Diana (Mrs. Peter) Halpern (Walter's step-daughter), Irma Mae Griffin (Roxbury's Town Historian),[17] Harold D. Williams (Colgate University Archivist Emeritus), and Samuel B. Stevens III (grandson of the Hon. Jim Stevens and, thus, Walter's cousin) of Poway, California.

Conversations with Elizabeth Starks (daughter of Elizabeth and Charles Hunt), Stephen Collins (Walter's stepson), Henry S. F. Cooper, and Ruth Dunn (who bought 27 Bank Street from Walter) and e-mail exchanges with Sylvia M. Blakeslee, granddaughter of Irvin Mead, were all helpful.

The access to Walter's files that Dorothy Brooks granted me was, of course, invaluable. I also had access to Walter's files at both Brandt & Brandt (his literary agents) and Knopf. Additionally, I found much useful information by conducting research at the following libraries: Colgate University and the public libraries of Rome, Roxbury, Rochester, and Hamilton, New York. The Field Library in Peekskill, New York, provided helpful information about the Mohegan Lake Academy, while the West Palm Beach, Florida, Public Library provided invaluable material about Lucy Stevens Kingsley Rutherford and her palatial home, La Bellucia. The Rome Historical Society was also an excellent source. Thanks to all.

---

17. Her book *History of the Town of Roxbury* (Roxbury: The Roxbury Library, 1995) is also extremely useful.

The following printed sources were consulted for individual chapters, as indicated.

CHAPTER 1

Bianco, Margery Williams. "To and Again," *The Three Owls, Second Book: Contemporary Criticism of Children's Books*. New York: Coward-McCann, 1928. 30–31.

Kunitz, Stanley J. and Howard Haycraft. *The Junior Book of Authors*. New York: H.W. Wilson, 1934.

King, Jessica. Review of *Freddy the Detective*. *Library Journal*, October 15, 1932: 865.

CHAPTER 2

Andrews, Prof. N. L. "Rev. Walter R. Brooks: An Appreciation." *The Madisonensis*, May 8, 1906: 229–34.

Baldwin, Ellis K. "Authors, Who Began Writing in Utica, Discuss Matters of Preparing Stories." *Utica* (NY) *Observer Dispatch*, February 1, 1938.

Beebe, Orsino. Letter to *Hamilton* (NY) *Republican*, n.d.

Brigham, Prof. Albert Perry. "Dr. Brooks as a Teacher." *The Madisonensis*, n.d. (1896). 238–39.

Brooks, Dr. Walter R. *God in Nature and Life*. New York: Anson D.F. Randolph & Co., 1889.

Clarke, W. N., D.D. "Memorial Sermon Concerning Walter R. Brooks, D.D. Delivered in the Baptist Church, Hamilton, N.Y., February 26, 1888." Hamilton, NY: Republican Print, 1888.

Cole, Aaron Hodgman, A.M. "Dr. Brooks as a Teacher." *The Madisonensis*, n.d. (1896): 239–40.

"Dr. Walter R. Brooks." *The Madisonensis*, November 11, 1902: 54–55. (Contains a report on the dedication of the memorial bust of Dr. Brooks.)

The First Half Century of Madison University (1819–1869) or The Jubilee Volume. New York: Sheldon & Company, 1872.

Hammond, L. M. *History of Madison County, State of New York*. Syracuse, New York: Truair, Smith & Co., 1872.

Interview with Harold D. Williams, Colgate University Archivist Emeritus, conducted October 9, 1985.

Letter from Walter R. Brooks to Louis E. Smith, City Clerk of Nelson, NY, August 2, 1933. Smith's undated reply is on the verso of this letter.

Smith, James H. *History of Madison County, New York*. Syracuse, NY: D. Mason & Co., 1880.

Smith, Malcolm K., M.D. Letter to Harold D. Williams, March 16, 1948.

"Snow" and "A Rare Celestial Sight," *Rome Sentinel*, January 9, 1886.

Tuttle, William H. *Names and Sketches of the Pioneer Settlers of Madison County, New York*. Interlaken, NY: Heart of the Lakes Publishing, n.d.

"Two Walter Rollin Brooks Babbling Way Through Life." *Waterbury* (CT) *American*, August 25, 1940. (A newspaper article by a journalist who shared Walter's name.)

Williams, Harold D. *A History of Colgate University 1819–1969*. New York: Van Nostrand Reinhold Company, 1969.

CHAPTER 3

"A Happy Occasion." *Rome Sentinel*, January 29, 1878.

"Among My Souvenirs." *Rome Sentinel*, September 27, 1947.

Beebee, Orsino. *Hamilton Republic*, n.d.

"Death at the Hands of Indians." *Rome Sentinel*, August 29, 1939.

Forbes, Dr. William M., ed. "Edward G. Stevens." *Annals and Recollections*. Rome: Rome Historical Society, January 1992.

"Henry T. Stevens." Obituary. *Rome Sentinel*, August 22, 1876.

History of Oneida County. Vols. 1 and 2. Chicago: The S. J. Clarke Publishing Company, 1912.

"Hon. Jim Stevens." Obituary. *Rome Sentinel*, June 14, 1912.

Marcosson, Isaac F. *Industrial Main Street*. New York: Dodd, Mead, 1953.

Wager, Daniel E. *Our City and Its People*. Boston: The Boston History Company, Publishers, 1896.

"William Stevens Dead." *Rome Sentinel*, October 21, 1901.

CHAPTER 4

"Death of Mrs. Brooks." *Rome Sentinel*, May 21, 1901.

"Death of Squire Stevens." *Rome Sentinel*, May 14, 1884. (Samuel Barron Stevens's will is on file in the Oneida County Courthouse in Utica, New York.)

History of Oneida County. Vol. 2. Chicago: The S. J. Clarke Publishing Company, 1912.

"Hon. Jim Stevens." Obituary. *Rome Sentinel*, June 14, 1912.

"Mrs. S.B. Stevens. Death on Tuesday of One of the Oldest Residents in the City." *Rome Sentinel*. July 1, 1896.

Stevens Mansion informational flier prepared by Veterans of Foreign Wars, Post 2246.

"Stevens Mansion in Gay Nineties Was Elegant Setting for Parties." *Rome Sentinel*, n.d.

Wednesday Morning Club *Minute Book, 1900-1902*. 26.

"William Stevens Dead." *Rome Sentinel*, October 21, 1901.

"The Work of Death. Prof. William W. Brooks Passes Away." *Rome Sentinel*, February 16, 1890.

CHAPTER 5

"A Children's Story Author Brings His Childhood Into Play." (Written to accompany the *Saturday Evening Post* story "Second Chance" by Walter Brooks, this three-column piece seems never to have been published.)

Bellamy Frances Rufus. "They Write for Us." *Commentator,* October 1939.

Brooks, Walter R. "Second Chance." *Saturday Evening Post*, February 14, 1948: 24.

Brooks, Walter R. Entry in *Junior Book of Authors*, second edition, revised. Edited by Stanley J. Kunitz and Howard Haycraft. New York: H.W. Wilson, 1951.

"Stevens." Obituary of Lucy Chamberlain Stevens. *Rome Sentinel*, January 12, 1911. (A copy of Lucy C. Stevens's will is on file at the Oneida County Courthouse in Utica, New York.)

"Stevens." Obituary of Rhoda Stevens. *Rome Sentinel*, February 14, 1911. (Unlike her sister, Rhoda left no will.)

"Two Sisters Leave Estates of $276,834." *Utica Herald-Dispatch*, n.d.

CHAPTER 6

Brooks, Walter R. Walter's boyhood journal, a Christmas 1901 gift from Perry M. Armstrong, covers the period from January 1, 1902 to March 25, 1903.

Landis, Norm. "Ghost from city's silver past rolls into Rome this weekend." *Rome Sentinel*. September 29, 1986.

"Mohegan Lake School," *The Historic Hudson*, 3:3, n.d.: 47. (See also "An Illustrated History of Mohegan Lake," www.yorktownhistory.org/homepages/march00.htm.)

The Moheganite. Duane Howard Nash, '03, Editor-in-Chief. First Quarter, n.d.

"On an Author," *New York Herald Tribune Book Review*, November 15, 1953: 2.

"Perrin-Brooks." *Rome Sentinel*, August 14, 1901.

Promotional copy written by Walter for his literary agency Brandt & Brandt, n.d.

CHAPTER 7

Brooks, Walter R. "Remember Tomorrow." *Commentator,* January 1940.

Letter from "Lucy" (Cullen), January 6, 1928. (Walter continued to correspond sporadically with Mrs. Cullen until at least 1949.)

Mott, Frank Luther. *A History of American Magazines.* 4 volumes. Cambridge, MA: Harvard University, The Belknap Press, 1930–1957.

Roxbury correspondent. "Brooks and Friends." *Walton (NY) Reporter,* June 30, 1950.

"The Wilson Prize." *New York Herald Tribune,* December 30, 1927.

CHAPTER 8

Ehrmann, Herbert B. *The Case That Will Not Die: Commonwealth vs. Sacco and Vanzetti.* Boston: Little, Brown, 1969.

Peterson, Theodore. *Magazines in the Twentieth Century,* second edition. Urbana, IL: University of Illinois Press, 1975.

"The Wilson Prize Essay Contest." *The Outlook,* January 11, 1928.

CHAPTER 9

Brooks, Walter R. "Reviewing Made Easy." *Bookman,* June 1932.

Johnson, Diane. *Dashiell Hammett: A Life.* New York: Random House, 1983. (For more about Hammett, see Layman, Richard. *Shadow Man: The Life of Dashiell Hammett.* New York: Harcourt Brace Jovanovich, 1981.)

CHAPTER 10

Kinney, Harrison. *James Thurber: His Life and Times.* New York: Holt, 1995.

Letter from Walter R. Brooks to Miriam Sieve of Alfred A. Knopf, November 2, 1927.

Peet, Creighton. Review of *New York: An Intimate* Guide in *Outlook,* April 29, 1931: 600.

Unsigned reviews of *More To and Again* appeared in the *New York Times,* 9/14/30; *Boston Globe,* 8/23/30; and *Outlook,* 12/10/30.

Unsigned review of *New York: An Intimate Guide. Books,* May 17, 1931: 10.

Utica Observer Dispatch, February 1, 1938.

Wood, Sally, ed. *The Southern Mandarins: Letters of Caroline Gordon to*

Sally Wood, 1924–1937. Baton Rouge: Louisiana State University Press, 1984.

CHAPTER 11

Bell, Lisle. *Books*, March 12, 1935: 12

Brooks, Walter R. Author's note accompanying "Don't Give It a Thought," *College Humor*, October 1936.

Brooks, Walter R. "Believing's Seeing." *Esquire*, June 1938.

Brooks, Walter R. "The Elopement." *Breezy Stories*, January 1916.

Brooks, Walter R. "Everything Is Nothing." *Scribner's*, March 1938.

Unsigned review of *Ernestine Takes Over. New York Times*, February 24, 1935: 19.

CHAPTER 12

"Bellamy, Francis Rufus." Obituary. *Publishers Weekly.* February 28, 1972: 53.

"Francis Bellamy, Author." Obituary. *New York Times* (biographical edition). February 4, 1972: 254.

Brooks, Walter R. "In the Garden," *The Bystander*, June 17, 1936.

Brooks, Walter R. "Neck's Appeal." *College Humor*, July 1938.

Johnson, Shirley. *Palm Beach Houses*. New York: Rizzoli, 1991.

New York: A Guide to the Empire State (American Guide Series). New York: Oxford University Press, 1940.

Warfel, Harry B. *American Novelists of Today*. New York: American Book Company, 1951.

CHAPTER 13

Brooks, Walter R. "You Can Make Up a Story, Too." *Young Wings*. New York: Junior Literary Guild, July 1932: 12.

Goldsmith, Clifford. Correspondence. (Walter received seven letters from the dramatist over a period of twelve years. The first letter is dated June 5, 1945, and the last, November 9, 1957.)

Pooley, Robert C., ed. *Wide Wide World*. Chicago: Scott, Foresman, 1959.

Wood, Peggy. Correspondence. (Walter received three letters from the actress regarding the possible dramatization of "Miss Emmeline Takes Off." The first letter, dated September 12, 1945, has the fabled hotel "The Garden of Allah, Sunset Boulevard" as its return address. The second, from Rte #2 Stamford, CT, is dated October 29, 1945 and the third, from Rancho Yucca Loma, Victorville, CA, is dated May 9, 1946.)

CHAPTER 14

More, Caroline Evelyn and Irma Mae Griffin. *The History of the Town of Roxbury*. Walton, NY: The Reporter Company, Inc., 1953.

CHAPTER 15

The Borzoi Quarterly. The Fourth Quarter, 1958. Vol. 7: no. 4.

"Brooks and Friends." Article about Walter "from Roxbury correspondent." *Walton (NY) Reporter*, June 30, 1950.

Brooks, Walter R. "Occupational Hazard." *The Borzoi Battledore*, September 1945: 6–7.

Nalven, Nancy. *The Famous Mr. Ed, 30th Anniversary Collector's Edition*. New York: Warner Books, 1991.

"The Brooks Book Service." Unsigned article. *Walton Reporter*, n.d.

"The Contributor's Column." *Atlantic Monthly*, August 1937.

"Walter R. Brooks." Knopf promotional brochure, ca. 1945.